NEW LIFE CHURCH

OCEANS

A Year of Devotions Celebrating

OF

15 Years of God's Goodness

GRACE

BRADY BOYD

Senior Pastor, New Life Church

WITH PAM BOYD

To the New Lifers who have come together Sunday after Sunday, learning and growing as followers of Jesus, and discerning and evaluating everything that was being taught. The pulpit is sacred at New Life; thank you for trusting me to fill it these past fifteen years. You've made me better every time, and your encouragement continues to be fuel for the journey we share.

I really do love you. And I love being your pastor.

Table of Contents

Introduction

When I was twenty-years old, I'd just given my life to the Lord and was about to give it to Pam. She and I had been dating seriously, and I knew that I wanted to marry her. But I also knew I needed to get my heart right before popping the big question. I turned my attention to faith.

Back then she and I were part of a tiny church in Jonesboro, Louisiana, that had a wooden altar at the front of it that smelled like lemon furniture polish and aged tears. I know that because I spent a fair amount of time kneeling there, begging God to help me get things turned around. I'd been a devoted sinner; now I wanted to be a devoted follower of Christ. I remember feeling awestruck that God said yes to those prayers. The moment I turned my life over to Jesus, the Holy Spirit overwhelmed me and started infiltrating my world, ushering light into every dark corner, giving me hope where I'd lost the plot.

Years ago, Pam and I were on vacation in the Florida panhandle, and one afternoon, wanting a moment alone, I stood in the ocean a good way out with my back to the beach. Before me was the grand Gulf of Mexico, just nothing but blue-green expanse. All I could hear was the crashing of the waves; all I could sense was the presence of God.

Brady, he seemed to be whispering, *Look around you. See all this water? That's how much grace I have poured out onto your life. Whenever someone asks you for a cup of cold water, don't be stingy. Give lavishly, remembering that you're swimming in oceans of grace.*

I haven't always gotten it right on the generosity front, but if I had to name what my mission in life has been since those days when I first surrendered to the lordship of Jesus, that would be it: always give the cup of cold water—and do it lavishly—remembering that you're swimming in oceans of grace.

It has been my absolute honor to serve as your senior pastor for the past fifteen years, and I look forward to growing old at New Life, ministering here fifteen more years and then fifteen after that. If you've been with us a while, the content in these pages will be familiar to you, since each entry was taken from a sermon I preached to our church. Whoever you are, whatever you're going through, and wherever you are in your walk with God, I pray that each time you pick up this book, you receive a figurative cup of cold, refreshing water.

May God's presence and power strengthen you, uphold you, and draw you nearer to him.

A NOTE FROM PASTOR PAM

In days past, God sent a message to a priest named Aaron and his sons, who were also priests. They were to deliver a blessing to the Israelites, God's beloved people, to remind them of some important truths. The blessing became known as the Aaronic Blessing and says this: "The Lord bless you and keep you; the Lord make his face to shine upon you and be gracious to you; the Lord lift up his countenance upon you and give you peace," (Numbers 6:24-26).

They were to give this blessing over the people following daily prayer and after sacrificial services, which were held in the temple each morning. If you've been part of New Life for a while, then you may know that just before our pastors dismiss services on the weekend, they often speak these words over us as the congregation as well. Of all the aspects of our gatherings, that time of blessing is my favorite. I love being sent out from our time of worship filled with words of encouragement that God sees me, that he accepts me, that he loves me, and that he is committed to transforming me into the image of his Son, Jesus.

As you finish each day's reading in this devotional, you'll find a blessing from me to you. I hope those words help remind you of some fundamental truths—that God longs to relate intimately with you, that his grace is sufficient for your every need, and that his promise to you is peace.

JANUARY

"You can return to God, seek his wisdom on things, and gain the restart that he wants to provide. If you've wandered from God's plans and are in a spun-out state today, start by telling him so."

- Pastor Brady Boyd -

Time for a Reset

I praise you because I am fearfully and wonderfully made;
your works are wonderful, I know that full well.

PSALM 139:14

Given how tech-obsessed our culture is, you probably own a few devices. You probably also know that you can get your device's software so tangled up that the only solution is to restore it to its original factory specifications. You can keep pushing buttons and changing settings, but until you reset that device, it's never going to properly work.

You and I are far more valuable than a tablet or phone, but in the same way that software can get hung up, life can hang us up too. Life can be painful and hard. Rack up enough years on planet Earth and you might find yourself running a little sluggish too. Like a laptop stuck with that spinning circle whirling, you might find yourself a little unresponsive from time to time.

You can try to keep on keeping on, just plowing ahead with your day and your life as though nothing at all is wrong. But this option only delays the inevitable breakdown waiting for you, kind of like a computer that has irreparably crashed.

You too can be "restored to factory specifications"—to the Designer's original intent. You can return to God, seek his wisdom on things, and gain the restart that he alone can provide. If you've wandered from God's plans and are in a spun-out state today: simply tell him so. You can quietly pray this prayer: "Lord, set my eyes on your purpose for me today. I want your divine 'settings' reinstalled in my life, so that I can discern your presence, hear your voice, and do what you ask me to do."

A BLESSING FROM PAM

May you find courage to make this prayer your own
as you ask God for the reset you need.

Hearing God's Voice

My sheep listen to my voice;
I know them; and they follow me.

JOHN 10:27

A question I'm often asked is, *How does God speak to us?* If I'm in a playful mood, I'll say, "Pam and I have been married more than half our lives. When she calls and I answer and she says hi, how often do you think I respond with, 'Who *is* this?'"

The answer, of course, is *never*. I could be in a room stuffed with people and pick out Pam's voice from a hundred feet away. And it's not because she's loud. She's *not* loud; I'm just *trained*.

In the verse from John 10 above, we read that the shepherd's sheep knew his voice because they listened for it. They craned an ear to hear from him. They leaned in whenever he spoke.

If you want to hear from God, then elevate one of the following practices in your life. God *will* speak.

1. **Read God's Word.** God speaks to his followers through the holy Scriptures.

2. **Seek godly counsel.** If you face a weighty decision in life, look around for someone who is more mature in his or her faith than you and ask if you can buy them a cup of coffee and get their input on something.

3. **Pay attention to peace.** If you are faithfully practicing the disciplines of Bible reading, prayer, and walking in community with wise people, then rest assured that as God leads you, he will simultaneously give you peace.

Train yourself today to listen for the voice of your heavenly Father. He knows you by name! And he longs to communicate with you.

A BLESSING FROM PAM

May you learn what God's voice sounds like.
And today, may you find the direction you seek.

Motivated by Love

Surely he took up our infirmities and carried our sorrows, yet we considered him stricken by God, smitten by him, and afflicted. But he was pierced for our transgressions, he was crushed for our iniquities; the punishment that brought us peace was upon him, and by his wounds we are healed. We all, like sheep, have gone astray, each of us has turned to his own way; and the Lord has laid on him the iniquity of us all.

ISAIAH 53:4-6

At the start of every New Year, if I'm not careful I can start feeling terrible about myself. Based on the world's rampant "new year, new you" messaging, I can become discontent with every aspect of life in the blink of an eye. My inner monologue then tanks:

"Shape up, Brady!"

"Get it together, Brady!"

"Set some goals, why don't you?"

Left unchecked, this type of self-talk can leave me sulking in a pit of despair. Which is proof that shame and accusation aren't the most efficient ways to motivate a person to change.

Want a far better way? It's *love*.

The words of the prophet Isaiah here are profound. They remind us that even before we were sick, Jesus took our infirmities. Before we were afraid, he purchased our peace. Long before we knew we were lost, he came running to find us. He offered help before we knew we were in need.

Not once did Jesus take us in and say, "Shape up, would you?" in response. Not once did he shout, "Get it together!" Not once did he shame or accuse us. He simply came. And died. Out of love.

A BLESSING FROM PAM

Today, may you know that you're loved. May you believe that you're loved.
May you live as though you are loved.

Who God Says You Are

But you are a chosen people, a royal priesthood, a holy nation,
God's special possession, that you may declare the praises
of him who called you out of darkness into his wonderful light.

1 PETER 2:9

Labels are sticky. I don't know which labels you've affixed to yourself along the way, or which labels others have affixed to you—that you are not smart enough or not skilled enough or not talented enough ... that you are unattractive or unreliable or weak. But I do know that those labels tend to hang around—that is, until we find some new ones to stick to our lives.

As I matured in my faith in my twenties, I noticed that the way God talked about me as his son was far different from how I once thought of myself. I came across the verse above, from 1 Peter 2, during that era and was floored. I was chosen? I was royal? I was special ... to *God?*

The answer was yes. Also true: he views you the very same way. God values you. In fact, God thinks you are *so valuable* that he sacrificed his own Son for you. He thinks you are valuable enough to call you out from the world as one of his "holy" ones. He thinks you are valuable enough to invest in, so that someday you will look just like Christ.

To be found *valuable* by the Creator of the universe is no small thing. And yet that is how God views you and me. He holds us like precious gems.

A BLESSING FROM PAM

When you look in the mirror today, may you see yourself as God sees you:
wise, wonderful, worthy of his attention and care. As you interact with others today,
may you reflect that same level of divine acceptance and admiration to them.

Practicing Well

Then Jesus was led by the Spirit into the desert to be tempted by the devil.
After fasting forty days and forty nights, he was hungry. The tempter came to him
and said, "If you are the Son of God, tell these stones to become bread." Jesus
answered, "It is written: 'Man does not live on bread alone, but on every
word that comes from the mouth of God.'"

MATTHEW 4:1-4

For decades now, I have prioritized daily Bible reading. Every morning, I get alone with God. I read his Word. I underline things that catch my attention. I turn a few verses into a prayer back to him. I think and journal about what I've read.

I don't uphold this habit out of a sense of duty or obligation. I uphold it because I recognize that I am the sum of what I practice each day, and I want God's presence, power, and perspective to inform those things.

Immediately after Jesus was baptized by John the Baptist at the beginning of his earthly ministry, he was led into the wilderness to endure temptation from the enemy. The story started above continues with Satan challenging Jesus twice more, and to both temptations Jesus simply claimed truth from the Scriptures he knew and loved. In the end the enemy was found impotent. In the end, Satan left Jesus alone.

Jesus prioritized the Word of God long before temptation came his way such that during that temptation, obedience to how his Father would want him to respond was reflexive, natural, and sure. Which begs the question of you and me both: What are we prioritizing today?

A BLESSING FROM PAM

Today, may you know the absolute relief of relying not on your own ideas, your own imagination, perspective, will, or ways, but rather on the unparalleled power of the Word of God.

A Constant Communion Carriage

I am the vine; you are the branches. If you remain in me and I in you,
you will bear much fruit; apart from me you can do nothing.

JOHN 15:5

We take Communion most weeks at New Life, and the elements of bread and wine—or juice, in our case—remind us all of Christ's great sacrifice: his body broken, his blood spilled out, his vast love for us as daughters and sons. The bread always makes me think about the part of the Lord's Prayer that says we should ask God for our "daily bread," for sustenance along this journey of life. Whenever I bite into that tiny wafer, I realize afresh that I'm generally at my holiest, most-whole self just after I partake. Right after Communion, I am a person at peace. Whatever was irritating me or distracting me before Communion is momentarily suspended by the sheer force of communing with Love, with Grace. Right after Communion, I'm relaxed. I'm calm. I'm at rest. And I'm kind. By the time I close the service and step out of the worship auditorium, my irritations and distractions are starting to vie for attention again, but *immediately after* Communion, God is having his way in my life. Which is making me start to wonder, what if this "Communion carriage" could be true of me all the time?

What if I carried myself with peace and grace and kindness not just on the heels of the sacrament, but on Monday through Saturday too? What if *you* did the same—can you imagine the good that would do?

We say the wrong thing so much of the time because we're trying to satisfy our craving for the bread of heaven with the cheap-flour bread of earth. Jesus says, "Ask *me* for your daily bread, to survive what this day will hold," to which we say, "Nah, but thanks for the offer, Jesus. I'll just whip up some loaves on my own."

Jesus says, "Abide in me, and I'll abide in you, and you'll keep yourself out of trouble and your foot out of your mouth," to which we grin in patronizing fashion, thinking, "That Jesus. He's a persistent one. Doesn't he know I've already kneaded the dough?"

I can always tell when I'm refusing to feast on the sustenance Jesus offers, instead of preparing provisions on my own. I overreact to some usual life circumstance; I fire back at someone with my words; I power up over one of the staff members I'm called to lead; I try to pocket my sinfulness, hoping God isn't looking and therefore won't see—I say and do any of a thousand things, all in the name of nourishing myself.

God whispers my way, in attempt to catch my attention, to speak to me, to offer me some direction and help, but I don't hear a word of it over the clanging in the kitchen, where I'm busily baking bread.

But the flip-side is equally true: Whenever you and I choose to satisfy our appetites with the bread of heaven, we will tend toward spiritual sanity in every aspect of life: Our actions will reflect level-headedness; our posture will reveal peace; our words will carry weight and wisdom; our entire *being* will be rooted in Christ. We will come to every conversation as people whose core needs have been met, which means we won't need the other person to resolve any deep-seated aches in our hearts. Those aches will have already been set right by God, and now we can fully and freely engage.

That kind of life would be *delicious*, don't you think? No better bread to be found.

A BLESSING FROM PAM

Even if you're not literally taking Communion today, may you choose to commune with God somehow. And may the peace and comfort you know in that exchange stick with you all day long.

Who's Ruling You?

*When that day comes, you will cry out for relief from the
king you have chosen, but the Lord will not answer you in that day.*

1 SAMUEL 8:18

In the book of 1 Samuel, the nation Israel demanded an earthly king. Until then, the Israelites had been led by God, and by a series of judges he'd appointed to rule on his behalf. But God's leadership was becoming bothersome to them. "Make us a king to judge us like all the nations!" they said, their fists raised in opposition to God.[1]

God warned them about what would happen: The king would reign over them, conscript them for military service, make them laborers for his cause, and take the best of their possessions and redistribute them to his staff. "You will cry out in that day because of the king whom you have chosen for yourself," God promised (1 Samuel 8: 18), "and the LORD will not hear you in that day."

Let me be your King, God begged them.

I have your best interest at heart.

But the nation Israel was resolute, and nothing could stop them now.

We don't want your leadership, God.

Step aside. Let us do our own thing.

So, God delivered them a king. And the devastating effects took hold.

We can't run toward God when we're preoccupied with running away. And so, whether our disobedience looks like outright rebellion, as was the case for the Israelites, or whether it looks like negligence in carrying out his plans, we do well to stop, turn around, and race as fast as we can back to God, whenever we detect that we've bumped him off the throne of our lives.

A BLESSING FROM PAM

*May you rest in God's perfect provision today, with fresh awareness
of his goodness, his graciousness, and his commitment to leading you well.*

---

[1] *See 1 Samuel 8.5.*

Hitting the Jackpocket

If you then, though you are evil, know how to give good gifts to your children,
how much more will your Father in heaven give the Holy Spirit to those who ask him?

LUKE 11:13

When Abram and Callie were little, Pam's mom would send them a giant box of goodies every Easter. Toys, plush animals, tons of candy—those care packages were the highlight of every spring.

One year that box showed up, and after Callie and her brother tore through the contents, she looked at Pam and me and with a wide smile yelled, "Wow! We hit the *jackpocket!*"

The phrase stuck, and to this day, whenever something fortuitous happens around the Boyd household, someone will say, "We hit the jackpocket!"

This same sense of elation is what overtakes me whenever I come across these words from Luke 11:13. Jesus was teaching his disciples how to pray. He had already given them specific words to say, but now he wanted to convey the *heart* of God. "Ask and it will be given to you," he said; "seek and you will find; knock and the door will be opened to you. For everyone who asks receives; the one who seeks finds; and to the one who knocks, the door will be opened," (vv. 9-10).

Your Father is *good*, he was telling them. He's *generous*. He loves to *give you gifts*.

In Christ, you and I have already hit the jackpocket. We are hitting the jackpocket still today. And we will spend an eternity living lavishly, at the side of the one true King.

A BLESSING FROM PAM

May you be reminded that you serve a good Father, a Father who loves
to lavish you with good gifts. May you know that as you rely on his
strength and guidance, by his Spirit he will always provide.

What are You Waiting For?

Now there was a man in Jerusalem called Simeon, who was righteous and devout.
He was waiting for the consolation of Israel, and the Holy Spirit was on him.

LUKE 2:25

I love the Bible story about the devout man Simeon. Simeon had been told by the Holy Spirit that he would not die before he had seen the Lord's Messiah and was determined to take God at his word.

Which begs the question: Do you and I do the same?

Throughout Scripture, God promises that as we hope in him, he will renew our strength, (Isaiah 40:31); that when we come to him, he will give us rest, (Matthew 11:28-30); that because we are his children, his steadfast love will never depart from us, (Isaiah 54:10), just to name a few.

We know many of his promises. We probably like his promises to us. And yet how often do we take matters into our own hands instead of trusting that his promises are true?

We build our own form of strength instead of relying on the power of God.

We look to self-made forms of escapism instead of relying on God for rest.

We pursue facsimiles of love in all the wrong places instead of relying on the Creator of love.

To which I imagine God whispering, "Hey. Wait a second."

Or a minute. Or six months. Or six *decades*, if need be.

Wait until God gives us what we need.

Be known as ones who can wait.

A BLESSING FROM PAM

Like Simeon, may you be at peace today as you wait on the Lord.
The acceptance or love or satisfaction or financial breakthrough will be far,
far better when it comes to you via the hand of the Lord.

The Blessings of Perseverance

Consider it pure joy, my brothers and sisters, whenever you face trials of many kinds, because you know that the testing of your faith produces perseverance. Let perseverance finish its work so that you may be mature and complete, not lacking anything.

JAMES 1:2-4

Years ago, Pam and I lost a friend to cancer. She was fifty-seven years old. That turn of events would have been enough to bear on its own; still worse was that two days before her death, our community lost a young sheriff's deputy who was killed in the line of duty. And two days *after* her death seventeen students were gunned down in a Florida school. It has been said that grief comes in waves. That week, life felt like a tsunami destroying everything in its path.

During the ensuing weeks, our church hosted two funerals for our fallen brother, Pam and I grieved the death of our dear friend, and our country mourned as another school shooting took too many lives. It was a sorrowful time. And yet it was also a time of hope.

This world is broken, sinful, and bleak. And yet a new world awaits us, a world where there will be no more suffering or pain. If you and I can set our sights on that new reality, even as we agonize over school shootings and friends dying too young, we can help to usher in that future world—right here, right now, today.

Considering a trial "joyful" doesn't have to be an exercise in self-flagellation. It can instead be a tangible reminder to direct our attention to God. We may not understand the pain. We may not like the loss. But we can remain faithful to the One who holds the world in his hands, and who has promised to see us through.

A BLESSING FROM PAM

May you be comforted by the God of all comfort in the imperfections of life today.

JANUARY 11

Getting Past Our Past

Therefore, there is now no condemnation for
those who are in Christ Jesus.

ROMANS 8:1

I was nearly an adult when I finally surrendered my life in full to the lordship of Jesus Christ, which meant I'd done some living—some living that wasn't honoring to God. Once I was "in Christ," I had a sinking feeling: *Ugh. If only I could undo some of the awful things I did ...*

Can you relate? Do you too have some things in your past that you desperately wish you could get past?

In Romans 8:1, the language used by the apostle Paul refers not to believers having been paroled, but to our having been *pardoned*: In Christ, our record is wiped totally clean, which should come as very good news.

I suspect you and I both would find it ridiculous for a prisoner who has been pardoned to continue living in a prison cell, and yet that's exactly what you and I are doing when we insist on identifying more readily with the pain and mistakes of our past than with the future that has been secured for us in Christ.

God never condemned you. He condemned the sin that was *destroying* you. But because of Jesus' sacrifice, there is now *no condemnation for us*. We have been freed. We now can live free. The door to the cell that has us living in bondage has been swung open wide, and God is whispering, "Go! Go and live!"

A BLESSING FROM PAM

Today may you trust God to erase all evidence of bondage and
lead you to the freedom he has in store for you.

Humility First

As a prisoner for the Lord, then, I urge you to live a life worthy of the calling you have received. Be completely humble and gentle; be patient, bearing with one another in love. Make every effort to keep the unity of the Spirit through the bond of peace.

EPHESIANS 4:1-3

Years ago, a colleague and I had a disagreement, and as we parted ways that day, my stomach churned. Our relationship had been fractured, and I wasn't sure it would ever be repaired.

Later that evening, I went outside to think. I needed to pray. I needed to gain insight on how to proceed.

Unfortunately, that's not what I did.

Instead of thinking, praying, or gaining insight, I fumed.

Before I headed back inside, I sensed God trying to get my attention. It was as if he said, "Our time is up already? Brady, I had direction to offer to you, but you were so distracted being angry that you couldn't detect my voice."

Whenever I come across Paul's words in Ephesians 4:1-3—especially the part about being "completely humble"—I think about that night.

When you and I face a challenge in life, we have two choices: we can look for the Holy Spirit, or we can look for a fight. We can't do both simultaneously, and only one of those paths will point us toward peace.

If we want the presence of God's Spirit, we must assume a posture of humility first. We can't elbow our way into God's presence, and fuming doesn't welcome him in. As we let ourselves become smaller, we invite God to become bigger. And from that place of strength our heavenly Father begins to set all things in our world right.

A BLESSING FROM PAM

Whatever has you feeling stirred up today, may you choose humility as the first action you take.

Three Key Words

There are different kinds of gifts, but the same Spirit distributes them.
There are different kinds of service, but the same Lord. There are different kinds
of working, but in all of them and in everyone it is the same God at work.

1 CORINTHIANS 12:4-6

I've known people who during midlife spiritually gave up. They barely went to church anymore. They were no longer involved in helping meet the needs of people in their city who were struggling. Their prayer life was anemic at best.

Around my fiftieth birthday I made a decision that has served me well to this day. I decided that as soon as I woke each morning, I'd pray a simple prayer: "Come, Holy Spirit."

It was my shorthand way of saying, "God, it is only by your Spirit that I have spiritual gifts to offer this world in need. It is only by your Spirit that I can be motivated to serve. And it is only by your Spirit that the work you long to do in and through me can occur. So before anything else happens today, I welcome the activity of your Spirit. I surrender to your leadership all over again."

Regardless of your age or stage in life, if you are feeling spiritually stuck, may I humbly exhort you to pray this three-word prayer each day and see what God chooses to do?

Come, Holy Spirit.

Come awaken our hearts to your will, your wishes, your ways.

Come give us passion for your name, for your mission, for the people your Son came to save.

Come help us run our race and not grow tired.

Come, Holy Spirit.

Come.

A BLESSING FROM PAM

As you face each sunrise to come, may you push aside all other distractions
and willingly invite God's Spirit to come, to move, to live, and to breathe.

Laying Ourselves Bare

How can a young man keep his way pure? By living according to your word.
I seek you with all my heart; do not let me stray from your commands.
I have hidden your word in my heart that I might not sin against you.

PSALM 119:9-11

Serious-minded Christ followers long to honor God.

They long to honor God with their attitude. They want to hold onto hope even when circumstances seem hopeless and bleak.

They long to honor God with their words. They want the words they speak to be true words, life-giving words, loving words.

They long to honor God with their actions. They want to consider others' needs ahead of their own.

But despite all those noble intentions, sometimes it's hard to be the people we long to be. We get tired. We get hungry. We get annoyed. We get sick. And before we know it, we think and say and do exactly what we wish we hadn't thought and said and done.

It's here that we need the promise of Psalm 119, which says that if we hide God's word in our hearts, being careful to live according to the instruction we find there, we will keep our way "pure."

When we let Scripture determine our lives, our attitude will be kept pure, our words will be kept pure, and our actions will be kept pure.

How can we know if our lives are honoring the God we say we serve? Our lives must be determined by his unfailing Word.

A BLESSING FROM PAM

Today, I give you a blessing based on the apostle Paul's encouragement to believers in Colossae more than two thousand years ago: "Whatever you do, in word or deed, do everything in the name of the Lord Jesus, giving thanks to God the Father through him," (Colossians 3:17).

A Personal Pursuit

Suppose one of you has a hundred sheep and loses one of them. Does he not leave the ninety-nine in the open country and go after the lost sheep until he finds it?

LUKE 15:4

One of my friends wanted to make a good impression on his first date with the woman who would one day become his wife. Given that his definition of "gourmet" revolved around pickle-flavored potato chips, he really upped his game. He purchased a picnic basket, fancy nuts, cheeses, breads, and fruit. He then bought a leather-bound copy of poems written by her favorite poet and read the entire book before the date to find just the poem to read to her that afternoon. He picked out a perfect spot near the river's edge, and to nobody's surprise, that date lasted *ten full hours*.

That woman wanted to stay there in that place, doing her best to freeze the moment in time, because she felt seen and cared for in a deeply personal way.

It is no stretch to say that our heavenly Father pursues his children in the same personal way. If the entire population of the world were accounted for while you aimlessly strayed from his sight, just like the shepherd in the parable we read above, he would *leave them to come find you*.

He sees you. He values you. He knows you deeply and loves you still.

You are not lost in the crowd. Your Father is looking for you as an individual. He is pursuing you—for *you*.

A BLESSING FROM PAM

It's easy to feel lost in the crowd, to feel unseen by everyone—including God. Today, may you realize with fresh understanding that God is near to you, that he adores you, and that his pursuit of you will never come to an end.

Healing Words

*The mouth of the righteous is a fountain of life, but
the mouth of the wicked conceals violence.*

PROVERBS 10:11

Remember the playground chant, "Sticks and stones may break my bones, but words will never hurt me"? Whoever came up with that line has never conversed with a human being. I know this because of all the pain I've sustained in life, some of the deepest pain came via someone else's *words*.

Words are powerful.

Words are weighty.

How we use our words matters deeply to God.

In Proverbs 10:11 we see that one delineation between righteous people and wicked people is simply the words they choose to speak. If we want to be righteous, then we will choose to speak words that teach, that encourage, that heal. If we want to be wicked, then we will choose to speak words that deceive, that discourage, that harm.

Jesus chose righteousness every time. His words were always thoughtful, carefully placed, wise. He drew people to his Father with his words instead of repelling them, shaming them, indicting them, belittling them, or powering up over them.

What a *fantastic* way to live.

I'm still learning how to use my words well, but I'm better than I used to be. Hard words point to a hard heart. I don't want my heart to be hard.

I'm guessing the same is true for you.

A BLESSING FROM PAM

*As you talk with others today, may God gently remind you that he longs to communicate
through you to a world deeply in need of acceptance, grace, and love.*

Fruitful Friction

How good and pleasant it is when brothers live together in unity!
It is like precious oil poured on the head, running down the beard, running
down on Aaron's beard, down upon the collar of his robes.

PSALM 133:1-2

Out of curiosity, what bugs you?

I'll tell you what bugs me.

It bugs me when someone I'm talking to starts texting someone else. So rude.

It bugs me when people drive slowly in the passing lane.

Coffee breath *really* bugs me.

Guess what? To live in this world is to be bugged.

Here's a humbling thought: Who is bugged by *you*? This works both ways, you know.

I don't mind aging if I'm "sage-ing" too." It's okay to get older if we're also getting wiser, and here's something wise people do: They take others' annoyances in stride. "Iron sharpens iron," Proverbs 27:17 says, which means that if we want to stay sharp in life, we'll need to invite friction—useful friction. Fruitful friction.

The work of the Holy Spirit is always most evident in environments not of annoyance and judgment, but of contentment, generosity, peace.

Just for today, choose not to be annoyed. Choose to let the ministry of God's Spirit flow freely through you so that you can enable, not thwart, his work.

If you don't, just know I'll be bugged.

A BLESSING FROM PAM

Whenever I'm annoyed by other people's words or actions, I take five seconds to ask how
I might "bear with" that person instead of judging them for their annoying behavior. It's all the time
God needs to recenter me and begin to work through me. May you take as many five-second pauses
today as are necessary. May you be a conduit of love and peace.

Where Does Your Loyalty Lie?

*For the eyes of the Lord run to and fro throughout the whole earth to show
himself strong on behalf of those whose heart is loyal to him.*

2 CHRONICLES 16:9

Back when major corporations paid for full-season sponsorships of NASCAR teams, many fans of the sport made buying decisions based solely on which company was behind "their guy." In the home-improvement space, for example, fans of Tony Stewart only shopped at Home Depot, while fans of Jimmie Johnson only shopped at Lowe's. A buddy of mine used to drive past three Home Depot stores on his way to the nearest Lowe's. He could need a five-dollar plumbing part, and still he'd make that extended drive.

The guy was loyal.

Sometimes that silly story comes to mind when I happen upon this verse from 2 Chronicles 16, which says that God is in the heavens searching the planet for one who is loyal to him. God is impressed with loyalty.

Loyalty to God means we "drive past" all other distractions, all other idols, all other things that vie for our allegiance. It means we yield *only and ever* to him.

In essence, here is what God says: "As you are loyal to me, I will show myself strong on your behalf," (2 Chron. 16:9). To have God's strength operating in our favor is the greatest imaginable gift. Think of all you could do, if only you had an infusion of divine power and strength! You could hope without wavering. You could love without needing. You could serve without getting. You could live with absolutely no lack.

Choose today your loyalty.

Choose today to attach your loyalty to God.

A BLESSING FROM PAM

*As God searches the whole earth today
for one who is loyal to him, may his gaze rest on you.*

The Faithfulness of a Friend

A friend loves at all times, and a
brother is born for a time of adversity.

PROVERBS 17:17

My younger brother Dave and I went to school in East Texas, and to get there we'd ride the bus. There was a boy on our route named Sammy who was the classic bully at our school: a big, mean dude who loved to stir up trouble.

These days my brother is six-foot-two and very strong, but at age twelve and thirteen, he was a little scrawny and kind of a loner—the perfect target for Sammy.

One day I was sitting near the front of the bus when I heard a scuffle toward the rear. I turned to see Sammy wailing on my brother, and something in me snapped. I fell upon that kid like David on the Philistines, and I beat the tar out of Sammy.

It was a bad day. But while I deeply regret the violence, there was something beautiful about that wretched experience: my brother knew that no matter what unfolded, I had his back.

A brother is born for adversity.

A sister, too.

We are called to be faithful in friendship, fighting not *with* them but *for* them.

I wonder, how faithful are you as a friend? Do you fight spiritually for those you love?

A BLESSING FROM PAM

May God bring to mind in this moment a friend you need to thank today.
And may he give you every resource you need to be a faithful friend in return.

Fearless

Even though I walk through the
darkest valley, I will fear no evil, for you are with
me; your rod and your staff, they comfort me.

PSALM 23:4

I have a congenital heart condition that necessitates open-heart surgery every few years, and a decade ago, when facing one of those surgeries, I was struck by a spirit of fear. I went through surgery fine, but five days post-op my doctor said, "You still have some potentially fatal rhythms in your heart." Sobering news for sure.

In the end, my doctor surgically implanted a defibrillator so that I could live life for at least another twenty years. But between the bad news and the life-saving intervention, there was nothing but fear. I was forty-four with a wife and two young kids. I was part of a thriving ministry. "Potentially fatal rhythms" didn't fit into my plan.

For eight days, I lay in a hospital bed, praying the same line to God a thousand times: "Lord, I'm grateful you're near to me." In my fear, I was glad he was there.

"Even though I walk through the darkest valley," the psalmist wrote, "I will fear no evil."

He didn't have a choice about whether to walk through the valley, but he did have a choice about how he'd respond.

So do we.

When we choose to arrest fear and live by faith in God instead, we can do *anything*. Because God is near, we can hope. Because God is near, we can love. Because God is near, we can serve. Because God is near, we can laugh. Because God is near, we can rest assured that fear won't take us down.

A BLESSING FROM PAM

Regardless of the chaos swirling around your life right now,
may you know that the God of the universe is near to you.

The Case for Kindness

*When a Samaritan woman came to draw water, Jesus said to her, "Will you give
me a drink?" (His disciples had gone into town to buy food.) The Samaritan woman
said to him, "You are a Jew and I am a Samaritan woman. How can you ask
me for a drink?" (For Jews do not associate with Samaritans.) Jesus answered
her, "If you knew the gift of God and who it is that asks you for a drink,
you would have asked him and he would have given you living water.*

JOHN 4:7-10

It was a typical day for the woman living in Samaria, who needed to frequent the
communal well to draw water to drink.

As she arrived, Jesus was already sitting there. Rather scandalously, as the text above
reveals, he engaged her in a spiritual conversation. The outcome? The woman was
utterly *compelled.*

"Sir, give me this water so that I won't get thirsty and have to keep coming here to draw
water," she said, (v. 15).

In other words: *Salvation.* Let it be mine!

The lesson here for us is this: Whenever we are fortunate enough to engage in a
spiritual conversation with someone who doesn't yet know Jesus, we must keep the
main thing the main thing. The other person may have faulty logic, mixed-up doctrine,
and wrong assumptions about God. Even so, let truth, love, and tenderness override
your need to debate.

I get it: It feels good to win an argument, doesn't it?

You know what feels even better? Winning the heart of a friend.

A BLESSING FROM PAM

*Today, may you lay down the burden you feel to have all the answers
and instead focus all your attention of listening and loving well.*

How People Grow

*Follow my example, as I follow
the example of Christ.*

1 CORINTHIANS 11:1

One of the most succinct definitions of discipleship was written from the apostle Paul to believers in Corinth: "Follow my example, as I follow the example of Christ," he said.

That's discipleship: *Follow me as I follow Jesus.*

Trust me as I trust him. Serve as I serve. Love as I love. Live as I live.

Pam and I have been part of five churches throughout the thirty-plus years we've been married. And as I look back on each, I realize that the reason she and I know how to be faithful Christians today is because people in those places taught us how.

We learned how to be parents by watching other parents get it right.

We learned how to worship by watching other worshipers worship God.

We learned how to pray by being around serious prayer warriors.

It strikes me afresh as I think about it now that the most important life lessons I've picked up along the way I picked up inside the Church. I learned them in Christian community.

These lessons are what bind us together as believers: how to relate lovingly with God, how to relate lovingly with one another, how to bring people up in the faith. If you consider the two parts to the word *community*, you'll see that "common unity" is our ultimate goal. Politics can't unify us. Education can't unify us. Religion can't unify us. Only the person of Jesus can unify us. It's only by following Jesus—and then teaching others to do the same—that we'll ever realize our potential ... that we'll ever truly grow up.

A BLESSING FROM PAM

*May you find the examples of godliness you long for as you walk through this year.
And may you be a godly example for others.*

Give and Take

*All the believers were one in heart and mind. No one claimed that
any of their possessions was their own, but they shared everything they had.*

ACTS 4:32-33

When I was sixteen, my parents lost everything: their house, their business, everything. I understand what it feels like to be a "taker." When you are destitute financially, you simply have nothing to give.

Flash forward to today. Each year, Pam and I give a little extra money to scholarship kids who want to come to Desperation but whose families can't afford it. So, by God's grace and a little financial self-control through the years, I also know what it feels like to be a "giver." I now know the joy of being able to give.

Every weekend, our church is filled both with people whose faith is hanging on by a thread and with those who are bubbling over with trust in God. It's filled both with people who are feeling vibrant and strong and with those who received a devastating diagnosis just yesterday. It's filled with those whose marriages are thriving and with those who fought viciously in the car on the way. Anytime we gather as a church, we have both givers and takers in our midst.

Here's what this means: If you are a giver today, give! And if because of circumstance you are a taker, please ask for what you need. If you have excess, I guarantee someone in need could use it. If you are the one in need, I guarantee someone has a little extra right now. Give as you are able. Receive as needs arise. And no one will be in need.

A BLESSING FROM PAM

*Today may you honestly assess your level of need
and give or take while trusting in God.*

What Must Go, When Jesus Comes

But who can endure the day of his coming? Who can stand when he appears?
For he will be like a refiner's fire or a launderer's soap.

MALACHI 3:2-3

Our greatest aim as believers is intimacy with God because it's how we become more like Jesus. If our longings tell us anything, they tell us that we want Jesus.

> More of Jesus.
> All of Jesus.
> Jesus at every turn.
> And yet, can we really *withstand* the presence of holy God?
> Because when Jesus *comes in*, some things must *go out*.
> Pride comes to mind.
> Lust. Greed. Spite. Hopelessness. Senselessness. Rage.

Jesus presents a crossroads, every time he appears. We can continue in our worldliness, or we can join him in his cause. We can't do both. Also true: we can't do neither. He issues a choice: A or B.

And yet talk to anyone who has been following Jesus for any length of time, and you'll come to understand that there is no better way than the way of Christ. There is no better life to live. Which is why we welcome him with open arms. "Disturb us, O Lord," 16th-century English explorer and fellow believe Sir Francis Drake once wrote, "when with the abundance of things possessed, we lose our thirst for the Water of Life; When, having fallen in love with time, we have ceased to dream of Eternity; And our efforts to build a new earth have allowed Your vision for a new heaven to grow dim."

A BLESSING FROM PAM

As you encounter the choice throughout today—the way of Jesus,
or the way of the world?—may you insist on Jesus every time.

In It But Not Of It

Do not love the world
or anything in the world.

1 JOHN 2:15

There are many things about this world that I love. Gardening comes to mind. Freshly fallen snow. Traveling.

You might love riding motorcycles on Saturday mornings with your friends. Or ballroom dancing. Or throwing hatchets at trees. Truly there are as many things to love as there are people to love them. This world can be a magnificent place. But God's Word is clear that despite all the beauty and grandeur and wonderful things to do that this world offers us, we aren't to love it more than we love God.

His Word reminds us that we can never be our own god. "For there is one God and one mediator between God and mankind," 1 Timothy 2:5 says, "the man Christ Jesus."

His Word asserts that his truth is the only truth there is. "Your word is truth," John 17:17 says. Which means that anything that contradicts God's Word by definition is not the truth.

If you're wondering whether you've become unwittingly captivated by the world, ask yourself these two questions:

1. Is there anything in my life that is keeping me from fully enjoying God's love?

2. Is there anything in my life that I love more than discovering and doing the will of God?

Only one thing will truly satisfy, and that thing is not of this world but of God. It is him, in fact—his presence, his affection, his attention, his grace. If any appetite in your life is out of control, let it be only your appetite for him.

A BLESSING FROM PAM

May everything you enjoy in creation today point you directly
back to the Creator—to God himself, the One who made all things.

Build Up and Benefit

Do not let any unwholesome talk come out of your mouths, but only what is helpful for building others up according to their needs, that it may benefit those who listen.

EPHESIANS 4:29

For years, Abram and I went to breakfast nearly every Saturday morning, usually to McDonald's. On one of those outings, after unpacking our food I realized the cashier had given us the wrong meals. My nonverbals were shouting as I headed back toward the counter, *What kind of idiot can't get a simple breakfast order right?*

Fortunately the Lord arrested my attitude before awful words came out of my mouth, and by the time I reached the counter and plunked the food down, I was able to speak with gentleness and grace. "Ma'am," I said, "I think my son and I got someone else's order by mistake."

And as I heard her reply I thanked God that he'd saved me from myself. "Oh!" she said. "Let me fix that for you. And by the way, *my family and I love being part of New Life.*"

Gulp. Close call.

This reminder from the apostle Paul should be viewed as nothing short of a *gift* by you and me. To recap: we should speak only what is helpful for building others up according to their needs, and we should be sure that every word that proceeds from our mouths benefits the person we're speaking to. *Build up and benefit.* Build up and benefit with every word that we speak.

A BLESSING FROM PAM

Today, if you are tempted to lash out at someone, by God's insight and power may you choose to "build up and benefit" instead.

The Law of the Farm: Preparation

*He taught them many things by parables, and in his teaching
said: "Listen! A farmer went out to sow his seed."*

MARK 4:2-3

I grew up in northwest Louisiana in an 800-square-foot house that my mom and dad built with their own hands. My dad worked at a poultry plant as a factory worker but was also a farmer who kept vegetables on the two acres behind our home.

Dad would hitch our bare-bones plow to the neck of his horse, Ranger, head out to the field, and start carving long, straight rows. After the rows were cut, Dad and we boys would head to the feed store to buy seeds. Corn. Okra. Purple-hull peas. We'd dig little holes, drop the seeds in, and wait. And then sure enough, the following summer we'd have barrels of fresh vegetables. The law of the farm was formed in me as a boy: If we wanted to eat, we first had to prepare.

Spiritually speaking, if you and I hope to see God produce anything worthwhile in our lives, we must prepare the soil of our lives. Throughout Scripture, soil is symbolic of the human heart. If a heart is bitter, unforgiving, or given to perpetual sin, God may use that heart to accomplish his purposes, but it won't be enjoyable for the person to whom that heart belongs.

On the flip side, when a person chooses to have a humble heart, a tender heart, a heart that is quick to obey God, God will entrust that person with exciting assignments. He will grow great things in that soil.

A BLESSING FROM PAM

*May you slow down today to consider the state of your heart,
setting down offenses and regrets, picking up godliness and excellence instead.*

The Law of the Farm: Seed-Sowing

*As he was scattering the seed, some fell along the
path, and the birds came and ate it up.*

MARK 4:4

If we want God to produce something fruitful in our lives, we first must prepare the soil of our hearts; only then can seed be sown. The "seed" is the Word of God, and unlike other seed that may sprout once and then decompose, this seed is continuously articulate—it never stops talking, never stops communicating, never stops producing. In this way, the Scriptures are no less than *alive*. "Living and active"—that's how the writer of Hebrews describes God's Word, (Hebrews 4:12).

So if the Scriptures are living and breathing and moving and are able to produce fruit in our lives each time we read them, why do so many believers struggle to live in any sort of fruitful way?

I've often said that one of the real dangers of having been a follower of Jesus for a long time is that we already know how every Bible story ends. We know that Moses and his people get across the Red Sea before Pharaoh captures them. We know that Jesus makes it out of the tomb. We know that Goliath gets a rock to the forehead. We can become so acquainted with these stories that we effectually silence them. They hold no mystery for us any longer. We breeze past them, thinking, *Yeah, yeah, I remember this one. What else you got?*

Is the soil of your heart ready for God to plant new seed? If so, commit now to coming to the Word of God with fresh eyes, eager to see what God wants to show you *today*.

A BLESSING FROM PAM

*May you come to God's Word today
ready to learn something new of him.*

The Law of the Farm: Watering

*Some fell on rocky places, where it did not have much soil. It sprang up
quickly, because the soil was shallow. But when the sun came up, the plants
were scorched, and they withered because they had no root.*

MARK 4:5-6

We prepare the soil of our hearts. We welcome the seed God longs to plant. And
then this: we invite the watering of the Spirit of God.

In the Bible, water is synonymous with the activity of the Holy Spirit. In the same
way that God's Word is living and active, the Spirit of God is living and active,
flowing, streaming, coursing through our lives.

When I was a kid, once my dad had prepared the soil and lain down seed, his
thoughts turned to rain. I pastored for a time in the farming town of Hereford,
Texas, and one September, we got a steady rain that lasted for days. "Brady," one
guy told me, "that out there's a million-dollar rain."

That three-day rain event all but secured the October harvest. Our community
was *thrilled*.

You and I don't want a deluge of God's Spirit. It would wipe us out! No, we want
what Hereford enjoyed that year: a slow drip for days on end. Just a bit today, a
bit tomorrow, a bit the day after that. A lifestyle, you might say, of rain.

As with rain encountering soil, when the Spirit of God hits our lives, something
miraculous happens. It's unseen, below the surface of life. But it's preparatory
for something incredible to burst through. It's growth—spiritual growth. It's
transformation from what *was* to what God *intends you to be*.

A BLESSING FROM PAM

*May the activity of God's Spirit fill you to overflowing today. May you know
that God is nearby. May you know that transformation can be yours.*

The Law of the Farm: Weed-Pulling

*Other seed fell among thorns, which grew up and choked
the plants, so that they did not bear grain.*

MARK 4:7

The soil is prepared, the seeds are sown, the plot is watered, and things are starting to happen underground. But in addition to the seed emerging, weeds will also sprout. For that tiny bud to turn into anything truly fruitful, weeding must occur.

Weeds are things that consume time, energy, creativity, or money and keep us from bearing godly fruit. As I write this, people are gearing up for March Madness, and it's all I can do to put my bracket away and focus on anything else. March Madness isn't evil. Having fun filling in a bracket isn't evil. But the moment my obsession with March Madness overtakes my obsession with encountering the living God, I've got a problem on my hands.

When looking for weeds, watch for anything that keeps you from fully enjoying God. Leave those weeds untended, and they will overtake the whole scene.

I wonder, what are the weeds threatening to choke growth in your life today? Are you giving more energy to a dysfunctional friendship than to daily prayer? Are you spending so much time at the gym that have nothing left for God? These things aren't inherently bad. It's just that they're keeping you from ultimate good.

My advice: get in there and get those weeds out. Even if it's just for a season, never knowingly let a weed stick around.

A BLESSING FROM PAM

*Today, may you know the satisfaction of enjoying a freshly weeded garden.
There's nothing better than seeing nothing but beautiful green buds set
against jet-black soil. That scene says health. It says growth. It says life.*

The Law of the Farm: Waiting

Still other seed fell on good soil. It came up, grew and produced
a crop, some multiplying thirty, some sixty, some a hundred times.

MARK 4:8

After my dad had completed the steps of preparing the soil and planting and watering the seed, never once did he step back and said, "Hmph. It's been fifteen minutes, and still: *nothing*. Must just be bad seed."

Yet often, that's the exact posture we assume before God. "God," we say, "I prayed fifteen minutes ago, and still: *nothing*. Don't you have an answer for me yet?"

We get frustrated that the payment hasn't come through. Or the child hasn't shaped up. Or the diagnosis hasn't changed. And while I understand these frustrations and experience them myself from time to time, when we have put our trust in God, just because we can't see what's happening doesn't mean that nothing is.

Dad knew that twelve or thirteen days after getting seed into the ground, green shoots of life would finally break through. He couldn't predict it. He couldn't control it. But it happened every time. This was the law of the farm.

I don't know what you're praying for these days, but if you are a follower of Jesus, I guarantee that God is working on your behalf to grow good things in your life. Anticipate divine activity in your future. Keep your heart pure. Let God's Spirit flow through your life. Work diligently to pull up every last weed. And then trust that God is at work, germinating, germinating, germinating until the day when *pop*, those shoots appear.

A BLESSING FROM PAM

May you know that God will make good on his promise to finish what he has started in you.
Growth may be happening under the surface of your life, but for the believer it's always there.

FEBRUARY

"What knots are you struggling to untie these days? Have you sought help from your heavenly Father? He longs for you to walk in wisdom! He'll share his wisdom with you."

- Pastor Brady Boyd -

The Necessity of Rest

When the devil had finished all this tempting, he left
him [Jesus] until an opportune time.

LUKE 4:13

When I first started pastoring I noticed that if I wasn't careful about managing my work hours and my rest, I'd get irritable, selfish, impatient, and annoyed. And once those things show up, they're tough to evict. Over the years I've reflected on Jesus' time in the wilderness as Jesus' earthly ministry was being launched. After the devil tried (and failed) three times to compel Jesus to sin, Luke 4:13 says that he "left him [Jesus] until an opportune time."

The devil is a *strategist*. He knows when we are hungry, when we're dehydrated, when we have been sitting in front of a computer for too long, and also when we're tired, and he chooses then to pounce.

When we're tired, we think everything is falling apart. Our health is crumbling. Our marriage is in crisis. Our kids have become vagrants. Our job is for the birds. But then we get a solid night's sleep, and *poof*! Our better selves emerge.

If you are weary today, please rest. Do not give Satan the satisfaction of taking you down when you're tired. Pull away, just as Jesus was known to do. Quiet your mind's spin cycle. Stop talking until you can use your words to build up instead of tear down. Ask your heavenly Father for help, and expect him to provide it. He loves to restore his followers—mind, body, spirit, strength, and soul.

A BLESSING FROM PAM

Today, may you rest. And may you return to your obligations with fresh perspective,
renewed energy, and a sense of strength to accomplish the work at hand.

First, the Going

All authority in heaven and on earth has been given to me. Therefore
go and make disciples of all nations, baptizing them in the name of the Father
and of the Son and of the Holy Spirit, and teaching them to obey everything I have
commanded you. And surely I am with you always, to the very end of the age.

MATTHEW 28:18-20

Before Jesus left his earthly ministry, he issued a mandate to his followers for how they would behave in the world. His disciples were fretful over his departure, so these instructions, called the Great Commission, were intended to clarify the plan.

These commands are straightforward, yet somehow as believers we tend to complicate things. Instead of going, we stay put. Instead of making disciples, we criticize sinners for their sin. Instead of inviting people into the waters of baptism, we indict them for their wayward lifestyles. Instead of teaching people everything Jesus has taught us, we take them to task in Jesus' name.

Let's keep it simple, just as Jesus did.

Let's start by *going*. Let's step outside our safe circles of comfort and reach out to someone "out there." We can ask an earnest question, we can tug the ear bud from our ear and listen attentively to the answer, we can ask a follow-up question after that. We can look someone in the eye. We can convey the care of Jesus. We can open our minds and hearts. We can do what God has asked us to do.

A BLESSING FROM PAM

May you be empowered and emboldened today to go; to engage someone in conversation that may turn spiritual; to speak the name of Jesus as you tell your story; to trust that as you make yourself available to God, God will avail much in and through you.

Flawed but Faithful

"Simon, Simon, Satan has asked to sift all of you as wheat.
But I have prayed for you, Simon, that your faith may not fail.
And when you have turned back, strengthen your brothers.".

LUKE 22:31-32

It was Jesus, live and in person, standing before him, daunting news on his lips. "Satan has asked for you," he said to Simon, "that he may sift all of you as wheat."

Can you imagine how sobering it would feel to have Jesus say those words to you?

Fill in your name, and see how it feels. *Satan has asked for you, to sift all of you as wheat.*

Can't you just say no to the ask??

Jesus wasn't tricking Simon here; he was prophesying to him. He was saying, "Simon, you are about to make a huge mistake. But even in your misstep, you don't have to fall away from your faith."

Jesus wanted Simon to know that even before Satan had tempted Simon, even before Simon had failed, Jesus had been interceding on his behalf. Did you know that right now, as you're reading these words, Jesus is interceding to the Father on your behalf?

Yes, he knows that we are flawed and that our faith will falter from time to time.

But because we are his beloved children, Jesus believes for our eventual return.

Jesus is faithful to us, even when we are not faithful to him.

Don't lose your faith as you falter. Life doesn't have to go that way. Borrow Jesus' belief in your ability to come home again ... to return to the lover of your soul.

A BLESSING FROM PAM

Today, may you persevere, so that when you have done the will of God,
you will receive what he has promised.

41

Divine Insight

*Call to me and I will answer you and tell you great
and unsearchable things you do not know.*

JEREMIAH 33:3

One evening when Abram was a teenager, I noticed that he was quieter than usual. I asked him what was up, but he blew me off. "I'm okay," he said.

I knew that wasn't the case, so I asked God for help. "What's going on with Abram?" I asked, to which God inaudibly responded, *It's his relationships.*

I prayed until I gained clarity on what the nature of the problem was, and then I said to Abram, "If I can tell you exactly what's bugging you, will you agree to talk with me about it?"

He was intrigued and nodded his head.

I laid out three big situations that were troubling him, Abram's eyes growing wider with each one, and when I was done with my little spiel, he said, "Dad, how did you do that?"

"It's not a party trick," I said. "It's the wisdom of the Lord."

I could have racked my brain for hours and not gained an ounce of insight regarding what was wrong in my son's life. But after one earnest prayer, I had wisdom from on high.

What knots are you struggling to untie today? Have you sought wisdom on those knots from God? Your heavenly Father longs for you to walk in wisdom! The last thing he will do is hide that wisdom from you. Quiet yourself. Get rid of all distractions for a moment. Humble yourself before God. And ask him for the direction you need. He loves to answer that prayer with insight that you simply can't get anywhere else.

A BLESSING FROM PAM

*May you come quickly before God, lay out your struggle,
and trust that he will gladly guide your steps.*

How to Know When You've Forgiven

Therefore, as God's chosen people, holy and dearly loved, clothe yourselves with compassion, kindness, humility, gentleness, and patience. Bear with each other and forgive one another if any of you has a grievance against someone. Forgive as the Lord forgave you. And over all these virtues put on love, which binds them all together in perfect unity.

COLOSSIANS 3:12-14

I've been in pastoral ministry for more than three decades now, and if I had to make a list of the topics I'm most often asked about regarding how to live the Christian life, among the top ten would definitely be *forgiveness*. People want to know why they have to forgive. They want to know how many times they need to forgive. They want to know what words to use when forgiving another person. And then there's this one: "How do I know if I've truly forgiven the person who wronged me?"

That's what we'll address today.

If you wonder if you've truly forgiven another person, there are two tests I'd ask you to run. If you can say the following two statements and mean them from the bottom of your heart, then in my estimation you have truly forgiven, in accordance with what the Bible asks us to do: "Forgive us our debts," Jesus taught his disciples to pray in Matthew 6:12-15, "as we also have forgiven our debtors."

Here are the two statements:

1. **"Nothing is owed."**

2. **"Nothing is claimed."**

If someone has wronged you and you have truly forgiven him or her, then you can say honestly, "Nothing further is owed." That person doesn't owe you an apology, an act of contrition, or any other form of recompense. You have chosen to forgive the offense, and you have moved forward in peace. *Nothing further is owed.*

Whenever I run this test in my own life, I am reminded of the words of 1 Peter 2:23, which says, "When they [Jesus' accusers] hurled their insults at him [Jesus], he did not retaliate; when he suffered, he made no threats. Instead, he entrusted himself to him who judges justly."

That last part is key, when we're talking about forgiveness from one person to another: rather than fighting for vengeance or seeking retribution, we must learn to entrust ourselves to our heavenly Father, who always judges justly.

And then there's the test of saying (and meaning) this statement: "Nothing is claimed." When you hold fast to bitterness over a wrong done to you, the person who wronged you is claiming space in your mind and heart. In the frontier days of our country, people would hold "claims" to parcels of land, which meant that nobody else could squat there and call the space their own. Similarly, when you and I allow someone else to "claim" space in our thoughts and emotions, other residents—joy, orderliness, contentment, peace—can't simultaneously call that space home. To say that "nothing is claimed" simply means that you cease handing over space to the issue—and to the person who caused the issue to emerge. You reclaim that territory as your own, inviting God's Spirit to take up residence there and help you to move forward by grace.

I need to remind you—and me as well—that we simply can't make these declarations apart from the power of God. It's not natural to be offended and then to say things like, "I forgive you. Nothing is owed. Nothing is claimed." This is a *supernatural* response. But by God's grace and by his power, you can say—and mean—these things.

A BLESSING FROM PAM

One of my all-time favorite quotes from Jesus was spoken when he was hanging on the cross, preparing to die. He said, "Father, forgive them, for they do not know what they are doing," (Luke 23:34). Forgiveness was a reflexive response from our Savior. May it be your reflexive response too.

The Restoration of Awe

When Jesus saw their faith, he said,
"Friend, your sins are forgiven."

LUKE 5:20

Luke 5:17-19 says, "One day Jesus was teaching, and Pharisees and teachers of the law were sitting there. They had come from every village of Galilee and from Judea and Jerusalem. And the power of the Lord was with Jesus to heal the sick. Some men came carrying a paralyzed man on a mat and tried to take him into the house to lay him before Jesus. When they could not find a way to do this because of the crowd, they went up on the roof and lowered him on his mat through the tiles into the middle of the crowd, right in front of Jesus."

When Jesus saw their faith, he forgave the man and said to him, "I tell you, get up, take your mat and go home," (v. 24).

And the man stood, he picked up his mat, and he walked—on his own two legs—all the way home praising God.

He couldn't *help* but praise God as he went. And he wasn't the only one. Verse 26 says, "Everyone was amazed and gave praise to God. They were filled with awe and said, 'We have seen remarkable things today.'"

One of my favorite things about our congregation is that we both *see* and *are amazed* by remarkable things. My hope is that we always are marked by the sense, the awareness, that God is among us, making something beautiful, bringing healing to broken limbs, tenderizing hearts that were previously hardened, welcoming us into his redemptive work.

And that our response to these things would be *awe*.

A BLESSING FROM PAM

May you have eyes to see the activity of God in and around you today.
And may you have the softness of spirit to receive that activity with awe.

The Glad Heart

This is what I have observed to be good: that it is appropriate for a person to eat, to drink and to find satisfaction in their toilsome labor under the sun during the few days of life God has given them—for this is their lot. Moreover, when God gives someone wealth and possessions, and the ability to enjoy them, to accept their lot and be happy in their toil—this is a gift of God. They seldom reflect on the days of their life, because God keeps them occupied with gladness of heart.

ECCLESIASTES 5:18-20

In my experience, we're all approaching our earthly existence in one of three ways:

1. We are living in willful defiance of and disobedience to God's will and ways.

2. We are living oblivious to the fact that there is a God and that he cares deeply about us.

3. We are living absolutely convinced that our only hope is for God to involve himself in every aspect of our lives.

For earnest followers of Jesus, the heart's desire is that third option, the one where we trust God solely to direct and sustain our lives. The writer of Ecclesiastes had a phrase to describe such people: he called them "occupied with gladness of heart," (Ecclesiastes 5:20).

As you move through your day today, try keeping two ideas top of mind. First, remember that *God is with you.*

And then this one: *God is good.*

God is with you.

God is good.

The only occupation you need to fuss with today is that of practicing gladness of heart.

A BLESSING FROM PAM

May you rest today in God's presence,
and also in his abiding love.

Foretaste of Glory

Then I saw "a new heaven and a new earth," for the first heaven and the first earth had passed away, and there was no longer any sea. I saw the Holy City, the new Jerusalem, coming down out of heaven from God, prepared as a bride beautifully dressed for her husband. And I heard a loud voice from the throne saying, "Look! God's dwelling place is now among the people, and he will dwell with them. They will be his people, and God himself will be with them and be their God. 'He will wipe every tear from their eyes. There will be no more death' or mourning or crying or pain, for the old order of things has passed away."

REVELATION 21:1-4

The hymn writer Fanny Crosby, who was born blind because of improper medical care, wrote one of my all-time favorite hymns titled, "Blessed Assurance." And in my view one of the best lines in the whole song is the one where she refers to the assurance of knowing Jesus as a "foretaste of glory divine."

Every time I sing that song, I think about how badly we all need a foretaste of divine glory. For all its beauty and magnificence, this world can be a tough place to be! There are pains on every side: emotional pain, mental pain, physical pain, spiritual pain, relational pain, financial pain, and more. We're all in a struggle of some sort, but the great news of the gospel is that in Jesus, all obstacles are overcome.

This passage from Revelation helps us to take heart that a better day will someday dawn, that a better reality will someday be ours. And so while we are pressed on every side with disappointments, challenges, and struggles, we can take heart that this earth and all its agonies will one day pass away.

You and I are headed for a Holy City, a new dwelling "coming down out of heaven from God," (Revelation 21:2).

There, the old order will be ushered out.

There, we will be made new.

A BLESSING FROM PAM

Today, may you see clearly all that is old as that which will someday be made new.

Quiet Words of the Wise

*I also saw under the sun this example of wisdom that greatly impressed me:
There was once a small city with only a few people in it. And a powerful king came
against it, surrounded it and built huge siege works against it. Now there lived in
that city a man poor but wise, and he saved the city by his wisdom. But nobody
remembered that poor man. So I said, "Wisdom is better than strength." But the poor
man's wisdom is despised, and his words are no longer heeded. The quiet words of the
wise are more to be heeded than the shouts of a ruler of fools.*

ECCLESIASTES 9:13-17

While it's easy to think of "wisdom" as a sweeping characteristic that we either
possess or don't possess, in reality wisdom is demonstrated one decision at a time.
When we make a singular decision to practice patience, for example, instead of losing
our cool, we're letting wisdom have its way. When we say something encouraging
and hold our tongue on all the other comments floating through our mind, we're
letting wisdom have its way. When we take a few minutes to welcome the Holy Spirit
at the start of each day, we're letting wisdom have its way.

I've joked over the years that equally as destructive as the "DUI" that stands for
"driving under the influence" is the one that means "*deciding* under our own
influence." If we're in control of our lives, then every decision we make will be
suspect, and our wisdom will be compromised. But if we allow the Holy Spirit to
carry sole influence over our minds and hearts, then our choices will be sound,
and wisdom will prevail.

In the story told by Solomon above, we see an entire city saved by one man's
wisdom. Which leads me to wonder, *What will you and I save by our wisdom today?*

A BLESSING FROM PAM

*Nothing compares with God's wisdom. Nothing. First Corinthians 1:25 says
that even the "foolishness of God is wiser than man's wisdom," if you can wrap
your mind around that. Today, may you absolutely refuse to look to your own
wisdom for guidance. Instead, may you look to God.*

The One Who Fulfills

Then Jesus declared, "I am the bread of life. Whoever comes to me will never go hungry, and whoever believes in me will never be thirsty."

JOHN 6:35

You and I have four basic needs:

1. **Identity.** We need to know who we are.

2. **Acceptance.** We need to know that we are seen and loved.

3. **Security.** We need access to food, water, shelter, and clothing.

4. **Purpose.** We need a sense of significance in this life.

Something else that is true:

> Our friends can't fulfill us.
> Our spouses and children can't fulfill us.
> Our jobs can't fulfill us.
> Our bank accounts, even if they were bulging with savings, can't fulfill us.

Nothing in this world that we can see, touch, and control will ever be able to meet the needs that cry out for attention in us.

Only Jesus can fulfill us. Only when we find our identity in him, only when we seek his acceptance more than the acceptance from anyone else, only when we look to him for our daily provision and lifelong purpose will we be fulfilled.

Jesus is the bread that satisfies our hunger. He is the Living Water that quenches our thirst. And so, a challenge for this day: peek behind everything else you think you want or crave or need to find your desire for Jesus standing there. He is what you are seeking. He is all that you need.

A BLESSING FROM PAM

Based on Psalm 37:3-5, today may you trust in the Lord and do good. May you dwell in the land and enjoy safe pasture. May you delight only in the Lord, so that he can give you the desires of your heart. May you commit your ways to him today, trusting in him to provide all that you need.

The Untroubled Heart

Do not let your hearts be troubled.
You believe in God; believe also in me.

JOHN 14:1

When I was seven years old, my mom and dad took my brother, my sister, and me camping. They borrowed an ancient tent that had never been waterproofed, which made our first night on a tiny plot of land beside the Sabine River pretty exciting.

The storm had kicked up at two a.m., and after half of hour of the sky unleashing itself and the water level inside the tent rising to unsafe heights, my dad said, "We've got to get out of here."

We heaved gear into the bed of his truck and took off. As my dad drove toward our town, his eyes wide as saucers, lightning cut the clouds above and thunder rocked the earth.

Looking back on that night, despite the harrowing circumstances I remember feeling at ease as we made our way out of the woods. My dad had grown up on the Sabine River. He'd walked and hunted every inch of those woods. He'd seen storms like that one his entire life. Most importantly, he knew the way home.

Whenever I read this verse in John 14, where Jesus tells us not to let our hearts be troubled, I think about that foiled camping trip. I think about how Dad expertly navigated us back to the safety of our home. And I think about Jesus standing in the storms of our everyday lives saying, "Don't worry. I know the way home."

Follow Jesus. He knows the way home. And he is committed to getting you there, where you'll be eternally safe and sound.

A BLESSING FROM PAM

May you trust the unfailing navigational skills of Jesus today, the One who knows which way to turn at every intersection and who will impart that wisdom to you.

On Greatness

*Blessed is anyone who does not
stumble on account of me.*

LUKE 7:23

You aren't all that great.

(Clearly it's time for me to re-read *How to Win Friends and Influence People*.)

You aren't all that great, and neither am I. But let me tell you why this is not discouraging, but *encouraging*, news: because we don't need to be great. We simply need to serve the God who is.

In Luke 7:23, Jesus delivered a blessing to his followers, the exact people who would fall away. He said this: "Blessed is anyone who does not stumble on account of me."

Now, why would he do this? Why would he taunt these fall-away-ers with the notion of being blessed for *not* falling away?

Here is what Jesus was saying: He did not need for his followers to be spectacular. He is the One who is spectacular. And his plan from the beginning of time was to use ordinary, frail, fallible human beings to deliver his good news of grace to the ends of the earth. You and I—in all our not-greatness—are the carriers of God's love to everyone we come across. Even when we momentarily fall away by becoming fearful and losing hope, Jesus never falls away from us.

A BLESSING FROM PAM

Today, regardless of how strong you feel in your faith, may you know the sure, steady presence of your Father, who will neither leave you nor forsake you—even for a moment's time.

At Home in the Things of God

But when he, the Spirit of truth, comes, he will guide you into all the truth. He will not speak on his own; he will speak only what he hears, and he will tell you what is yet to come.

JOHN 16:13

For years, I've loved ministering to pastors in Wales, even as something always feels off when I'm there. It's not that they drive on the wrong side of the road or refuse to season their food. It's more than that. It's an *unsettledness of spirit*, you might say.

Maybe you can relate to a foreign locale seeming "off" to you somehow. It's that feeling that says, "You don't belong here. You're not of this place."

In John 16:13, Jesus promises his followers the coming of his Spirit—the Spirit of truth, he calls him. Three things are promised with the coming of the Spirit: He will guide us into all the truth. He will speak that which he hears from God. And he will tell us what is yet to come. You and I cannot follow Jesus without the empowering work of his Spirit. But when we yield to the input of the Holy Spirit, we are able to follow Jesus successfully. We are able to love God well.

When we walk by the Spirit, we feel settled in the things of God. The things of the world start to seem "off" to us, in the same way that unseasoned fish and chips make me squirm. Darkness doesn't seem so appealing anymore. Rebellion is no longer fun.

Are you feeling more settled these days in the ways of the world or in the righteous ways of God? The Spirit longs to direct you. The Spirit longs to settle your soul.

A BLESSING FROM PAM

May your soul be settled by Jesus alone today.

Passion Pursuit

"Or suppose a woman has ten silver coins and loses one. Doesn't she light a lamp, sweep the house and search carefully until she finds it? And when she finds it, she calls her friends and neighbors together and says, 'Rejoice with me; I have found my lost coin.' In th same way, I tell you, there is rejoicing in the presence of the angels of God over one sinner who repents."

LUKE 15:8-10

Have you ever lost something important to you? You could drop a crumb or a paper clip or a penny, and maybe you'd give the floor a quick glance to see if the item were easy to spot and pick up. But are you going to scour the place looking for it? My guess is probably not.

But now replace those incidental items with something more valuable: the last piece to a 1,000-piece puzzle, the engagement ring you plan to give your girlfriend, your smart phone (gasp!). You will turn the place upside-down looking for the thing, right? You will go crazy until it's found.

Let's up the ante further still: let's say you're in God's shoes, seated on his throne in heaven, and you are the one who is lost. Well, call off all other plans, because an all-out search will need to commence.

You may not think that much of your value, but God knows the truth of your worth. Furthermore, he knows how futile your life will be until you enter into an intimate relationship with him.

He is committed to finding you.

He is committed to fulfilling you.

He is committed to funding the heavenly celebration that will erupt when you return.

I don't know where your agenda has you going today, but no destination could possibly be more important than straight into the presence of God. Let yourself be found by your heavenly Father. He's waiting. He's looking. He's at hand.

A BLESSING FROM PAM

Every mama relates to this image of God searching carefully for each of his kids. Today, may you make that search straightforward, as you come joyfully into the presence of God.

The Empire that Endures

*Do not store up for yourselves treasures on earth, where moths
and vermin destroy, and where thieves break in and steal.*

MATTHEW 6:19

I've been to Jerusalem and have seen the site where Solomon's lavish and seemingly impenetrable temple was built, Mount Moriah. Guess what's there now? The same thing that dots the landscape of every other human-built empire: a pile of rocks.

Jesus delivered the counsel we find in Matthew 6:19 during his Sermon on the Mount, saying, "Do not store up for yourselves treasures on earth, where moths and vermin destroy; and where thieves break in and steal."

I know it's tempting to pursue power and glory and all the things the world says are cool, he seemed to say, *but trust me, friends, those empires someday will fall.*

What, then, *were* they to do? Here's verse 20: "But store up for yourselves treasures in heaven, where moths and vermin do not destroy, and where thieves do not break in and steal."

Jesus' way contradicted the world's way. The world says, "Accumulate as much money and power as you can, and do whatever you need to do to get it."

Jesus' way said, "Whatever resources you find in your hands, invest them on behalf of others. Use your power to bless others. Use your money to bless others. Take care of people. Serve people. Tend to other people's needs. This is how to get wealthy, in the truest sense of the word."

The only empire that will endure is the one you and I can help build today. It is the kingdom of God, the kingdom that has no end.

A BLESSING FROM PAM

*Today may you experience the incomparable peace that comes from knowing
that in following Jesus—his leadership, his character, his way—you are building
the only kingdom in history that cannot and will not fall.*

Life Together

A father to the fatherless, a defender of widows, is God in his holy dwelling.
God sets the lonely in families, he leads out the prisoners with singing; but
the rebellious live in a sun-scorched land.

PSALM 68:5-6

If you're like most people, both your greatest pain and your greatest joy have come through the relationships in your life.

In Psalm 68, the psalmist reminds us that you and I were built for relationships, for friendships, for families. And while there are real risks involved when engaging with other people—disappointment and heartbreak, to name two—the upside of doing life in the context of community is limitless in its scope.

For many years now, I have had a singular goal on Sunday mornings, as I show up at New Life to preach. Yes, I want to deal rightly with the Scriptures so that people can grow in their faith. But more specifically, I long to engage with just one person—to make him or her feel seen and included and loved. We forget that everyone we meet has a struggle of some sort, and that a simple smile and word of encouragement could be the difference between life and death.

Today, I hope you'll be a life-saver for someone. Smile. Stick out your hand. Make the introduction. Speak kind words on behalf of God. Risk being a people person. Be "family" to one who's alone.

A BLESSING FROM PAM

My hope for you today is that you would lift your eyes from your own concerns to
find people all around you in need of care. May you be the answer to their prayers.

The Good Stored Up

*Make a tree good and its fruit will be good, or make a tree bad and its fruit will be bad,
for a tree is recognized by its fruit. You brood of vipers, how can you who are evil say anything
good? For the mouth speaks what the heart is full of. A good man brings good things out of
the good stored up in him, and an evil man brings evil things out of the evil stored up in him.*

MATTHEW 12:33-35

Years ago I came across one of the most comprehensive longitudinal marriage studies ever conducted, this one out of the University of Washington. It tracked several hundred couples across a period of years, recording through wearable devices every word spoken between them.

Of the 90 percent of the couples in that study who wound up divorcing, a singular common denominator existed: criticism.

At some point, one or both members of the partnership began criticizing the other one, and this eventually led to divorce.

When I meet with couples for counseling, the critical spouses are always shocked to learn that they are critical, as if they don't hear themselves making all those derogatory remarks.

What do I advise them to do? *Start storing up better things.*

When we overwhelm our thoughts with God's Word, we begin storing up "good" in our hearts. And since our words flow from what is stored up in our heart, what we speak will begin to change.

When we have a problem with our words, we have a problem with our heart—it's as simple as that. From the overflow of the heart, the mouth speaks. Let's guard our hearts today.

A BLESSING FROM PAM

*May you enjoy a rich encounter with God and with his truth today,
and may each word that you speak reflect it.*

Praying the Psalms

God is our refuge and strength,
an ever-present help in trouble.

PSALM 46:1

A favorite approach to prayer is praying a personalized psalm back to God, such as this one, from Psalm 46:1-7. Read the psalm aloud, responding to the prompts as you go. Then, consider adopting this approach as part of your usual prayer life, declaring God's characteristics back to him while reminding yourself of the promises he's made.

"God, you are my refuge and my strength, an ever-present help in trouble."
The troubles I see as I survey my life today include …

"Therefore I will not fear, though the earth give way and the mountains fall into the heart of the sea, though its waters roar and foam and the mountains quake with their surging."
I need this reminder today, because the fear is real. My biggest fears are that …

"There is a river whose streams make glad the city of God, the holy place where the Most High dwells. God is within her, she will not fall; God will help her at break of day. Nations are in uproar, kingdoms fall; he lifts his voice, the earth melts. The LORD Almighty is with me; the God of Jacob is my fortress."
Please show up in my situation with this kind of divine power, God. Please show yourself strong in these specific circumstances:

In Jesus' holy name,
Amen.

A BLESSING FROM PAM

Today, as you speak God's words back to him,
may his purposes be accomplished in your life.

Surer than Sure

*Fix these words of mine in your hearts and minds; tie them as
symbols on your hands and bind them on your foreheads.*

DEUTERONOMY 11:18

There's a phrase found in Deuteronomy 11:18 that can carry great power in our lives.
There, we read instructions from Moses to, "fix these words of mine [God's words] in
your hearts and minds; tie them as symbols on your hands and bind them on your
foreheads."

Fix God's words in our hearts and minds—there's permanence to the language
Moses chose. Immovability. Certainty.

There are many things we can fix our hearts and minds to in this life—appearance,
accomplishment, aspiration, material possessions that we adore. But only one fixation
will yield positive results in our lives, and that is a fixation on the words of God.

We can be sure that God is who he says he is. We can be sure that God will do what
he says he will do. We can be sure that God will provide for us. We can be sure that
his presence is near. And all of this certainty comes from reading his Word, from
fixing his word in our hearts and minds. So much about life is uncertain these days,
but our faith? It can be surer than sure.

A BLESSING FROM PAM

*Today, may you indulge one fixation, and one fixation only:
the fixing of God's words to your heart and mind.*

Wanting Wellness

*Some time later, Jesus went up to Jerusalem for one of the Jewish festivals. Now there is
in Jerusalem near the Sheep Gate a pool, which in Aramaic is called Bethesda and which
is surrounded by five covered colonnades. Here a great number of disabled people used to
lie—the blind, the lame, the paralyzed. One who was there had been an invalid for thirty-eight
years. When Jesus saw him lying there and learned that he had been in this condition for a
long time, he asked him, "Do you want to get well?"*

JOHN 5:1-6

Do you want to be well?

I'm asking earnestly: *do you want to be well?*

Those parts of your life that aren't working right ... the distance between you and
your spouse, your frustration over your wayward kid, your wild amount of consumer
debt, the fear that maybe you really are addicted to that substance you keep
swearing has no control over you ... do you want those to be made well?

We might read this account from John 5 and assume that he doesn't actually
expect a response from the man who has been ill for nearly four decades, that he's
somehow just making small talk.

He's not.

Ask any counselor or therapist, and that person will tell you that the first step to
helping anyone move past any dysfunction is gaining consent from the suffering
person that he or she does, in fact, want to be well.

It's a question worth pondering, I think: do we want to be well today? That longing—
the simple longing to live life well—is the best possible starting point for finding
healing, whatever that healing might involve for you.

A BLESSING FROM PAM

*May you find courage today to long for wellness—in mind, body,
spirit, emotions, and life. And to bring that longing to God.*

The Soul Finds Healing First

*"Sir," the invalid replied, "I have no one to help me into the pool when the water
is stirred. While I am trying to get in, someone else goes down ahead of me."
Then Jesus said to him, "Get up! Pick up your mat and walk."*

JOHN 5:7-8

Our text continues here, with Jesus telling the disabled man, "Get up! Pick up your
mat and walk."

While it's true that the man in the story was physically healed, there is a critical
takeaway for you and me both: God cares about our disease-free bodies, but he
cares more about our divinely healed hearts.

When Jesus gives the man those three commands—get up, pick up your mat, walk—
he's not only speaking literally to the man. He's speaking spiritually to you and me too.

Get up. Yes, God initiates salvation in our lives, but he only comes so far before we
must open the door of our heart and invite him to come in.

Pick up your mat. That old way of life we've been living no longer fits, once we
surrender our growth to God. It's time to fold it up and throw it away.

Walk. Once we are new creations in Christ, it's time to get moving in this new way of
life. It's time to forge ahead in faith.

Yes, we long for every aspect of our lives to be made right in the power of Jesus'
name. And on many occasions, for the purpose of gathering glory up for himself,
God will choose to heal those very things. But I ask you: in the meantime, what's the
state of your soul? Are you choosing to live *spiritually* whole?

A BLESSING FROM PAM

*Today, may you be totally and completely consumed
by having your soul made healthy first.*

Give Your Gift

We have different gifts, according to the grace given to each of us. If your gift is
prophesying, then prophesy in accordance with your faith; if it is serving, then serve; if it
is teaching, then teach; if it is to encourage, then give encouragement; if it is giving, then
give generously; if it is to lead, do it diligently; if it is to show mercy, do it cheerfully.

ROMANS 12:6-8

If you're feeling detached these days from our congregation, let me give you three words of encouragement. First: Come home. You cannot receive the benefits of church life by continuing to stay away from church. Second and third: As you reengage at New Life, watch for ways that others' gifts are a blessing to you, and then look for ways to employ the gifts that God has given to you.

God has given each of his children a gift. To some, he has given the gift of prophesy. To others, service. To some, teaching or encouragement, giving or leadership or mercy. As you interact with people, think about these gifts. Which ones do you spot? Might you tell that person so?

Then, pay attention to God's promptings. Is he prompting you to give financially or putting specific words on your tongue to speak to someone else? Is he helping you see gaps in the strategy of a system, ministry, or effort? God has gifted you so that you can be a blessing to the body! As you use your gifts, and as you acknowledge the gifts you see in others, you are honoring the gift-giver, God.

A BLESSING FROM PAM

Today, may you reconnect with the gifts that make you distinctly you. And may
you employ them not for the sake of yourself, but for the magnificent glory of God.

Wisdom Swap

*Don't be harsh or impatient with an older man. Talk to him as you would
your own father, and to the younger men as your brothers. Reverently honor an older
woman as you would your mother, and the younger women as sisters.*

1 TIMOTHY 5:1-2 MSG

Pam and I have always sought out friends and mentors twenty years older than we are. We just wanted to be around them, to hear how they processed life, to see how they lived life, to absorb as much of their wisdom as we could.

Now that I'm in my early fifties, I'm standing between two generations. I'm seeing people fifteen or twenty years older than I am retiring and winding down, and I'm seeing people fifteen or twenty years younger than I am chasing their tails as we all seem to do when we're building careers and marriages and families. And I'm seeing far too few people in all three groups—my age group included—live out the words of 1 Timothy 5. We are to behave as a family with other believers—deferring to those who are older, honoring those who are younger. We are to engage with each other so that our burdens are lightened and our path is made more predictably straight.

If you are in your twenties or thirties, who is mentoring you?

If you are in your sixties or seventies, who are *you* mentoring?

If you are in those midlife years, I'd ask *both* questions of you.

There is hard-won wisdom in every elder.

There are questions brimming in every Millennial and Gen-Z soul.

It's time we came together to share what we wonder and what we know.

A BLESSING FROM PAM

*May God direct you today to one who is wiser than you
and to one who needs the wisdom you already possess.*

Christology First

Jesus went throughout Galilee, teaching in their synagogues, proclaiming the good news of the kingdom, and healing every disease and sickness among the people. News about him spread all over Syria, and people brought to him all who were ill with various diseases, those suffering severe pain, the demon-possessed, those having seizures, and the paralyzed; and he healed them. Large crowds from Galilee, the Decapolis, Jerusalem, Judea and the region across the Jordan followed him.

MATTHEW 4:23-25

If you've been around New Life for some time, you have probably noticed that everything we do centers on the person of Jesus. Our teaching, our worship, our prayers, our ministry efforts—everything we are about must begin with Christology, which is the subset of theology concerning the person, nature, and role of Christ in our church and in our lives.

And so today, I come to you with a challenge, of sorts. I invite you to read the entire Sermon on the Mount, Matthew chapters 5, 6, and 7. It will take you about eighteen minutes to read, but the profound insights you gain there will fuel you for a lifetime, if you let them.

You will never make a better decision in life than the decision to model yourself after Jesus—his motivation, his priorities, his habits, his peace. Begin with him, and go from there. And prepare to find joy in life.

A BLESSING FROM PAM

May you boldly conform yourself to the example of Jesus today and let all other conformity fall away.

Seeing the Heart Rightly

The heart is deceitful above all things and
beyond cure. Who can understand it?

JEREMIAH 17:9

One of the greatest byproducts of surrendering our lives to Jesus is that our hearts undergo a transformation from being tainted by sin to being trustworthy and sure. Before we knew Jesus as Savior, our hearts were "deceitful," as the prophet Jeremiah describes them, and "beyond cure." But by the power of God, once we yield ourselves to his will, his ways, his whims, the Holy Spirit moves into our hearts and starts renovating them, room by room. We begin to be able to weigh our motives, to assess our actions, to judge the impact we're having on others, and to pursue right relationship with God.

As you begin your day today, place your hand on your heart and consider before your heavenly Father how you might answer questions such as these:

Am I living in true surrender to you, God?
Do I long to do your will above my own?
Am I open to your assessment of my attitudes and actions?
Will I conform myself to your standard of holiness today?

Let the Holy Spirit have free rein in your heart. Hold nothing back from his tender, loving care. Invite him to change you, to mold you, to release you, to transform you, as you seek to live more like God's Son. Ask God to remove every last ounce of deception from your inner world so that you can more fully glorify him.

A BLESSING FROM PAM

May you rest in the knowledge today that as believers our hearts
have been made pure. May you continue to look to the Holy Spirit
to guide you into goodness, gratitude, and righteousness.

Unseen Generosity

*Be careful not to practice your righteousness in front of others to be seen
by them. If you do, you will have no reward from your Father in heaven.*

MATTHEW 6:1

With the arrival of social media came the prevalence of the "humble brag." Humble bragging is posting something like, "Landed first book deal today ... six-figure advance ... any advice on how to be an author??"

We like to believe we'd never be so obnoxious, but then comes the true test: can we do something kind, something helpful, something generous, and *not say a word about* it to anyone else?

That verse from Matthew 6 continues with this counsel from Jesus himself: "So when you give to the needy, do not announce it with trumpets, as the hypocrites do in the synagogues and on the streets, to be honored by others. Truly I tell you, they have received their reward in full. But when you give to the needy, do not let your left hand know what your right hand is doing, so that your giving may be in secret. Then your Father, who sees what is done in secret, will reward you," (vv. 2-4).

To be a follower of Jesus is to be a helper, a servant, a giver. To be a *true* follower of Jesus is to live this sort of life without trumpeting it for all the world to hear.

As you move through your day today, remember that God is with you, and that his Spirit is empowering you to do good in your corner of the world. As you follow his promptings to help, to give, to serve, return to him for your reward.

Let your reward come only from him.

A BLESSING FROM PAM

*May God's pleasure be enough for you today,
as you bless those you come across.*

A Word on Going It Alone

Though one may be overpowered, two can defend themselves.
A cord of three strands is not quickly broken.

ECCLESIASTES 4:12

My best guess as to why so many of us are going it alone in life is that somewhere along the way we were hurt by someone we counted as a friend, and from that moment forward, we decided we'd never do that again. We make a sort of inner vow, declaring *that* we'll never be vulnerable with a friend again. Yeah, we may stick out our hand for an introduction, but that's as close as that person ever will get. Our guard is up now. Our heart is walled-off. We know better this time around.

If you've fallen prey to the belief that you can go it alone in life and flourish as a result, may I ask a straightforward question? How is that working for you so far?

Maybe there's a part of your life today that feels a little overpowered, a little broken down, a little disappointing or hopeless or flat. While it's true that your heavenly Father sees you and is committing to providing for you in your time of need, a very real way that that provision may be headed your way is through the eyes and hands and feet and prayers and acts of service of a *friend*.

Take the risk today of asking for help where you need it. Admit that you have been trying to fly solo but are crashing and burning as a result. Trust that by engaging others in your struggle, you'll see the hand of God at work.

A BLESSING FROM PAM

Today, may God remind you of the friends who have been faithful in your life.
And may you prove to be a faithful friend to someone who is lonely and afraid.

Table of Grace

For I received from the Lord what I also passed on to you: The Lord Jesus, on the night he was betrayed, took bread, and when he had given thanks, he broke it and said, "This is my body, which is for you; do this in remembrance of me." In the same way, after supper he took the cup saying, "This cup is the new covenant in my blood; do this, whenever you drink it, in remembrance of me."

1 CORINTHIANS 11:23-24

In the church I grew up in, the center aisle and pews on either side all faced a wooden table that had engraved in it these words: "This Do in Remembrance of Me." Once a month, communion elements would magically appear on that table, and our entire church would partake.

Years later the idea of taking communion became far more important to me, and it was because of Paul's words here.

From that moment forward, the staff and I began prioritizing the taking of Communion, and in the years since, we've only *not* had Communion offered following a worship service on a handful of occasions. If you've been around New Life these past several years, you've probably noticed the shift. Our worship services all but center on this meal, on coming as a body to this table of grace.

My invitation to you is this: resist letting Communion breeze by you as you take the elements each week. Let everything else fall away as you focus on just two themes: *grace*, and *thanksgiving*.

Christ's body, broken for us.

Christ's blood, spilled for us.

The centerpiece of our faith.

A BLESSING FROM PAM

May you live undone by the goodness of God's grace today.

Set Apart

The LORD said to Moses, "Speak to the Israelites and
say to them: 'I am the LORD your God.'"

LEVITICUS 18:1-2

Once, God asked Moses to say to his people, "You must not do as they do in Egypt, where you used to live, and you must not do as they do in the land of Canaan, where I am bringing you. Do not follow their practices. You must obey my laws and be careful to follow my decrees. I am the LORD your God. Keep my decrees and laws, for the person who obeys them will live by them. I am the LORD," (vv. 3-5).

To tell his people that they were no longer in "Egypt" would have been to remind them that they were no longer under the control of the most prosperous military superpower of the day. To tell his people that they were not to conform to the customs of "Canaan" was to tell them not to be swayed by the deplorably trends they saw all around them, including incest, prostitution, child sacrifice, and bestiality.

To be sure, we could draw up a similar set of temptations in our world today. We live in the most prosperous military superpower the world has ever known, and with that allegiance comes the real danger that it's our government—and not God—that protects us. We also live in a sexually deviant culture. Without the careful guarding of our hearts, we will certainly be led astray.

The prayer I pray over my own heart, my own life, my own family, my own church, is the same one I invite you to pray each day: It's the simple declaration to our heavenly Father, "You are the Lord, my God."

You, alone, are God.

A BLESSING FROM PAM

May you both prepare yourself for and practically
live a life set apart for God today.

MARCH

"If you will find your security not in your spotless home, your soaring career, or your stellar marriage, but instead in the person and preeminence of Christ, you will live constantly connected to joy."

- Pastor Brady Boyd -

One for All

*So in Christ we, though many, form one body, and
each member belongs to all the others.*

ROMANS 12:5

We learn in the book of Matthew that Jesus himself built the Church and that it was through the Church that he would accomplish God's redemptive mission in the earth. Despite her imperfections even the "gates of Hades" would not be able to overcome it, Matthew 16:18 says, a truth that over the years I've been immensely grateful for. The Church is God's idea. The Church is a good idea. The Church as a body will always prevail.

This begs a couple of questions. Do you believe in the idea of the Church? As you read through the Scriptures, are you convinced that Jesus intended for his followers to gather together to learn what his Word says and to worship God and to share resources and to pray? If your answer is yes to these questions, then consider for a moment that while the way in which we have "done church" may have been wrong from time to time, the idea of Church itself is not wrong.

I've carried a fundamental belief for decades now, which is that only lovers of the Church will get to heal the Church. Cynics of the Church will not.

Be one who loves the Church of Jesus Christ. Serve her. Deal tenderly with her. Encourage her. Be faithful to her. She is your Savior's beloved bride, the one for whom he came to die.

A BLESSING FROM PAM

*May you be awakened today to the beauty of the Church
and to the necessity of your involvement in it.*

Who He Is

So Moses chiseled out two stone tablets like the first ones and went up Mount Sinai early in the morning, as the LORD had commanded him; and he carried the two stone tablets in his hands. Then the LORD came down in the cloud and stood there with him and proclaimed his name, the LORD. And he passed in front of Moses proclaiming, "The LORD, the LORD, the compassionate and gracious God, slow to anger, abounding in love and faithfulness, maintaining love to thousands, and forgiving wickedness, rebellion and sin."

EXODUS 34:4-7A

In Exodus 34, Moses receives a second batch of stone tablets, on which are written the Ten Commandments from God. (He destroyed the first set when he descended the mountain where he'd received them and found his people worshiping idols they'd fashioned from gold.) Once Moses has completed the chiseling of the second set, God reveals himself to Moses in a cloud and says a few things about himself.

If I could sit with you and tell you anything about God, I would flip to this passage in Exodus and recount for you what God has said about himself.

Your heavenly Father is compassionate.
He is *gracious*.
He is slow to anger.
He is abounding in love.
He is also abounding in faithfulness; he cannot *not* be faithful to the promises he has made.
He maintains love to thousands.
He forgives wickedness.
He forgives rebellion.
He forgives sin.

What a *relief*. What a total and utter relief. When God chose to offer a picture to Moses of who he was at his core, this is the picture he gave. This is what he wants you to know.

A BLESSING FROM PAM

*May you be awakened today to the beauty of the Church
and to the necessity of your involvement in it.*

It Stops Here

Thou shalt not bow down thyself to them, nor serve them: for I the Lord thy God am a jealous God, visiting the iniquity of the fathers upon the children unto the third and fourth generation of them that hate me ...

EXODUS 20:5 KJV

For the first handful of years that Pam and I were in Colorado, we lived in a neighborhood on the Palmer Divide, and because the lot had no real landscaping to speak of, one of our first efforts was to plant a row of trees. That first winter, the wind was generally coming from the north, which meant that our tiny, vulnerable trees grew not straight toward the sky but bent toward the south. That "bent" or propensity is what Exodus 20:5 is talking about when it refers to *iniquity*. An iniquity is an internal influence that causes us to behave in a certain way.

I grew up in Northwest Louisiana and was in the first racially integrated class in the history of the school I went to. I'll always be proud of my heritage, but one trend I am not proud of was the rampant racism in the community in which my family lived. Racist comments and jokes flew around like seeds on the wind, and as they took root in the hearts of our people, ugliness began to grow. It's no exaggeration that for my entire childhood I was a little racist boy.

When I became a believer in Jesus in my late teens, it's as if I could see clearly for the first time what my upbringing had done to me in forming degrading thoughts and assumptions about people of color, and so I set about the task of systematically evicting those things one by one. More accurately, God removed those things for me. The turning point was when God sent Pam and me to serve every week in a part of Shreveport, where we were living, populated entirely by African American women, men, and children. We fell in love with those people, and with each relationship formed something awful broke off of my heart, something I was all too eager to let go.

The only humans ever to live free from iniquity were Adam and Eve. Beginning with their offspring, every person ever to live has been born with a bent, a propensity, toward a particular sin. This is in part why the prophet Isaiah reminded us in Isaiah 53:5 that Jesus was "crushed for our iniquities." A big reason Jesus suffered death on a cross was to empower us to live free from the waywardness we've indulged.

His crucifixion and ensuing resurrection said to us, "You don't have to live under the obligation to that way of life. You can live free from iniquity and sin."

What does this mean for you? It means that beginning today—this minute—by the power of God living inside of you, you can break free from the iniquity you were born into. The immorality. The cycle of abuse. The alcoholism. The trend toward divorce. The materialism. The legalism. The workaholism. The racism. The substance misuse. The spiritual lethargy. The inability to hold down a job. The lack of appreciation for education. The harshness with your kids.

You can be freed from these things right now. The pattern can stop with you. Claim the power of Jesus in your life and in the life of your family. Declare what your legacy will be. Quit caving to the iniquity you were handed. Rise and walk in newness of life.

A BLESSING FROM PAM

Today may you realize just how powerful God is to heal you from the patterns of unfaithfulness that have held you back from pure devotion to him.

Untangled

*Get rid of bitterness, rage and anger, brawling and slander, along with
every form of malice. Be kind and compassionate to one another, forgiving
each other, just as in Christ God forgave you.*

EPHESIANS 4:31-32

I once knew a man who was critical. He and his family had been part of the church where I was pastoring, and while I'd had many meetings with him and had prayed for him and had worked up a plan for helping him control his slander and rage, nothing seemed to work. It was time for him to go.

He came to the meeting having written up a pages-long accusation of me, and as he rattled off the offenses, God prompted me: "Brady, if you want to help him, I will show you the root of bitterness that is causing this harm."

"Let me say something, please," I said. "When I look at you, I see a boy cowering underneath your childhood bed, hoping that your father doesn't come into the room and beat you senseless again. What does that vision mean to you?"

That fully grown man fell, weeping, to the floor. He'd made a vow as a boy that he would never trust a man in authority again, and he'd kept that vow all these years.

Long after I'd left that church and transitioned to New Life, I returned there to preach one weekend. Afterward, the man surfaced. "Hey, Pastor Brady!" he called. "So good to see you, man."

It was good to finally see him too. The *real* him. The him untangled from bitterness's root.

You can hang onto unforgiveness, or you can hang onto the provision of God. But you can't have both simultaneously. Today, you've got to choose.

A BLESSING FROM PAM

*May you be willing today to release the offense you've been carrying,
and to release the offender who's been held hostage in your heart.*

The Lord Bless and Keep You

The LORD said to Moses, "Tell Aaron and his sons, 'This is how you are to bless the Israelites. Say to them: "The LORD bless you and keep you; the LORD make his face shine on you and be gracious to you; the LORD turn his face toward you and give you peace."'"

NUMBERS 6:22-26

On a Saturday night in 1988, I was driving home after having dropped Pam off at her house. I was in love with her and wanted to spend the rest of my life with her, but I wasn't the man I needed to be. I needed to surrender my life to God, so on that short drive home, I did just that.

To save money, I was living with my parents as I finished college, and the next morning, I said to them, "Hey, I want to go to church with you."

My mom was suspicious.

"Last night, I turned my life over to God," I explained, to which she said, "I knew that already. Just by looking at you, I could tell."

Nearly every Sunday around New Life, we send you out with this blessing from Numbers 6:24-26, a passage you may now know by heart. You may recall that when Moses encountered God at the giving of the second set of the Ten Commandments, his face "was radiant because he had spoken with the LORD," (Exodus 34:29).

Encounters with God tend to do that, which is why we pray those words over you. We long for you to bear the radiance of Christ, the glow that says you've encountered God.

A BLESSING FROM PAM

Today may all other obligations and to-do's
take second place to carving out time for him.

Called Out

I pray that the eyes of your heart may be enlightened in order that you may know the hope to which he has called you, the riches of his glorious inheritance in his holy people.

EPHESIANS 1:18

Do you remember the season of life or maybe even the exact day when Jesus called you out of darkness into his wonderful light?

Over the years I've asked people to tell me their dark-to-light stories, and the answers are always the same: We were going our own way and then realized that we make *horrible* gods. We were entranced by sin and then realized that sin makes a *horrible* master. We were chasing all that the world had to offer and then realized that those things could never fulfill. We were colossally distracted and then realized we'd veered tragically off-course.

But then ... Jesus.

Jesus came into view, and we couldn't resist him.

Jesus came into view, and we couldn't refute him.

Jesus came into view, and we knew we'd never be the same again.

I look back on the person I was before I loved Jesus, and I don't even recognize that guy. What I used to crave, I no longer crave. What I used to pursue, I no longer pursue. I have been called out of that lifestyle into a totally new one, and I will never be the same.

True for you, as well?

If we have indeed been called from darkness into light, then one way that reality gets manifested is that we *know hope*. Today, consider doing just that: Tell someone about the person you once were, and about who you are today, and about the hope in you as a result.

A BLESSING FROM PAM

May you walk and love and live
in the light of Jesus today.

All Because of Love

By this everyone will know that you are my disciples,
if you love one another.

JOHN 13:35

In ancient Greece, military leaders established a battle formation known as the *hoplite phalanx* that was nearly impossible to take down. Hoplites were armed middle-class citizen-soldiers who'd been employed for battle for two years, and to ensure that they actually lived for the entire term of their service, commanders taught them how to leverage the larger group to protect each individual man. The fighters would line up shoulder-to-shoulder, forming a wall of shields and spears, which made enemies' frontal assaults far less effective in war. On his own, a given soldier would have been vulnerable to attack, but together the wall was impenetrable—as long as the formation didn't break.

In the same way that those fighters aligned themselves to each other and gained energy from each other's strength, we as the Church are to fight with and for each other as we work to push back darkness in the world. We're to lock arms. To stay present. To look out for each other. To advance against our enemy's schemes. We're to encourage each other. And prompt good in each other. And keep each other from doing life alone.

If I have one goal for New Life Church, it's that the watching world would peek in on us from time to time and say, "What on earth are they *doing*? Why are they helping each other? And serving each other? And sharing resources with each other? Why are they praying for each other and treating each other so well?"

The answer, of course, will be *love*.

We're doing these things because of love.

A BLESSING FROM PAM

Live loved this day. You are loved! You are loved by Love himself
and can therefore be a conduit of love to others today.

Comfort in Prayer

*... for your Father knows what you need
before you ask him.*

MATTHEW 6:8

Let's say that Pam came out to the garage one afternoon and found me looking under the hood of my truck saying, "Yep, should have known it was the flux capacitor."

My wife is endlessly supportive, but she would burst out laughing. "There is no *way* you have any idea what you're talking about," she would say.

And she'd be right.

Porting this dynamic into the spiritual realm, too many of us as believers treat prayer like an automotive problem to be solved. We pop the hood on our deepest needs and stand there saying, "Yep ... looks like if we just attach the adoration to the confession and the confession to the intercession, we'll be good to go."

Here is where Matthew 6:8 comes in. Just before Jesus lays out what we now refer to as the Lord's Prayer, he offers up a profound insight. It's as if he knows that we'll be tempted to make his sample prayer some sort of magic formula and chooses to head that off at the pass. He says this: "Your Father knows what you need before you ask him."

Isn't that comforting to know?

Yes, we are to come to God with our heartfelt confession as well as our earnest requests. But before we ever utter a word, he knows precisely what we need.

Pray.

Pray without ceasing, in fact. (See 1 Thessalonians 5:16.)

Just remember that your Father is one step ahead of you. He's aware of the burdens you're bearing and is committed to lifting each one in turn.

A BLESSING FROM PAM

*May your prayers reflect the comfort, ease, and sheer joy
God hopes we'll manifest as we come into his presence today.*

The Family of Believers

Be alert and of sober mind. Your enemy the devil prowls around like a roaring lion looking for someone to devour. Resist him, standing firm in the faith, because you know that the family of believers throughout the world is undergoing the same kind of sufferings.

1 PETER 5:8-9

It's not uncommon during an average day that I pause for a minute or two and think about small groups of believers half a world away—in Iran, in Afghanistan, all throughout Asia—who are gathering under the cover of nightfall to covertly hold church services, aware that at any moment they could be arrested and even killed. The stories that we hear week after week from our global-ministries team often leave me shaking my head in disbelief and counting my blessings that in this country we still can freely worship God.

It would be easy to stop there, in that spirit of thankfulness, forgetting that those worshipers who are suffering persecution for the sake of the gospel are sisters and brothers of mine. Of ours. Which means that their suffering is our suffering; their pain is our pain.

When I was growing up, I often heard pastors say that while Satan indeed was prowling around like a roaring lion, because of the gospel, that lion had no teeth. But that's not how I read Peter's counsel above. Satan is prowling around looking for someone to devour. I probably don't have to tell you that he can, in fact, devour. And in the wild, guess who hungry lions go after? The vulnerable. The exposed. The weak. These sisters and brothers of ours in countries all over the world who are remaining faithful to the gospel despite threats to their well-being and their very lives are vulnerable. Today, may we take time out of our day to ask for God's protection over their minds, their hearts, and their lives.

A BLESSING FROM PAM

May your heart be captured today by God's affection for all his followers, both here and in far-flung places around the world.

Finishing Strong

In all this you greatly rejoice, though now for a little while you may have had to suffer grief in all kinds of trials. These have come so that the proven genuineness of your faith—of greater worth than gold, which perishes even though refined by fire— may result in praise, glory and honor when Jesus Christ is revealed.

1 PETER 1:6-7

Of all the people in Scripture, the one I most relate to is Peter. Peter was one of Jesus' three closest friends. And it was on Peter that Jesus said he would build his Church. But also true was that Peter denied Jesus three times immediately after boasting that he'd *never* abandon Christ.

I've told New Life for years that my singular goal now that I'm entering my mid-fifties is to finish strong. I want to be the old grandpa guy you can't get rid of, the one who tells the same stories over and over and thinks they're equally funny every time. I want to keep growing in Christlikeness, becoming wiser and kinder and more compassionate year by year.

Peter is a guy who finished strong.

In the passage above we find a much older, much more mature version of the prideful hothead who couldn't keep his word. Most scholars believe that when Peter wrote 1 Peter and 2 Peter, he was approximately 64 years old. He's thoughtful now. Pensive. Reflective. Wise.

It's worth noting that as Peter reminds believers of their inheritance in Christ, he's about to be martyred for that same faith. He spends his final days and months and years praising God, celebrating the joy we have in Christ, and putting earthly suffering in its place. *This* is how to age gracefully.

A BLESSING FROM PAM

For today, may you know laser-like focus as you reflect Jesus to those you meet.

Again and Again and Again

Then Peter came to Jesus and asked, "Lord, how many times shall I forgive
my brother or sister who sins against me? Up to seven times?"
Jesus answered, "I tell you, not seven times, but seventy-seven times."

MATTHEW 18:21-22

Have you ever had the same person commit an offense against you time and time again? If you're married, then you're probably nodding your head yes. I know Pam would be. There are a few issues regarding my part of our marriage where that forgiveness count of seventy-seven, as noted in Matthew 18:22, doesn't seem that far off. (In the King James Version of this verse, the last two words are transposed, which seems to indicate we are to forgive the same person not just seventy-seven times, but seventy times seven times, or 490 times in full. For the sake of our marriage, I think I'll ask Pam to memorize that translation of the verse.)

Whether we're talking about seventy-seven or seventy times seventy volitional acts of forgiveness, the point here is this: the number is more than we think. Jesus isn't wanting us to get fixated on the amount but on the approach. In other words, we are to forgive as often as it takes.

I would ask you and me both: whom can we forgive today?

Given this injunction from Jesus, what are we waiting for?

A BLESSING FROM PAM

May you come to the end of your entitlement today and choose instead to forgive.
Fully, completely, joyfully, may forgiveness be swift and sweet.

Victorious in the End

For everyone born of God overcomes the world. This is the
victory that has overcome the world, even our faith.

1 JOHN 5:4

We all feel insecure from time to time, but based on the testimony of Scripture, "insecure" isn't at all how God wants us to live.

John the apostle reminds us in John 4:4 that we "are from God and have overcome them [the spirits not of Christ]," because the one who is in us "is greater than the one who is in the world." Further, writing to believers living in Corinth, the apostle Paul thanked God, saying, "He gives us the victory through our Lord Jesus Christ," (1 Corinthians 15:57).

If we are *in Christ*, then we are *ensured* victory. Yes, we might struggle and strain every day of our lives, but in Jesus, we win in the end.

The day that I preached these concepts, I remember that our worship team led us in that great old hymn, "Turn Your Eyes Upon Jesus." Can I remind you of the truth of that song? The chorus says this: "Turn your eyes upon Jesus // Look full in His wonderful face // And the things of earth will grow strangely dim // In the light of His glory and grace."

What things of this earth need to grow dim for you today, so that you can focus on the divine victory that is to come?

I can promise you this: If you will find your security today not in your spotless home, your soaring career, your sweet marriage, but instead in the person and preeminence of Christ, you will reconnect with your joy.

You will know beautiful, deep-seated joy.

A BLESSING FROM PAM

May you not feel ashamed today for your insecurities but instead feel compelled to bring
them to God. There, they will be overwhelmed by his goodness, his sufficiency, his grace.

Divine Increase

Then the church throughout Judea, Galilee and Samaria enjoyed a time of peace and was strengthened. Living in the fear of the Lord and encouraged by the Holy Spirit, it increased in numbers.

ACTS 9:31

A decade ago, Pastor Glenn and I began praying about launching a New Life campus downtown. We talked, prayed, and dreamed together, and when it became clear that God was laying the same vision on both of our hearts, we went to New Life's elders and asked them to help us move ahead.

For years, many people in our congregation had let us know that given their residence ten or twenty miles south of our north campus, it was tough for them to plug into our church. They wanted to participate. They just didn't have the bandwidth in their schedules to accommodate the lengthy round-trips. Furthermore, given the city council's regenerative development plans for the downtown area, a local campus there would help us reach hundreds more for Christ

After gaining clearance from our elders, our staff, and you, our congregation, we decided to take the leap, and now that downtown communities is but one of eight congregations meeting in six distinct locations that are flourishing by the grace of God.

In our reading today, Luke was clear that as the early church was faithful to practice the disciplines God had laid on their hearts—learning the Scriptures, praying and fasting together, worshiping God regularly, sharing their resources with those in need—God would be faithful to grow them up and also grow their numbers in their midst.

A BLESSING FROM PAM

Today, may you be prompted to pray for the Church of risen Christ, that she would know peace today, that she would know prosperity today, that she would know increase today, and that today she would know strength.

The Worthiest Pursuit

Flee the evil desires of youth and pursue righteousness, faith, love and peace,
along with those who call on the Lord out of a pure heart.

2 TIMOTHY 2:22

After having countless conversations with people who have been stymied by Satan, I've come to believe that the most common trap he sets is the trap of sexual temptation.

Do you remember the story of Joseph in the Old Testament book of Genesis, who was sold into slavery by his brothers but ended up being given a powerful role in the house of Potiphar, who was one of Pharaoh's officials? Genesis 39:6 says that Joseph was well-built and handsome, characteristics Potiphar's wife must have noticed too because in the following verse she wasted no time inviting Joseph to come sleep with her.

Joseph raced from Potiphar's wife's presence so quickly after she reached for him that the woman was left holding a corner of Joseph's cloak in her hand.

I think about that singular image on occasion, and about what a fitting response it was to sexual temptation, and about how you and I would be wise to do the same.

There are some temptations that we can subtly resist, and we'll be okay. But whenever sexual temptation is part of the deal, I think the better option is to flee. To run away as fast as we can. To high-tail it out of there—fast.

If you've been thinking sexually inappropriate thoughts or typing sexually inappropriate texts or speaking sexually inappropriate words or watching sexually inappropriate shows or committing sexually inappropriate acts, stop.

Stop now.

Stop now, and flee the scene.

Ask God to forgive your misstep, and begin pursuing right living today.

A BLESSING FROM PAM

May all that has been tainted in your sight, in your mind,
and in your heart be made beautifully pure today.

Where Your Loyalties Lie

But Ruth replied, "Don't urge me to leave you or to turn back from you. Where you go I will go, and where you stay I will stay. Your people will be my people and your God my God. Where you die, I will die and there I will be buried."

RUTH 1:16-17

One of the most moving scenes in all of Scripture unfolds as Ruth, a young widow, says to her mother-in-law, who is departing their land to take up residence in a foreign land, "I'm going with you." In that one move, she determined to leave all that was familiar to her, the family who loved her, and the rhythms that made home *home*.

Coming with Naomi meant certain struggle, as Ruth would be a pagan Moabite woman making her home among Israelites. She would be a foreigner, an outcast. But Ruth could not be swayed. And in what I believe was a work of the Holy Spirit, she left.

Nobody could have foreseen all that would unfold in Ruth's life as she made her way in the new, strange land. She met a man named Boaz, who would become her husband. She birthed Obed, who fathered Jesse, who fathered David, the greatest king Israel ever would know. From David's lineage came our Lord Jesus—just a staggering turn of events. And it all can be traced back to one simple woman making one difficult decision to remain loyal when logic said to run.

Rarely will you and I regret remaining faithful to the important people God has placed on our paths. There's a real void of faithfulness, of loyalty among friends and family these days. Maybe you and I can help turn the tide.

A BLESSING FROM PAM

Right here, right now, in your distinct circle of influence,
may you find a practical way to prove yourself faithful to someone today.

Something Altogether New

He is not here; he has risen, just as he said.
Come and see the place where he lay.

MATTHEW 28:6

Jesus' first followers had expectations of what it would mean to follow him, and then Good Friday came. You and I can engage in Good Friday services these days and enter into the bleakness of the scene because we know that bleakness won't last forever. We know that Easter Sunday is on its way. But back then, Jesus' followers had no clue that "the end" wasn't really the end. They followed Jesus to the mount where they saw their Messiah hanged on a cross, and all they knew was disbelief.

These disciples had listened and learned and sold and given and sacrificed and followed and adored. And all that it got them was ... this? A dead Messiah, there on a cross?

Nothing could have prepared Jesus' followers for what they would find on Easter morning. Resurrection had happened—that was the only explanation. Jesus had risen from the dead.

You understand that nothing like this had ever happened before. Resuscitations had happened—sure ... people were brought back to life before they eventually went on to die. But to have someone raised from the dead to new and eternal life? This would make headlines for sure.

In the same way that those who blasted tunnels in mountains that once thwarted forward progress along early-frontier paths, with his Son's resurrection God was saying in esssence, "I'm not settling for a way around this situation. I'm doing something explosive in their midst."

A highway right through the mountain of death—that's what the resurrection is.

The most explosive thing the world has ever known.

A BLESSING FROM PAM

May you view the central event of our faith, the resurrection of Jesus,
with fresh appreciation ... with awe ... today.

The One Who Has Been There Too

Then he said to Thomas, "Put your finger here; see my hands. Reach out your hand and put it into my side. Stop doubting and believe."

JOHN 20:27

After Jesus was resurrected he appeared to his disciples to show them that it was really him—that he really had defeated the awfulness of death. He appeared to most of those men at once, who were all gathered together on the night that Jesus showed up. But one disciple wasn't there: Thomas.

In John 20, we read this from Thomas: "Unless I see the nail marks in his hands and put my finger where the nails were, and put my hand into his side, I will not believe," (v. 25b).

The passage in John tells us that a full week passed before Thomas could be reunited with Jesus. But Jesus came into the room and, knowing of Thomas's doubts said, "Put your finger here; see my hands. Reach out your hand and put it into my side. Stop doubting and believe," (v. 27).

Jesus didn't come to Thomas with apologetics regarding the death, burial, and resurrection of himself. He came to him with his incarnation and nothing else. No philosophical arguments. No theological grandstanding. No logical schemes. Just, "put your finger here."

Jesus issues the same invitation to you.

Are you broken by the world's brokenness today? Here he stands, saying in all genuineness, "I get it. I've been there. I suffered, I bled, and I died. Put your finger here, for proof. Reach out. Touch my side."

A BLESSING FROM PAM

May you take comfort today in the presence of a God who understands. He has been where you are and emerged from that place victorious. And he offers that victory to you.

Come and Eat

Jesus said to them, "Come and have breakfast." None of the disciples
dared ask him, "Who are you?" They knew it was the Lord.

JOHN 21:12

In John 21, the disciples went out fishing and were demoralized when their nets came up empty time and again. The next morning, Jesus appeared on the shoreline, asking, "Friends, haven't you any fish?" (v. 5), to which the disciples in sad, sorry unison said only one word: "No."

"Throw your net on the right side of the boat, and you will find some," Jesus said, (v. 6), and despite what the disciples may have been thinking about how futile that ridiculous shift would surely be, they did as they were told. And the haul they took in was nearly too heavy for the net to stay intact.

After wrangling the slippery creatures onto the boat and rowing back to shore, the disciples emerged to find that Jesus had already started a fire. He'd placed fish on the fire and had bread as well. "Come and have breakfast," he said, (v. 12).

It's tempting to see the disciples' failure and to see Jesus' arrival on the scene and to think, *Ah, I get it. God is a God of second chances. That's it! Once those disciples had a second chance, they were successful in their work!*

This is the wrong takeaway.

The lesson we learn from this scene on the water is that on our own, we can't even feed ourselves, but divine breakfast is waiting for us.

That picture of Jesus cooking fish on the beach, a piping-hot loaf of bread in hand, reminds us that he is the daily nourishment we need, that he is the One who provides.

A BLESSING FROM PAM

May you entrust all of your needs to the Lord Jesus today,
believing that he is delighted to care for you.

Mover of Mountains

" ... Truly I tell you, if you have faith as small as a mustard seed, you can say to this mountain, 'Move from here to there,' and it will move. Nothing will be impossible for you."

MATTHEW 17:20B

Ten years ago, when our church was $23 million in debt, I was standing in the World Prayer Center with ministry leaders from our staff during a midday prayer time. Our worship team was leading us in the song, "Mighty to Save," and as we got to that line, "Savior, you can move the mountain ..." I stared at the top of Pikes Peak in all her grandeur and thought, *You really can move the mountain, Father. You can move our mountain of debt.*

I will move that mountain of debt, Brady, I sensed God saying, *but first I want to know something: If I release all those funds into the church that are being used right now to service your debt, what will you do with that money? How will you glorify me?*

I decided that as our church made our way out from underneath that heavy financial burden, we would use that money to support international missionaries and purchase apartment complexes to renovate for single moms and provide assistance to families in our city who were struggling just to survive. That debt is a quarter of what it used to be now, and each time we've gotten a little bump financially that's exactly what we've done.

James 4:3 says it this way: "When you ask, you do not receive, because you ask with wrong motives, that you may spend what you get on your pleasures."

It's on *his* pleasures that we're to spend our resources.

It's God's pleasure we're living for.

A BLESSING FROM PAM

May you courageously align your motives with the motives of God today, joining him in his redemptive work in the world.

Center of Our World

*And the one who sat there had the appearance of jasper and ruby. A rainbow
that shone like an emerald encircled the throne. Surrounding the throne were
twenty-four other thrones, and seated on them were twenty-four elders. They
were dressed in white and had crowns of gold on their heads. From the throne
came flashes of lightning, rumblings and peals of thunder. In front of the
throne, seven lamps were blazing. These are the seven spirits of God.*

REVELATION 4:3-5

I wonder if upon catching this revelation, John realized that he wasn't the center of
his world after all. And that for all its power and prowess, Rome wasn't the center
either. Remember, as John experienced this vision he was stranded on the island of
Patmos, placed there by Roman officials who figured if they could just isolate this
radical follower of Christ's, he'd be rendered ineffective in spreading the gospel. God
clearly had a different plan. And every time you or I read the book of Revelation still
today, we are bearing testimony to the effectiveness of that plan.

Today, natural disasters abound. Rioting continues in major cities all over our country.
Racial injustice still has us in a vise grip. Political divisiveness is at an all-time high.
People are leaving the church in droves. What a *gift* to know that God is in charge.
The world cannot give us lasting peace, but he can. And he does.

Close your eyes and pictures the scene John details above, from Revelation 4:3-5.
We're headed to a place of protection and peace, friend, a place where God is in
perfect control.

A BLESSING FROM PAM

*May you rest in the comfort that a beautiful day is dawning soon,
a day when all that is wrong will be made right.*

Jesus Holds It All

In him you were also circumcised with a circumcision not performed by human hands. Your whole self ruled by the flesh was put off when you were circumcised by Christ, having been buried with him in baptism, in which you were also raised with him through your faith in the working of God, who raised him from the dead. When you were dead in your sins and in the uncircumcision of your flesh, God made you alive with Christ. He forgave us all our sins, having canceled the charge of our legal indebtedness, which stood against us and condemned us; he has taken it away, nailing it to the cross. And having disarmed the powers and authorities, he made a public spectacle of them, triumphing over them by the cross.

COLOSSIANS 2:11-15

I've often been asked why I am so "fanatical" about Jesus Christ, and if this death-to-life idea doesn't help that fanaticism make sense, nothing will. Listen, I remember what it was like to be dead in sin. You may remember, too. It was agonizing. Exhausting. Desperate. Into that scene God sent his Son, Jesus. For the explicit purpose of giving me ... and you ... a fresh start.

And how are we access this fresh start? Simply by believing. By trusting. By yielding to the work of Jesus, both in and through our lives.

Maybe today this news can penetrate the walls you've built around your heart and life. I pray so. I pray that today, you'll accept that fresh start.

That you'll trade in your sin—your ugly, deplorable sin—for the goodness of God.

That you'll trade in death for life.

A BLESSING FROM PAM

Today may you be reminded of the sweetest exchange we could know: our sin for the righteousness of Jesus. Our pain for comfort from him.

Problems We're Called to Solve

The Spirit of the sovereign LORD is on me, because the LORD
has anointed me to proclaim good news to the poor.

ISAIAH 61:1

For many years a team of people from New Life has been driving down to Trinidad Correctional Facility to minister to men who are incarcerated there, but when the pandemic hit, we were unable to gain entry into the prison and were feeling set adrift.

The leaders of that ministry called their chaplain, Rick, and together they realized that while our people couldn't come, our people's contributions still could. That team rallied a bunch of other New Lifers, and together they assembled more than five hundred care packs for people who were still incarcerated and dozens of life-mentoring curriculum packets for people who had been paroled.

Not long after those care packs were delivered, we received an envelope from an inmate in Trinidad. Inside was a tithe check made out for ten dollars and a note that said, "Dear New Life, Your thoughts and generous actions have touched my heart and erased these long, long hours."

This passage from Isaiah is chock-full of really big efforts that we can be part of: proclaiming good news to the poor, binding up the brokenhearted, proclaiming freedom for the captives, releasing prisoners from darkness, comforting all who mourn, providing for those who grieve, and more.

How I pray we continue to make this choice, New Life, this choice to use our resources for good, for God, for the sake of freedom everywhere.

A BLESSING FROM PAM

May you know the joy today of carrying one who can't carry himself or herself,
of meeting one with comfort who is otherwise facing despair.

Divine Gathering

"At that time men will see the Son of Man coming in clouds with
great power and glory. And he will send his angels and gather his elect from
the four winds, from the ends of the earth to the ends of the heavens."

MARK 13:26-27

We're two years into the pandemic now, and still, things are rough. For several months we couldn't worship together in person. For a longer period still, we all were relegated to our homes—working from home, schooling from home, living 24/7 together from home. And while the novelty of that might seem delightful, over time it wore us all out.

These days, air travel has kicked back in. Restaurants have reopened in-dining service. Grocery stores no longer require masks. Schools are holding classes in person again. Some businesses are foregoing Zoom and getting together face to face. Undeniably things are better, but those experiences left a mark. We wanted to get back to normal for so long, even as there is no "normal" to return to. We'll never go back to where we were before because that place no longer exists. Change changes us. Change changes the world as we know it, which is exactly what happened here.

I take comfort in the words of Mark 13:26-27, which promises that at Jesus' second coming, the primary action he will undertake is to *gather* the lovers of God. Isn't that a magnificent word? *Gather.* To come together. To unify. To draw in. To pull us close and hold us tight and welcome us in as one.

If you are feeling scattered today, be reminded that if you are following Jesus, you are following the greatest Gatherer the world has ever known. You don't have to live scattered today. In Jesus we find unity, and order, and peace.

A BLESSING FROM PAM

May the God of all steadfastness hold you fast today.

Necessary Silence

*"Come to me, all you who are weary and
burdened, and I will give you rest."*

MATTHEW 11:28

When was the last time you tugged your ear buds out of your ear, stowed your digital devices in some other room, and sat or walked in silence long enough to actually have a string of coherent, God-directed thoughts? I'm telling you, this simple ability is getting rarer and rarer in our culture, the ability to pull away from technology and think. And pray. And listen to God.

Frequently on a Sunday evening, I will end the day by heading outside without my phone (gasp) and sitting in absolute silence. I'll watch the stars appear. I'll pray. And then I'll head back in to go to bed. Any guesses as to how I sleep, when I close out a day in that way?

In a word: *soundly.*

This invitation from Jesus is perhaps the most declined invitation in the history of the world—and by his own followers, no less! If we want to be technical, it's not even an invitation, but a command. He is using imperative language there: "Come to me!" Meaning, "*You*, come to me!"

That's right: he's talking to us.

He knows that left to our stubborn, activity-obsessed human nature, we will never slow, never pause, never rest. And so for our own good, and for the good of our relationship with him, he says, "Stop. You're looking for something in all that activity that activity can never fulfill. The rest your soul is craving will come only from fellowship with me."

Are you weary today?

Are you heavy-burdened?

Rest is waiting for you.

A BLESSING FROM PAM

*Today, may you sense your Father's restorative presence
as you bring your weariness to him.*

"I Did That One Time, Too"

Therefore confess your sins to each other and pray for each other so that you may be healed. The prayer of a righteous person is powerful and effective.

JAMES 5:16

When our kids were young, Pam and I noticed that while many of the disciplinary measures our kids were made to suffer were met with whining, complaining, and sometimes outright defiance, there was one response to their misbehavior that actually reeled them in instead of pushing them away: *empathy.*

Once they were out of the tantrum-prone toddler years and had achieved a measure of interpersonal savvy, we learned that the easiest way to hold their attention—and the surest way to drive home our point regarding why their wrongdoing was wrong—was not to preach or teach but rather to whisper, "I did that one time, too."

Upon hearing those words, Abram's and Callie's eyes would widen. They would lean in. The tears of shame and contrition would stop flowing as rapt attention took control. "Really?" they'd say. *"You?"*

By this point they'd nearly be salivating. "Tell us more!" they'd cheer.

There's a reason the journalism industry has the long-standing saying, "if it bleeds, it leads." We love hearing of others' misbehavior, don't we? We can't get enough of the scandalous, the salacious, the spicy. And yet there is also a beautiful aspect to this trend of confessing our sins one to another: James says that in those confessions, *we are healed.*

Drag your sin into the light, my friend.

Tell another believer of the wrong you've done.

Ask him or her to pray for you, and in so doing, may you be healed.

A BLESSING FROM PAM

May you find courage to quit hiding your sin. May you admit it.
May you boldly speak it out. And may you know healing at a soul level today.

Well Pleased

As soon as Jesus was baptized, he went up out of the water. At that moment heaven was
opened, and he saw the Spirit of God descending like a dove and alighting on him. And a
voice from heaven said, "This is my Son, whom I love; with him I am well pleased."

MATTHEW 3:16-17

Years ago I told the congregation about an occasion in our college-student ministry that sticks with me still today. Aaron Stern, who pastored that group and then turned the ministry into a New Life church plant in Fort Collins, Colorado, had noticed a real void in our college students' lives. They were wonderful young women and men, but way too many of them had never been encouraged by an older, wiser believer in Christ. They lacked the input from spiritual moms and spiritual dads that is necessary to every Christian's growth. As a first step in filling this gap, Aaron invited fifty-five mature followers of Christ to the group's weekly gathering, and toward the end of the worship service he called those folks to the front of the stage. He asked his four young sons to join him and then prayed a blessing over each of them as he laid hands on them and wrapped loving arms around each one. He thanked God for their unique personalities and for their distinctive spiritual gifts. He praised them for honoring God with their choices and for being such great sons. He asked God to bless them and to accomplish his work in and through those boys' lives. He then prayed for each of his son's protection, for his safety, for his provision, for his peace. He finished by looking at them one at a time and saying, "You're an amazing young man! I'm so thankful for you, and I love you. I bless you in the name of Christ."

He then looked at the congregation and said, "I know that many of you have never had a father say things like this to you, and so tonight, I have invited fifty-five spiritually mature men to stand here for as long as it takes and look at you and lay hands on you and hug you and encourage you in Christ."

Pastor Aaron closed his part of the service and invited people to come forward who wanted this type of ministry that night, and the room tipped over as young women and young men flooded the aisles and packed themselves ten-deep in front of the stage. They were sponges soaking up long-awaited care. They were orphans trying to come home.

Just before Jesus began his public ministry, he chose to be baptized by John to let onlookers know that he was devoted to following God's will rather than going the world's way with his life. And as soon as he was emerged from the waters of baptism, his Father expressed his delight. "This is my Son, whom I love," he said. "With him I am well pleased," (Matthew 3:17).

Do you know how drastically the crime rate in this country would drop and how many mental-illness issues could be resolved and how quickly we could engage this generation in the cause of Christ if every person walking the planet knew how deeply loved he or she was by God? .

Let's begin this shift with you. Friend, you are deeply loved by God. You are so loved by him, in fact, that he sent his Son to die a brutal death to rescue you.

You are seen by God.

You are loved by God.

With you, your Father is well pleased.

A BLESSING FROM PAM

*May you rest in the wild and wonderful acceptance
and adoration of your heavenly Father today.*

Choosing to Remain

Whoever dwells in the shelter of the Most High will rest in the shadow of the Almighty.
I will say of the LORD, "He is my refuge and my fortress, my God, in whom I trust."

PSALM 91:1-2

Pam and I married when we were twenty-two, and back then I was running my life at a breakneck pace. I taught junior- and senior-level English literature; coached both boys' and girls' varsity basketball, boys' JV basketball, junior-high basketball, high-school track and field; was the campus pastor for the entire school; and served as the volunteer youth pastor at the church that was attached to the school. All told, these commitments kept me busy from six in the morning until eleven at night, grading papers, holding parent-teacher conferences, tutoring students, leading practices, driving buses, coaching games, washing uniforms, and more.

Busyness equaled movement, and movement was necessary for me to get ahead.

I look back on those days and shake my head in mystified incredulity. What a miss it all proved to be. I missed out on the early days of my marriage. I missed out on forming habits that would have served me well for years and decades to come. And I missed out on time with God.

Jesus offers us a different way. "Remain in me," he promises in John 15:5, "and you will bear much fruit."

What I would give to go back to the early-twenty-something version of me, look him in the face, and say, "Brady, be very careful about where you choose to remain. Only one place gets top billing, and that place is in the presence of God."

A BLESSING FROM PAM

God will make good on his promise here:
remain in him, and your life will bear fruit.

Power in the Cross

For the message of the cross is foolishness to those who are perishing,
but to us who are being saved it is the power of God.

1 CORINTHIANS 1:18

A concern I carry is that as Christians, we have made the cross palatable. We decorate with it. We put flowers around it. We cast it in gold, thread a chain through it, and wear it around our necks. But to the apostle Paul, the cross represented serious business. This Roman method of execution was so tortuous that you never would have alluded to it in polite company, let alone glorified it.

Crucifixion was a shameful way to die, and nobody wanted to be reminded that the One they'd devoted their lives to had been murdered on a Roman cross. This was a culture that celebrated the successful and the strong. This image of a poor, weak, vulnerable Jesus being put to death in this manner went against everything they esteemed.

This is why Paul referred to the message of the cross as "foolishness to those who are perishing," (1 Corinthians 1:18). Who wanted a crucified Lord?

And yet to those who are being saved, Paul continued, "it is the power of God."

It is by the power of the cross that believers can live blamelessly.

It is by the power of the cross that churches can operate harmoniously.

It is by the power of the cross that humility can mark a human heart.

The apostle Paul knew that the practical shifts he was asking believers in Corinth to make would happen only by the power of the cross, and so he fixed his gaze on the old rugged cross, trusting that there, all wrongs would be made right.

A BLESSING FROM PAM

May you know the power of the cross of Christ today,
which carries with it the power to transform your life.

Divine Increase

Yet the news about him spread all the more, so that crowds of
people came to hear him and to be healed of their sicknesses.
But Jesus often withdrew to lonely places and prayed.

LUKE 5:15-16

The first time this pair of verses hit me in any sort of meaningful way, I remember being struck more by the fact that news about Jesus was spreading quickly than by the part about him withdrawing to pray. Interesting, isn't it? We're probably moved by one or the other; we're probably not moved by both.

In later years, after maturity had its way a bit, I was leveled by the fact that Jesus didn't withdraw to pray only when things were overwhelming and he was tired or facing burnout. No, the text refutes that with the little adverb, "often." He often withdrew. Even when things were going well.

It begs a question, I think: would those who know you well say that you often withdraw to pray?

My guess is that you're smart. And talented at something. And maybe even accomplished. I can guarantee you're interesting—I've never met a person who isn't. What I'm not so sure of is this: are you a person of faithful prayer?

Only one of those characteristics will bring daily peace to your soul.

Prayer, alone, is where peace gets found.

A BLESSING FROM PAM

May you set aside all other obligations for a few minutes today and come joyfully
before God in prayer. He is your Father, and he longs to spend time with you! He has
wisdom to impart to you that can be found nowhere else.

On Inheriting Eternal Life

On one occasion an expert in the law stood up to test Jesus.
"Teacher," he asked, "what must I do to inherit life?"

LUKE 10:25

The Parable of the Good Samaritan is the most famous one Jesus told. Found in Luke 10:30-37, it reads:

"A man was going down from Jerusalem to Jericho, when he was attacked by robbers. They stripped him of his clothes, beat him and went away, leaving him half dead. A priest happened to be going down the same road, and when he saw the man, he passed by on the other side. So too, a Levite, when he came to the place and saw him, passed by on the other side. But a Samaritan, as he traveled, came where the man was; and when he saw him, he took pity on him. He went to him and bandaged his wounds, pouring on oil and wine. Then he put the man on his own donkey, brought him to an inn and took care of him. The next day he took out two denarii and gave them to the innkeeper. 'Look after him,' he said, 'and when I return, I will reimburse you for any extra expense you may have.'

"Which of these three do you think was a neighbor to the man who fell into the hands of robbers?"

The expert in the law replied, "The one who had mercy on him."

Two phrases occur to me as I read this story: Love God, and love *like* God. That's what we're to do.

Love God.

Love *like* God.

That's what the Samaritan did.

"Go," Jesus said, "and do likewise." Those words weren't just for the teachers of the law, but for you and me as well.

A BLESSING FROM PAM

May you shine like light in the darkness for someone who needs your help today.

Careful with the Name

One day the evil spirit answered them,
"Jesus I know, and Paul I know about, but who are you?"

ACTS 19:15

There's nothing worse than a name dropper—especially when that name belongs to the Lord. In a remarkable story from the book of Acts, we learn that as God was "doing extraordinary miracles by the hands of Paul," (19:11), some were seeking to capitalize on this power. Acts 19:13-14 says that "some of the itinerant Jewish exorcists undertook to invoke the name of the Lord Jesus over those who had evil spirits, saying, 'I adjure you by the Jesus whom Paul proclaims.' Seven sons of a Jewish high priest named Sceva were doing this."

But then a truly astounding thing occurred. The next verse reports that one of the evil spirits had the audacity to talk back.

Can you imagine how freaked out you'd be?

"But the evil spirit answered them," Acts 19:15 says. (Ever wondered what an evil spirit says? Read on.) "'Jesus I know, and Paul I recognize, but who are you?'"

I love that line. *Who do you think you are, invoking the holy name of Christ?*

From there, Scripture says, "the man in whom was the evil spirit leaped on them, mastered all of them and overpowered them, so that they fled out of that house naked and wounded," (v. 16).

Why were they naked? Not sure either.

But the point of the story stands: We must be careful not to misuse the name of Jesus. If we want the power that he brings, we must have a personal relationship with him.

A BLESSING FROM PAM

Lean fully into your relationship with Jesus today!
Fellowship with him intimately, and know the power that is always at hand.

APRIL

"What has God been asking you to do that you've been avoiding day after day? Your Father is always pleased by action that's motivated by faith in him. Faithfulness nets real rewards."

- Pastor Brady Boyd -

A Bit of Faith

*And without faith it is impossible to please God, because
anyone who comes to him must believe that he exists and
that he rewards those who earnestly seek him.*

HEBREWS 11:6

A few years ago during one of our church's "First Wednesday" services, I received a prompting from God. *Take up an offering for those deputies*, he seemed to say.

Several weeks prior I'd had a conversation with our county's sheriff, during which he informed me that 155 of our city's deputies did not possess adequate tactical gear for managing hostile situations. They needed bulletproof vests, and yet there was no money to fund that need.

Pam is always a voice of reason in my life, so I leaned over and whispered to her about the deputies and what I'd heard, to which she said, "Do it. Do what God has asked you to do."

Still, I hesitated. Did Pam (or God?) have a clue how much each set cost? Fourteen hundred bucks a pop. Fourteen hundred times *155*.

My brain whirred to make sense of this. Upward of *$200,000*.

Here. Tonight. On a whim.

Despite the fear that creeped up my neck, I knew it was time to help.

More than $100,000—that's what came in that one night.

And scores of officers felt a level of safety and protection they had never, ever felt.

What is God asking you to do right now? What has he *been* asking you to do that you've been avoiding day after day? Your Father is always pleased by action motivated by faith in him. Faithfulness will *always* net a reward.

A BLESSING FROM PAM

*May you know the sheer joy of stepping out in obedience today, operating not according
to all that is seen and understood but according to simple, God-directed faith.*

Quiet Endurance

For this reason, since the day we heard about you, we have not stopped praying for you. We continually ask God to fill you with the knowledge of his will through all the wisdom and understanding that the Spirit gives, so that you may live a life worthy of the Lord and please him in every way: bearing fruit in every good work, growing in the knowledge of God, being strengthened with all power according to his glorious might so that you may have great endurance and patience, and giving joyful thanks to the Father, who has qualified you to share in the inheritance of his holy people in the kingdom of light.

COLOSSIANS 1:9-12

Have you ever wondered if it even matters that you live uprightly?

Paul wrote the book of Colossians to people who did. The Colossians were unnamed believers who were part of a fledging church living in a declining city nobody cared about. Did it even matter if they lived righteous lives? Paul had opinions about that.

If you're feeling small or insignificant today ... unseen even as you do good ... then let the words of Paul sink deeply into your spirit: the Lord indeed cares about your good works. He cares deeply that your life is bearing fruit. He cares deeply that you are growing in the knowledge of him. He cares deeply that you don't give up.

To look across the pages of Scripture is to see seasons of real anonymity in the lives of some of the greatest lovers of God ever to live—Moses, David, Jesus himself.

Your faithfulness? It may not get the attention of people. But it sure has the attention of God.

A BLESSING FROM PAM

*May your Father's pleasure be enough for you today
as you live a life worthy of his name.*

Reaching for the Power We Need

*Now when Jesus returned, a crowd welcomed him, for they were all expecting
him. Then a man named Jairus, a synagogue leader, came and fell at Jesus' feet,
pleading with him to come to his house because his only daughter, a girl of about
twelve, was dying. As Jesus was on his way, the crowds almost crushed him.
And a woman was there who had been subject to bleeding for twelve years, but no
one could heal her. She came up behind him and touched the edge of his cloak,
and immediately her bleeding stopped. "Who touched me?" Jesus asked. When they
all denied it, Peter said, "Master, the people are crowding and pressing
against you." But Jesus said, "Someone touched me; I know that power has gone
out from me." Then the woman, seeing that she could not go unnoticed, came
trembling and fell at his feet. In the presence of all the people, she told why she
had touched him and how she had been instantly healed. Then he said to her,
"Daughter, your faith has healed you. Go in peace."*

LUKE 8:40-48

When we read of Jesus stopping everything to head to Jairus's house to heal his
daughter, we nod our heads in understanding. Jairus was a leader in the church,
respected among his community, worthy of the aid he was about to receive.

But to see Jesus search high and low for one of society's lowest members—a
diseased woman who had been an outcast for more than a decade—we shake our
heads in awe.

Jesus has time for *her?*

Jesus has time for ... us?

A simple brush against his garment with her fingertips—that's all the faith it took
for her to be healed.

That same Healer stands before you now. What brokenness of yours needs to be
made whole?

A BLESSING FROM PAM

*Today, may you come to Jesus to find the healing he holds in his hands.
Come to him. Come trembling, if you must. Just come.*

Clean Hands, Pure Heart

*Who may ascend the mountain of the LORD? Who may stand in his holy place? The
one who has clean hands and a pure heart, who does not trust in an idol or swear by
a false god. They will receive blessing from the LORD and vindication from God their
Savior. Such is the generation of those who seek him, who seek your face, God of Jacob.*

PSALM 24:3-6

In ancient times lovers of God would travel up to the temple in Jerusalem to worship
him, and as they went, they would recite poetry, pray prayers, and sing songs to God.
I love picturing this scene—a throng of faithful ones, eager to get to the house of the
Lord, where they can be reminded that there is a God and that he is good.

As we step out in faith to come near to God—with blameless actions, with right
attitudes and motives—God comes near to us. When we come humbly, in other
words, he heartily steps toward us. Matthew 5:8 declares the pure in heart "blessed,"
reminding us that it is they who "will see God."

It's not that we have to clean ourselves up before we can come into God's
presence—that's the wrong takeaway here. God, by his Spirit's power and his Son's
sacrifice, is the only one who can declare us righteous, fit to share space with him.
No, it's that as we enter God's presence *with the motivation of surrendering to and
serving him alone,* we are welcomed in by him.

"Who may ascend the hill of the Lord?" What a good question to ask ourselves today.
What a perfect way to assess the current state of our hands and hearts.

A BLESSING FROM PAM

*May you listen closely for the voice of your heavenly Father today,
letting all other voices fall away.*

Returning to God

"I the LORD do not change. So you, the descendants of Jacob, are not destroyed.
Ever since the time of your ancestors you have turned away from my decrees and have
not kept them. Return to me, and I will return to you," says the LORD Almighty."

MALACHI 3:6-7

For nearly fifteen years I have prayed for New Life Church. During most of those prayer times, I am deeply encouraged as I lift up requests for your safety and provision, for your expansion and growth. But on two occasions—just two out of thousands and thousands of times—I have been sobered as I prayed, a specific burden weighing me down.

The burden I bore was this: "Father, as the things of this world start going well for some of us, please keep us from worshiping a cheap imitation of you."

Jesus told his followers that it is impossible to serve two masters. "Either you will hate the one and love the other, or you will be devoted to the one and despise the other. You cannot serve both God and money," (Luke 16:13). So while I am always grateful for economic conditions that allow us to experience financial prosperity, I'm also aware that earthly success has an allure to it. If we're not careful, it can cause us to start worshiping created things instead of the Creator God.

This is what the prophet Malachi was getting at, proving that this temptation we face today is absolutely nothing new. The answer for us is the same answer that stood for them: we must return to God.

Even when our bank account is bulging ...

Even when our business is booming ...

Even when the stars are all aligning ...

Especially then, we must return to God.

A BLESSING FROM PAM

May you find fulfillment today in the unparalleled fellowship of God.

Through Him and For Him

The Son is the image of the invisible God, the firstborn over all creation. For in him all things were created: things in heaven and on earth, visible and invisible, whether thrones or powers or rulers or authorities; all things have been created through him and for him. He is before all things, and in him all things hold together. And he is the head of the body, the church; he is the beginning and the firstborn from among the dead, so that in everything he might have the supremacy. For God was pleased to have all his fullness dwell in him, and through him to reconcile to himself all things, whether things on earth or things in heaven, by making peace through his blood, shed on a cross.

COLOSSIANS 1:15-20

This passage from Colossians is known as the Christ Hymn and is perhaps the greatest description of Jesus in the Bible. As you read these verses, be reminded of *who* Jesus is, of *where* he is, of *when* he is, of *how* he is. And then meditate on these words from the next three verses from Colossians 1, the so-what to the passage above:

"Once you were alienated from God and were enemies in your minds because of your evil behavior. But now he has reconciled you by Christ's physical body through death to present you holy in his sight, without blemish and free from accusation—if you continue in your faith, established and firm, and do not move from the hope held out in the gospel," (Colossians 1:21-23a).

This person of Jesus is our means for coming to God. He is our means for being found acceptable by God. He is our means for life that is truly life.

A BLESSING FROM PAM

May you live through Jesus and for Jesus today.

Persevering in Prayer

But many who heard the message believed; so the
number of men who believed grew to about five thousand.

ACTS 4:4

In the book of Acts, Luke recounts that the early church was inclined to pray. "They all joined together constantly in prayer," he wrote in Acts 1:14, "along with the women and Mary the mother of Jesus, and with his brothers."

In my estimation it is no coincidence that those believers saw miracles unfold in their midst, such as the outcome described here in Acts 4:4, where thousands came to faith in Christ.

The fact that this report shows up in our Bibles a page or two after we learn about the early church's prayer habit can cause us to think that the two events happened one after the other: pray, receive answer to prayer, like a magic trick, bing, bang, boom.

In reality, the miraculous acts of the apostles that we see unfold happen not instantaneously but across more than *twenty-five years*.

My point: the blessings of perseverance come only to those who persevere.

This is why we come together, believing.

This is why we pray.

A BLESSING FROM PAM

May God expand your belief today that he is who he says he is and that he will do what he says
he will do—in the manner of his own determining, and in the timing that he deems right.

Glimmer of God

Whoever oppresses the poor shows contempt for their Maker,
but whoever is kind to the needy honors God.

PROVERBS 14:31

A pastor I once served under had great vision for serving people who were poor. To combat the problems in our city of Shreveport—gang violence, crack use, increased murder rate—he wanted members of our church to connect personally with every resident in the zip codes, zip codes where most of the problems also lived.

Wanting to help out, I put together a team that for three months' time met regularly to log people's names, addresses, and needs. We connected people in our congregation with residents in those areas, adopting block by block, and began blanketing the neighborhoods with the love and peace of Jesus.

We'd go introduce ourselves to "our" residents. We'd come every Saturday before lunchtime to ask how we could pray for them. We'd sit on their porches, in their living rooms, on their back stoops. And we'd ask questions, and listen, and care. Pam and I served about twenty families those years, and I did weddings and funerals and baby dedications as those friends passed through various stages of life. We visited them when they were in the hospital. We brought food to them when they were hungry. We showed up when they felt all alone in the world. We loved them, and they loved us.

Still today, those faces will flash through my thoughts from time to time, those deep-water eyes, those wide smiles, those foreheads glistening with sweat. I see a glimmer of God in each gaze.

Where do you find a glimmer of God?

A BLESSING FROM PAM

May you pause your pursuits long enough today to see God in the needs of another.
And may you honor your heavenly Father by meeting the need you can meet.

Called to Serve

For even the Son of Man did not come to be served, but to serve,
and to give his life as a ransom for many.

MARK 10:45

Over the years I have talked with countless people who love God and who long to follow God but who seem disappointed that life isn't as exciting or adventuresome or stimulating as they hoped it would be. And on each of those occasions, my response has been the same: "The moment you decide that doing even some seemingly insignificant thing for God is more important to you than pursuing all the things that seem significant for you, that thrilling life will show up in a jiffy. You'll never be spiritually bored again."

You and I are called to serve. Furthermore, you and I are called to serve God's agenda in the world, not ours. Which means that we won't always understand the assignment he asks us to complete. My advice in these situations? *Complete it anyway.*

Do the thing God is asking you to do, even if it inconveniences you. Even if it embarrasses you. Even if it doesn't fit within your gifting. Even if it doesn't make sense. Do what he asks. Do it now. Do it joyfully. And get ready for quite a ride.

A BLESSING FROM PAM

May you whisper an immediate yes to God today.

Failing Forward

Now the LORD provided a huge fish to swallow Jonah, and Jonah was in the belly of the fish three days and three nights. From inside the fish Jonah prayed to the LORD his God. He said, "In my distress I called to the LORD, and he answered me. From deep in the realm of the dead I called for help, and you listened to my cry. You hurled me into the depths into the very heart of the seas, and the currents swirled about me; all your waves and breakers swept over me. I said, 'I have been banished from your sight; yet I will look again toward your holy temple.' The engulfing waters threatened me, the deep surrounded me; seaweed was wrapped around my head. To the roots of the mountains I sank down; the earth beneath barred me in forever. But you, Lord my God, brought my life up from the pit."

JONAH 1:17-2:6

You've probably heard the story of Jonah before, how he refused to do what God asked him to do in ministering to the people of Ninevah, instead running in the opposite direction and fleeing the presence of God. But unless you've looked at a map of this series of events, it's tough to get your arms around the sheer scope of this disobedient act. If you were to head to the far eastern edge of the Great Sea and then go inland about a thousand miles, you'd find the city of Ninevah, where Jonah was supposed to report. Where did he go instead? "He headed "for Tarshish," Jonah 1:3 says, all the way across the Mediterranean, to the farthest westernmost point.

Isn't that a great picture of what we do when we sin?

I'm outta here, we think. *Get me as far away from God as I can get.*

And yet as Jonah's testimony bears out, things never work out when we run.

The next time you fail God, keep one thing in mind: regardless of what you have done (or refused to do, as was the case for Jonah), repentance will place you back on God's path. Repentance—the simple turning from sin toward righteousness—is what allows us to return to God. Every spiritual advance begins with turning away from what's hindering obedience to him. Leave the sin, and you'll lean toward God, 100 percent of the time.

A BLESSING FROM PAM

Today, may you spare yourself the pain and agony of running away from God, instead choosing to plant your feet, take a deep breath, and do the thing that he's asked you to do.

Returning to God

Create in me a pure heart, O God, and renew a steadfast spirit within me.
Do not cast me from your presence or take your Holy Spirit from me. Restore to me the
joy of your salvation and grant me a willing spirit, to sustain me.

PSALM 51:10-12

What's sustaining you these days?

That's a good question, isn't it? We can look everywhere for things that we think will sustain us: that morning cup of coffee, our favorite snacks throughout the day, the attention and affection of a spouse or friend, accolades at work, a little "me" time, faithfulness to hitting the gym three times a week. We think if we just order our lives in a certain way, we will be sustained.

This never pans out to be true.

In this powerful psalm written by David after he sinned against God by sleeping with Bathsheba and then having her husband killed by placing him on the front lines of the war, you get the feeling he was a little more in touch than usual with where sustenance is actually found. In the passage above the final sentiment is key to the whole deal: It is when we have a willing spirit to pursue the things of God that those pursuits are met by him. It is a willing spirit that leads us to a pure heart. It is a willing spirit that leads us to renewed steadfastness. It is a willing spirit that leads us to restored joy.

When our spirit is willing, we will be fully sustained.

A BLESSING FROM PAM

May you be held in God sustaining promises today.

Always Seen and Intimately Known

You know when I sit and when I rise; you perceive my thoughts from afar.
You discern my going out and my lying down; you are familiar with all my ways.

PSALM 139:2-3

Civilla Durfee Martin is most famous for having written the lyrics to a hymn titled, "His Eye is on the Sparrow." One of the lines in that song says, "I sing because I'm happy!" and if we're not careful we might think that what Mrs. Martin meant was that she was singing because everything in life was going her way. That couldn't be further from the truth.

As the story goes, after Mrs. Martin and her husband befriended another couple, Mr. and Mrs. Doolittle, they learned that in addition to the wife having been bedridden for nearly twenty years, the husband was incurably disabled and had to prop himself up in a wheelchair all day long. The Doolittles had every reason to complain about life, but they chose a different path.

During a visit to the Doolittles' home, Mr. Martin commented to Mr. Doolittle on his "bright hopefulness" and asked what his secret to happiness was. Answering on her husband's behalf, Mrs. Doolittle pointed heavenward and said, "His eye is on the sparrow, and I know he watches me."

The brokenness of this world can weigh down even the most optimistic person, but the same God who raised his Son from the grave is watching you today. He sees you, and his heart is inclined toward you. That is what made Mrs. Martin happy, the knowledge that she was seen and known by God and that someday, when God set the entire world right, there would be pain and suffering no more.

A BLESSING FROM PAM

May you relax into the reality that you are seen today
by the only One who can inject hope into even hopeless situations.

Salt and Light

You are the salt of the earth ... You are the light of the world ...

MATTHEW 5:13, 14

A woman named Jessica was living with her boyfriend in Washington State, trying to find work while enduring a horribly abusive relationship. At seven months pregnant, Jessica found herself locked in a closet, bloodied and scared out of her mind. She was hungry, thirsty, cold, and alone. She had no idea when she'd get out of the cramped space or if her boyfriend was even still around.

From the floor of the closet Jessica traced the baseboards with her frail fingers until her hand happened upon a finishing tack. She worked that tack loose and then jimmied the door lock until she was free. Opening the door as quietly as she could, she slipped through the shadows, grabbed her purse from the kitchen counter, and silently left the dingy apartment through the front door.

I've got to get to Colorado, Jessica told herself. She'd always dreamed of living in Colorado, and now she had her chance. But with no money or gas, how would she make it there?

Twice en route to Colorado, Jessica stumbled upon local churches that outfitted her with donated clothing free of charge. "What else can we help you with before you head off?" a staff member at one of the churches had asked her, even as she filled a sack with a Bible and snacks for Jessica's next leg of the trip.

Eventually, Jessica made it to Colorado Springs, where she pieced together the money from so many strangers and rented a storage unit. Leveraging the portable restrooms at a nearby campground, as well as a creek that ran behind her "house," Jessica decorated her space from the dumpsters that were positioned all over the storage facility's campus. "People throw away the *most* amazing things," she said.

For the month leading up to her child's birth, Jessica collected enough odds and ends to begin something of a resale business. She'd find beat-up dressers or chairs that were missing a leg and restore them with dumpster supplies. Then she'd drive to the local library, where she had computer access, and post her custom pieces on sites like Craigslist. She was starting to turn a profit when her baby decided to come.

Once her contractions started, Jessica drove herself to the nearest hospital she could find. She feared the worst: when hospital staff discovered that she had no place of residence, no job, no bank account, no insurance, and an out-of-state driver's license, they would surely take her baby from her. Her child would become a ward of the state. By the time she reached the emergency entrance, Jessica was a wreck. She was crying so hysterically that triage nurses had trouble understanding why she was there.

One of the nurses tending to Jessica knew of Mary's Home, the supportive-housing community that New Life and other churches run on the south side of town for mothers and their children who are homeless, and excused herself to place a call. Jessica was accepted the next day.

Fast-forward two years, and Jessica had graduated from the Mary's Home program, relocated to northern Colorado, rented a one-bedroom apartment, and officially launched her online furniture shop. Today, she clears nearly $60,000 a year in income. She pays for her own insurance. She has money for food and gas. And she is involved in a local church, holding babies the same age as her own little girl each week while those babies' parents serve on the worship team.

For days after I heard Jessica's story, I looked at the people around me differently, the ones who were clearly in need. I saw "Jessicas" everywhere: people who needed a break, some food. I also thought about the people at the gas stations Jessica had stopped at, how they'd paused, and probed, and cared. And about the church staff who had welcomed her in, clothing her not just with shirts and jeans but also with Christlike love.

And I thought about that nurse who'd reached out to Mary's Home. Such a simple act that phone call was, and yet look where it ultimately led. I thought about the thousands of donors who had made Mary's Home possible in the first place, and of the staff there who always work hard to make new residents feel at home. I thought about how each of us is a scene in every stranger's story, and how we get to decide whether that scene will be marked by compassion, or if apathy will have its way.

A BLESSING FROM PAM

May you be one who helps a Jessica today.

Blessed to Bless God

*After Abram returned from defeating Kedorlaomer and the kings allied with him,
the king of Sodom came out to meet him in the Valley of Shaveh (that is, the King's
Valley). Then Melchizedek king of Salem brought out bread and wine. He was priest
of God Most High, and he blessed Abram, saying, "Blessed be Abram by God Most
High, Creator of heaven and earth. And praise be to God Most High, who delivered
your enemies into your hand." Then Abram gave him a tenth of everything.*

GENESIS 14:17-20

In this passage from Genesis, Abram returned from a military victory and was
received with deferential hospitality from Jerusalem's spiritual leader, the priest
Melchidezek. And yet both men recognized that despite their renown, it was God
who had yielded this blessing. And it was God who should be praised.

By offering Melchidezek "a tenth of everything," Abram was not only acknowledging
the authority and prowess of Melchizedek, but also declaring with his actions that he
chose to submit only to the authority of God.

Scholars have long held that Melchizedek is a type of Jesus Christ, who would later
be referred to as a "great high priest," (see Hebrews 4:14), so for us this passage
takes on greater meaning still. When we experience a positive outcome, are we
quick to honor God? With our words and with our actions, do we respond by
gathering up glory for him?

I've long held that based on the example of Jesus and on passages such as this one,
the only reason we experience blessing is to turn around and bless God's name.

It is from his hand that all blessing comes.

It is always the doing of God.

A BLESSING FROM PAM

*In Christ, you are richly blessed. May you be in touch with that blessed reality today,
and may you bless God for the goodness you've known.*

Waiting Well

*When the people saw that Moses was so long in coming down
from the mountain, they gathered around Aaron and said, "Come,
make us gods who will go before us. As for this fellow Moses who brought
us up out of Egypt, we don't know what has happened to him."*

EXODUS 32:1

In Exodus 32, we find Moses on top of Mount Sinai, receiving the second set of stone tablets from the Lord, on which God was inscribing the laws he expected his people to follow. Down below, the Israelites were getting antsy, having decided that forty days and forty nights was just too long to wait.

By the time of these events, God had already rescued his beloved people from slavery in Egypt, where they'd been imprisoned for generations. He'd parted the Red Sea for them. He'd sprinkled manna from heaven on them. Wanting them to be set apart for holiness, he'd given his Law to them. He'd been with them every step of the way. And yet when a delay little more than a month unfolded, they decided it was time to abandon God.

It's tempting to turn away from God when he acts in ways we don't understand. But to turn from God is to turn toward something else. And just as those man-made golden idols could give the Hebrew people nothing in return for their worship, anything you choose to worship but the one true God will be an object of futility at best.

Being faithful to God means staying faithful even in the waiting. It means forsaking the corrupt practices of our past once and for all and trusting that by the power of the Holy Spirit a path forward will be paved.

A BLESSING FROM PAM

*May you receive fresh perspective that your God has not forsaken you,
there in your waiting. May your faith in his goodness expand today.*

Where All Growth Begins

*Repent, then, and turn to God, so that your sins may be wiped out, that times of
refreshing may come from the Lord, and that he may send the Messiah,
who has been appointed for you—even Jesus.*

ACTS 3:19

Repentance is the key to every step of growth in your life. All spiritual advances begin here, with the decision to stop disobeying, to turn back to God, and to begin walking once more toward him.

Repentance is simply saying to God, "I was wrong. I made a mistake. I blame myself for where I've ended up. And now, I want to come home."

A note on this process, worthwhile though it is: repentance does not magically erase the consequences of our sin. There is a price to pay for disobedience, and despite Jesus having paid that price in an eternal sense before God, we may be made to "pay" for what we've done here on earth. If you break the law, you may have to stand trial. If you file inaccurate expense reports, you may lose your job. If you misuse a substance, you may suffer the agonies of detox. These natural results aren't indications that you're doing something wrong, that you're now headed in the wrong direction as you seek to correct your position before God. In fact, they're indications that you're doing something *right*. And truly, better to walk through those consequences with God cheering you on than to walk through them gravely alone.

If you long for growth today, repent.

Turn from your self-focused, self-referential attitudes and actions, and return to the Lover of your soul.

A BLESSING FROM PAM

May you take even one step toward God today.

On All Sides, God

At once I was in the Spirit, and there before me was a throne in heaven with someone sitting on it. And the one who sat there had the appearance of jasper and ruby. A rainbow that shone like an emerald encircled the throne. Surrounding the throne were twenty-four other elders. They were dressed in white and had crowns of gold on their heads. From the throne came flashes of lightning, rumblings and peals of thunder. In front of the throne, seven lamps were blazing. These are the seven spirits of God.

REVELATION 4:2-5

When I was a boy my mom and dad were always around. The world had its troubles, especially as I entered middle-school years. But no matter what happened "out there," inside my house, there was peace. My parents' presence was sure, and that presence had a settling effect on my soul.

When we read John's words in Revelation 4 about God's throne in heaven, we are meant to be similarly settled in our soul. In that future, glorified state, we will be utterly surrounded by the presence of God. When we look left, he will be there. When we look right, he will be there. When we look up and down and inward and outward, there our God will be. In the ultimate manifestation of what the psalmist calls being "hemmed in" behind and before, (Psalm 139), we will experience God on all sides, always.

Here's my encouragement along these lines: the next time you sing songs of worship to God, sing with this future image in mind. Refuse to let worship songs be mere words on a screen. Instead, practice relishing his nearness, his presence, lifeblood of all our coming days.

A BLESSING FROM PAM

May you rest in the approach of our
unapproachable Light today.

Real Rest

Then, because so many people were coming and going
that they did not even have a chance to eat, he [Jesus] said to them,
"Come with me by yourselves to a quiet place and get some rest."

MARK 6:31

During the early days of my marriage, when I was running too fast and pushing too hard, I found it difficult to "come down." And so I kept the pedal to the metal, upping my RPMs while praying each and every moment that I'd somehow avoid a crash.

But the reality is that we always have to come down. We can't stay up forever. And because I refused to learn how to slow myself in a healthy manner, I was forced to walk an unhealthy path, a path paved with Internet pornography. From a place of deep humility, I have shared with New Life how challenging it was to untangle myself from the grip of pornography across the span of several years in my twenties, but by God's grace, I did get free.

For years, I looked back on that stretch of sinfulness with disbelief; how could I stoop to that level? Things make more sense to me now. When you and I don't say yes to God's form of rest, we will say yes to a fraudulent form, cooked up by Satan himself. We will say yes to porn or to wine or to drugs or to gambling or to extravagant spending—all in the name of "unwinding." It's proof that real rest is opposed, that rest without God is not "rest" at all.

A BLESSING FROM PAM

May you find rest—real rest—in the presence of your heavenly Father today.

Standing with God

We do, however, speak a message of wisdom among the mature,
but not the wisdom of this age or of the rulers of this age, who are
coming to nothing. No, we declare God's wisdom, a mystery that has
been hidden and that God destined for our glory before time began.

1 CORINTHIANS 2:6-7

In Paul's letter to the church at Corinth, the apostle acknowledged that his message might read as foolishness to some of the believers gathered there. It is a message of wisdom, he said in 1 Corinthians 2:6, but "not the kind of wisdom that belongs to this world or to the rulers of this world." By definition, the "wisdom that belongs to the world" is any thinking that is apart from God.

To be fair, the Corinthian people had every reason to be impressed with themselves. They had settled in a new land and made a respectable name for themselves. Things were looking good, and the town's prosperity had them to thank. Paul didn't come to take any of those gains away from them; rather, he came to say that there's a wisdom that is greater still. Would they esteem themselves, or God?

At its core, Paul's ministry to the church at Corinth centered on a singular question: *Are you sure, Corinthian believers, that you want to stand by the choice you've made?*

This is a key point because, by extension, Paul's question begs an answer from you and me too. How will we respond to the pains of our age? And decades from now, as we look back on our lives, will we be pleased with the choice that we made?

A BLESSING FROM PAM

May you—may we all—speak and act today in a way that confirms the choice
we've made to be impressed not with ourselves but with Jesus Christ, our Lord.

Love's Starting Point

Love is patient,
love is kind.

1 CORINTHIANS 13:4A

The most famous passage of Scripture on the topic of love was written by the apostle Paul to the church at Corinth and begins this way: "Love is patient, love is kind," (1 Corinthians 13:4). In the Amplified Bible the verse reads this way: Love endures with patience and serenity, love is kind and thoughtful, (v. 4), and while these concepts may seem straightforward enough to us, to the people to whom Paul was writing they must have seemed an unattainable goal. Believers at Corinth were living under the shadow of a tyrannical Roman regime; they were supposed to be patient with and kind to *that*?

We tend to look at the landscape of our lives and ask the same question: We're supposed to be patient with and kind to *that*?

In terms of our posture toward all people, the answer to both is yes.

We begin from a place of patience.

We begin with kindness as our goal.

We approach every interaction, every situation, with divine love leading the way.

A BLESSING FROM PAM

Because you are richly loved, may you richly love today.

The Goodness of God

*The Lord is good to all; he has
compassion on all he has made.*

PSALM 145:9

Much is being written these days on younger generations fleeing the faith, leaving the church, and abandoning God. They grew up in Christian homes but aren't sure they believe what their parents believe anymore. "Nones," they're called, referring to the box they might tick on a healthcare application next to the prompt, "Religious Affiliation."

Or "deconstructionists," referring to their primary spiritual pastime at the moment.

This trend has older, more mature Christ followers understandably in a tizzy. What will become of the faith if our children and grandchildren don't believe?

There is a singular reason for this mass exodus, and it's this: young men and young women are not wanting to follow God because they're not convinced that he is good.

You can preach until you're blue in the face about God's power and wisdom, but still they will not follow. They want to know, Is he good?

If he is wise but not good, he is an egomaniac. If he is powerful but not good, he is a bully. If he is actually worth following, he simply must be good.

A good goal for us today: put the goodness of God on display. Anger and retaliation and spite do not demonstrate the goodness of God. Yes, we might win an argument, but we'll simultaneously lose a soul.

Humility puts God's goodness on display. Tenderness puts God's goodness on display. Patient listening puts God's goodness on display.

"How can I help?" is a question that puts God's goodness on display.

God is good. He is good to all. Our lives can demonstrate that goodness today.

A BLESSING FROM PAM

*May you be moved today to celebrate the glory of God's kingdom
that is to come and that is unfolded all around us day by day.*

Heard in Heaven

The smoke of the incense, together with the prayers of God's people,
went up before God from the angel's hand. Then the angel took the censer, filled it
with fire from the altar, and hurled it on the earth; and there came peals of thunder,
rumblings, flashes of lightning and an earthquake.

REVELATION 8:4-5

A few months into the pandemic, a woman from Guatemala reached out to me to alert me to a problem at the school that New Life supports near Guatemala City. She said, "Pastor Brady, before the pandemic, hundreds of children who come to our school received all their meals inside of our building. Now that we've shut down, our children are hungry. What are we to do?"

I remember thinking, "New Life is going to respond to the prayers of those children. God is going to answer their prayers through us."

I imagined God hearing hundreds of pleas, all spoken in Spanish, requesting him to come to their aid. "Please, God! We are hungry. Please, please send us food."

Those prayers were like a mist, a cloud, wafts of smoke reaching up to the ear of God.

And God heard. And God responded. And food was sent through our church.

There is a reminder here for us: every prayer we have ever prayed has been heard in heaven. Every. Single. One. No matter how feeble, no matter how fleeting. Every prayer we've prayed has been heard.

What's more: Every prayer has mattered to God.

When you are in need, when someone you know is in need, come boldly before God's throne and let that request be known. Let it rise like incense to God's ear. Let it activate his goodness on your behalf.

A BLESSING FROM PAM

May you invite God into your need today, laying down
your heavy burden for his burden, which is light.

Ready to Do Good

*Remind the people to be subject to rulers and authorities, to be obedient,
to be ready to do whatever is good, to slander no one, to be peaceable and
considerate, and always to be gentle toward everyone.*

TITUS 3:1-2

When Pam and I became parents, it became obvious to us that children are born into this world as sinners, desperately in need of forgiveness by God. We all come into this space depraved and broken and perfect candidates for salvation by grace, evidenced by the plentiful passages in Scripture aimed at reminding us how we are to live. What this meant for Pam and me was gathering up little Abram and little Callie and telling them time and again that they were not in charge of the family. God and their parents were.

We taught them from the youngest of ages to pray as soon as they knew how to speak. Why? So that prayer would become for them a second language, a language between them and God.

We taught them to obey us joyfully. Why? So that someday they'd joyfully obey God.

We taught them to tell the truth. Why? So that they would lay out their truth before God and trust that confession really was good for their souls.

We "bent" them toward goodness from the very beginning so that goodness would be their bent all their lives.

Now that they're adults, we see the fruit of all that labor. Still today, they're bent toward what's good.

It is said that the best time to make a wise decision in your life was twenty years ago, and that the second-best time is today. You can bend yourself toward goodness starting now.

A BLESSING FROM PAM

*As you prepare yourself for the day, may you establish
in your mind and heard a readiness to do good.*

Bearers of Good News

How beautiful on the mountains are the feet of those who bring good news,
who proclaim peace, who bring good tidings, who proclaim salvation,
who say to Zion, "Your God reigns!"

ISAIAH 52:7

For years flags from every country in the world have adorned the perimeter of our church's Living Room ceiling, and it's not uncommon on a Sunday morning during worship that my eye will be drawn to one country or another, and then my prayers are drawn there, too. This matters, I think, this allowance we give to the Holy Spirit to invite us into the redemption of people in every corner of the globe, and one of the primary ways we participate with him is by praying for people who don't yet have a relationship with God.

In this country, sometimes our biggest concern on a Sunday morning is arriving in time to grab a quick Dutch Bros before heading in. But this isn't the case in many parts of the world today. There, worshiping God is an all-out luxury. If government leaders found them gathering and praising Jehovah God, they'd be arrested or even killed. This threat to personal security doesn't help the cause of Christ in villages and cities where other religions already tempt people away from following God.

All to say, our prayers on a given Sunday morning *matter*. Our giving toward missionaries on the ground in these regions *matters*. Our willingness to go wherever God sends us—across the street, across town, or across an ocean—to bring good news to people who have not heard it *matters*.

These things are what bring heaven to planet Earth.

A BLESSING FROM PAM

May your life bear testimony today that despite the rampant struggles
of life in a fallen world, through Jesus' sacrifice God has gained victory.

The Sufficiency of Grace

When Jesus had finished saying all this to the people who were listening, he entered Capernaum. There a centurion's servant, whom his master valued highly, was sick and about to die. The centurion heard of Jesus and sent some elders of the Jews to him, asking him to come and heal his servant. When they came to Jesus, they pleaded earnestly with him, "This man deserves to have you do this, because he loves our nation and has built our synagogue."

LUKE 7:1-4

This story from Luke 7 has always been intriguing to me because it is every bit as relevant to our post-modern world as it was to those first-century ears.

This centurion is so concerned about the health of his slave that he urgently implores Jesus to help him out. But it's in that plea that we see the same errant thinking that many believers fall prey to today.

Do you see it peeking out from the language, the tit-for-tat with Christ? The slave had demonstrated good behavior; didn't Jesus owe him something in return?

Jesus did wind up healing that servant, and I'm sure the centurion exhaled a massive sigh of relief. But he altogether missed the point of grace.

Grace reminds us that regardless of whether God heals any aspect of our brokenness here in this reality, he has provided a *perfect reality* for us in the kingdom to come. Of course we pray for suffering to be alleviated in this reality. But ultimately we rest in the knowledge that his plans are unfolding just as they should.

By his grace he has already given us eternity. Nothing was or can be earned.

A BLESSING FROM PAM

May you know that God is working on your behalf today,
bringing all that was once dead back to life.

Gaze-worthy

One thing I ask from the LORD, this only do I seek: that I may dwell in the house
of the LORD all the days of my life, to gaze on the beauty
of the LORD and to seek him in his temple.

PSALM 27:4

It was a summertime night in 1986 when I invited Pam to join me for a dinner. I took her to a dive called Snuffy's, and we shared a pizza. As I gazed at her sitting there, I thought, *this is someone I want to know better. I want to spend more time with this girl.*

Most people who decide to follow God can recount a spiritual version of this scene. They might have "known" God for years, but still they recall a specific day or season when something shifted, and they saw God in a different light.

Pam and I have been married for more than thirty years, and still in our living room sits a throw pillow I gave her one Valentine's Day that has stitched on it this phrase: "It all began at Snuffy's."

Regarding your walk with Jesus, I wonder where it all began. Do you remember? Do you revisit that place from time to time in your mind?

I love the psalmist's plea in Psalm 27:4, when he says that really the only thing he wants or needs is to be able to sit across from God, so to speak, and stare at him for the rest of his life.

If you have never known this sort of intimacy with your heavenly Father, I invite you to enter into it today. You will never regret the moment you decide to go all-in with God, to say from the bottom of your heart that you're his.

A BLESSING FROM PAM

May every longing you experience today
point you back to your one true King.

The Sign You're Looking For

Then some of the Pharisees and teachers of the law said to him [Jesus], "Teacher, we want to see a sign from you." He answered, "A wicked and adulterous generation asks for a sign! But none will be given it except the sign of the prophet Jonah. For as Jonah was three days and three nights in the belly of a huge fish, so the Son of Man will be three days and three nights in the heart of the earth. The men of Ninevah will stand up at the judgment with this generation and condemn it; for they repented at the preaching of Jonah, and now something greater than Jonah is here.

MATTHEW 12:38-41

We looked briefly at the story of Jonah previously, but allow me one additional point.

There is a key parallel among the stories of Jonah and Jesus that ought to carry meaning for us today: While Jonah was forced to spend three days in a fish because of his disobedience in loving and serving the people God had asked him to love and serve, our Lord Jesus willingly spent three days in a borrowed tomb out of obedience to loving and serving the people God had asked him to love and serve.

"You want a sign?" Jesus questioned his disciples. This is the only sign you need.

I would ask us both to consider afresh whether we too are waiting on additional signs that Jesus is who he says he is and has done what he said he would do. The resurrection is the only proof we need for believing that God indeed accomplished his plan of salvation, and that death has forever been overcome.

A BLESSING FROM PAM

May you look with fresh eyes
upon the finished work of Christ today.

Refusing to Retaliate

Two other men, both criminals, were also led out with him to be executed.
When they came to the place called the Skull, they crucified him there, along
with the criminals—one on his right, the other on hi left. Jesus said, "Father,
forgive them, for they do not know what they are doing."

LUKE 23:32-33

A mob is ready to condemn Jesus. Religious leaders in the group will say to him, "He saved others. Let him save himself!" (Luke 23:35). Military leaders in the group will say to him, "If you are the king of the Jews, save yourself," (v. 37). Others in the group will place a written notice above Jesus' head that reads, "This is the King of the Jews," (v. 38). But before anyone says or does what they're about to say and do, Jesus prays.

Jesus bows his head, he inhales, and in an audible voice, he prays: "Father, forgive them, for they do not know what they are doing," (v. 33).

Before the sin occurs, Jesus claims forgiveness for the sinners.

"When they hurled sins at him," 1 Peter 2:23 says, "he [Jesus] did not retaliate, and when he suffered he made no threats."

What a radical way of responding, agreed?

What a remarkable way to live.

A BLESSING FROM PAM

Following the way of Jesus, may you advance
forgiveness to everyone you encounter today.

Growing Up in God

So Christ himself gave the apostles, the prophets, the evangelists, the pastors and teachers, to equip his people for works of service, so that the body of Christ may be built up until we all reach unity in the faith and in the knowledge of the Son of God and become mature, attaining to the whole measure of the fullness of Christ.

EPHESIANS 4:11-13

If you've ever been daunted by how difficult adulting can be, then you're catching Paul's vibe here in his encouragement to the Ephesian church. Spiritual adulting can seem just as overwhelming, but take heart: there is a way to grow up. It centers on a little give-and-take.

Well, take-and-give, to be precise.

First, to the "take." The surest way to mature in your faith is to find a spiritually mature person and hang around him or her for a while. Acknowledge and encourage them in their maturity. Ask them thoughtful questions about the practices that sustain their faith. Practice those same practices, asking for feedback as you go. Once you find a sense of stability in your walk with Jesus, then consider what you have to give.

Are you given to be an apostle, someone who brings order to ministry initiatives?

Are you given to be a prophet, someone who hears and teaches others to hear the whispers of God?

Maybe you're given to be an evangelist, someone who loves to share the good news of the gospel.

Or what about being a pastor who loves and nurtures people who are open to devoting themselves to God?

Receive wisdom and insight from others. Serve from the gifting God has ordained. And soon you will see maturity having its way in you as you grow yourself up in God.

A BLESSING FROM PAM

*May you echo your loving Father's commitment
to you to grow you up in him.*

The Hope of the Empty Tomb

At this, she turned around and saw Jesus standing there, but she did not realize that it was Jesus. He asked her, "Woman, why are you crying? Who is it you are looking for?" Thinking he was the gardener, she said, "Sir, if you have carried him away, tell me where you have put him, and I will get him."

Jesus said to her, "Mary."

She turned toward him and cried out in Aramaic, "Rabboni!"
(which means Teacher).

JOHN 20:14-16

You want to see his body just one more time. Need to see it, in fact. And so you stumble through the dense fog, making your way to the tomb. Scattered rocks threaten your surefootedness. Will you get there in one piece?

You recall that the tomb was heavily guarded ... will close access be attainable for you? And yet you trudge on, determined to see for yourself.

Such hope you held for a Messiah, for a political leader, for a brand new world to come! But look at how things unfolded. What a mockery—a total letdown.

You near the tomb—why is the stone that covered the opening now at its side? Closing the gap, you crane to look inside and find ... no body. There's nobody in this tomb.

You wonder if someone has moved the body, but no, this doesn't make sense.

A flurry of activity later, and the truth will get sorted out.

He is risen; he is risen, indeed.

The grave could not hold your God.

A BLESSING FROM PAM

May you rejoice today as if for the first time that death had no victory over Jesus, that death could hold no sting.

MAY

"Especially today, in the
face of such brokenness and
divisiveness, we must continue in
what we've learned and remain
diligent in the sight of God."

- Pastor Brady Boyd -

No Obligation to Sin

And if the Spirit of him who raised Jesus from the dead is living in you, he who raised Christ from the dead will also give life to your mortal bodies because of his Spirit who lives in you. Therefore brothers and sisters, we have an obligation—but it is not to the flesh, to live according to it. For if you live according to the flesh, you will die; but if by the Spirit you put to death the misdeeds of the body, you will live.

ROMANS 8:11-13

We tend to think of temptation as being a negative thing, but I'd like to draw your attention to a different perspective, one that helps me whenever I am about to step into sin.

It's true: we never sin without having first been tempted to sin, and so in this regard temptation is a dangerous thing. But also true is this: we never thwart the enemy's schemes for our lives without first having overcome temptation, and so temptation is also a *useful* thing. Temptation reminds us that we are overcomers in Christ.

Thirty years ago I was a very angry person. Anger mounted in me from the depth of my heart and I could erupt—*snap!*—just like that. Today? That's not who I am. Today, I'm a man of peace. Yes, I still sin. But anger is no longer my gig. I'm more in touch with my obligation to walk by the Spirit these days instead of feeling somehow obligated to sin.

If the Spirit of God is living in you, then you are being transformed day by day into the very image of God. Each time you take a pass on the sin that lurks behind temptation, you say yes to fullness of life.

A BLESSING FROM PAM

*May you feast on freedom today,
the freedom we know when we live as Christ lived.*

The Usefulness of God's Word

In fact, everyone who wants to live a godly life in Christ Jesus will be persecuted,
while evildoers and imposters will go from bad to worse, deceiving and being deceived.
But as for you, continue in what you have learned and have become convinced of,
because you know those from whom you learned it, and how from infancy you have
known the Holy Scriptures, which are able to make you wise for salvation through
faith in Christ Jesus. All Scripture is God-breathed and is useful for teaching, rebuking,
correcting and training in righteousness, so that the servant of God may be
thoroughly equipped for every good work.

2 TIMOTHY 3:12-17

Especially today, in the face of such brokenness and divisiveness and societal exhaustion, believers the world over need this reminder from Timothy to continue in what we have learned, to remain diligent in the sight of God, to joyfully persist in our faith. And how does this "continuing" occur? By prioritizing the Word of God.

It is by knowing, loving, and applying the Holy Scriptures that we live a godly life.

It is by knowing, loving, and applying the Holy Scriptures that we keep from being deceived.

It is by knowing, loving, and applying the Holy Scriptures that we are made wise for salvation in Christ.

It is by knowing, loving, and applying the Holy Scriptures that we are taught and rebuked and corrected and trained in the ways of God.

It is by knowing, loving, and applying the Holy Scriptures that we are equipped for every good work—*thoroughly* equipped, in fact.

All that we long for and all that we need is found in the infallible, indefatigable Word of God. Here is instruction for life.

A BLESSING FROM PAM

May you return again and again to the vibrancy of God's Word,
the means for our prosperity, the means for our good success.

Our Savior's Final Words

Jesus called out with a loud voice, "Father, into your hands I commit my spirit." When he had said this, he breathed his last.

LUKE 23:46

Last spring during our Good Friday service we revisited the last sayings of Christ, and if you need a refresher on the grandeur of the God we serve, you need look no further than those words.

Jesus had been led away by religious leaders to the site of his crucifixion. He had been ridiculed and insulted by people who questioned his authority, his authenticity, and his power. Now, he is about to be murdered. But before that happens, here is what Jesus said:

1. **"Father, forgive them, for they do not know what they do,"** (Luke 23:34).

2. **"Truly I tell you, today you will be with me in paradise,"** (Luke 23:43).

3. **"Woman, here is your son"; "Here is your mother,"** (John 19:26, 27). Ensuring that his mother, Mary, would be cared for upon his death, Jesus connected her to his beloved disciple John.

4. **"Eli, Eli, lema sabachthani?"** (meaning, "My God, my God, why have you forsaken me?").

5. **"I am thirsty,"** (John 19:28). Perhaps only to fulfill the prophesy noted in Psalm 69:21, which said, "They put gall in my food and gave me vinegar for my thirst," Jesus spoke this phrase. We also see his humanity surfacing during the spiritual agony he faced.

6. **"It is finished,"** (John 19:30).

7. **"Father, into your hands I commit my spirit,"** (Luke 23:46).

"So I'll cherish the old rugged cross," the old hymn goes, "till my trophies at last I lay down; I will cling to the old rugged cross and exchange it someday for a crown."

A BLESSING FROM PAM

May you be sobered today by Jesus' great love, his great sacrifice, his great grace.

MAY 4

Our Good Shepherd

*"I am the good shepherd. The good shepherd lays down his life for the sheep. The hired
hand is not the shepherd and does not own the sheep. So when he sees the wolf
coming, he abandons the sheep and runs away. Then the wolf attacks the flock and
scatters it. The man runs away because he is a hired hand and cares nothing for
the sheep. I am the good shepherd; I know my sheep and my sheep know me."*

JOHN 10:11-14

When I first heard this passage as a kid, I'd already been through the first of what
would be many open-heart surgeries and thus was already in touch with my
limitations in life. I remember hearing those words and thinking, *I cannot save myself.*

No matter what we are able to do in this life, this reality holds for us all: we cannot
save ourselves.

Whenever I pray with someone who wants to receive salvation, those are the exact
words I ask them to repeat: "Father, I am a sinner. I need to be saved from my sin.
And I cannot save myself ..."

In spite of your strength and creativity, you cannot save yourself.

In spite of your talent and ambitions, you cannot save yourself.

And the fact is, neither can I.

You and I both were born needing a shepherd, One who would lay his life down for
us. This good shepherd's name is Jesus, who knows us, who loves us, who cares. He
became what we were so that we could become what he is: holy, righteous, set apart
by a loving God.

A BLESSING FROM PAM

*May you be intimately aware today of your inability to rescue yourself
from the ravages of your waywardness and sin. And may you be comforted
by the good shepherd, Jesus, who guides us by his grace.*

United in Christ

*After this I looked, and there before me was a great multitude
that no one could count, from every nation, tribe, people and language, standing
before the throne and before the Lamb. They were wearing white robes
and were holding palm branches in their hands.*

REVELATION 7:9

Since my earliest days as your pastor, I've kept a vision alive in my heart. It centers on a bunch of people living life out in the world, oblivious to the fact that there is a God who cares about them. But then they happen by a place on the north side of town, a building with a giant blue roof, called New Life Church. They peek through the windows wondering what on earth this thing is about. And when they catch sight of what's going on inside, they are captivated, compelled, overwhelmed.

They see women and men, young and old, black and brown and white, Republicans and Democrats and Libertarians, rich and poor, Americans and those from other countries, extroverts and introverts, sinners of every possible stripe, raising one unified voice at the throne of King Jesus, celebrating God for all that he is. They see focused attention on the only thing that matters: intimacy with Jesus Christ.

They see joy in every countenance, despite our being hard-pressed on every side.

They see love in every interaction, as resources are freely shared.

They see resolve in every posture—to stay faithful, committed, true.

The best part of this vision? It plays out in reality around New Life, week after week. This is who we are. This is what we do. This is us, the Church, Christ's bride, practicing for what we'll do for all of eternity: worshiping with each other before the throne of grace.

A BLESSING FROM PAM

*May you be blessed today for your participation
with other believers in worshiping the one true God.*

Hungry for God

"At that time the kingdom of heaven will be like ten virgins who took their lamps and went out to meet the bridegroom. Five of them were foolish and five were wise. The foolish ones took their lamps but did not take any oil with them. The wise ones, however, took oil in jars along with their lamps. The bridegroom was a long time in coming, and they all became drowsy and fell asleep. At midnight the cry rang out: 'Here's the bridegroom! Come out to meet him!' Then all the virgins woke up and trimmed their lamps. The foolish ones said to the wise, 'Give us some of your oil; our lamps are going out.' 'No,' they replied, 'there may not be enough for both us and you. Instead, go to those who sell oil and buy some for yourselves.' But while they were on their way to buy the oil, the bridegroom arrived. The virgins who were ready went in with him to the wedding banquet. And the door was shut. Later the others also came. 'Lord, Lord,' they said, 'open the door for us!' But he replied, 'Truly I tell you, I don't know you.' Therefore keep watch, because you do not know the day or the hour."

MATTHEW 25:1-13

I was in Honduras speaking to a church of twelve thousand believers who convened three times weekly in a massive auditorium that had no air conditioning. The majority of congregants were poor—very poor. And to get to church they had to be bussed in from all across the countryside. On the day I was to preach, it was 85 degrees outside, the humidity level was hovering around 100 percent, and by noon the skies had opened wide and thrown down so much rain that you could barely see ten feet in front of you. Still, the people came.

They came knowing that it would take a sixty-minute bus ride to get there.

They came knowing that the rains would have washed out many of the roads en route.

They came knowing that once they arrived they'd be sitting in sweltering heat for hours on end.

They came knowing that unless they themselves took up an offering to pay the bus driver, that debt would not be relieved.

They came knowing that it would have been far easier to just stay home.

And yet as soon as I started preaching, I saw something I've never seen before: simultaneously, twelve thousand bodies *leaned in*. It was like an ocean wave, the sight of them all subtly shifting toward the stage, and I could have sworn I heard a slight whoosh. These followers of Jesus were hungry for teaching, hungry for preaching, hungry for an encounter with God. The whole time I spoke that day, I had the parable of the ten virgins sitting at the back of my mind.

In this parable from Matthew, we find foolish virgins who possess lampstands but have run out of oil for the lamps. They miss the arrival of their bridegroom because they cannot see in the dark.

On the contrary, we find wise virgins who are prepared for the coming of that long-awaited bridegroom and have oil in *abundance* at hand.

It's easy to believe that when you and I head to the developing world to minister, we are the ones doing the giving, but in my experience, worshipers in those villages and regions are always more eager to learn and yield and grow. We may be the owners of lampstands, but they are the ones with the oil.

My prayer for us as a church is that our passion and fervor for the things of God would not wane in these final days. I pray that we would be hungry for more of God, that whenever we come into his presence, we would collectively choose to lean in.

A BLESSING FROM PAM

May you be absolutely zealous for Jesus today.

All in Need

But God demonstrates his own love for us in this:
While we were still sinners, Christ died for us.

ROMANS 5:8

One of my favorite times at New Life each year is Baptism Sunday—mostly because of the sheer diversity of participants represented. The week after Easter I stood there and saw a man in his sixties get baptized. And then an elementary-school-aged girl. And then a woman in her forties. And then brothers, both in their teens. There were people with black skin and people with brown skin and people with white skin. People who looked like they might live at the gym and people who needed assistance coming out of the pool, lest they slip on the wet surface. There were people who had come prepared for the experience and those who were so moved in the moment that they decided then and there to get baptized that very day.

It doesn't matter where we come from, where we've been, or even where we're going. It doesn't matter how bad we've been or how good we've been. It doesn't matter if we're rich or poor, young or old, thin or heavyset. We all stand in need of a Savior, and Jesus's death was sufficient for us.

The waters of baptism remind us that it is only by identifying with Jesus that we have anything worthwhile to say. It is because of his power that we are powerful. It is because of his goodness that we can be made good. It is because of his righteousness that God sees us as righteous. It is because of his sacrifice that we can be saved.

All of life is found in the person of Jesus! When you and I were most in need, it was his love that rescued us.

A BLESSING FROM PAM

May you feel radically embraced
by your adoring Father in heaven today.

Hungry for God

For we know that if the earthly tent we live in is destroyed, we have a building from
God, an eternal house in heaven, not built by human hands. Meanwhile we groan,
longing to be clothed instead with our heavenly dwelling, because when we are clothed,
we will not be found naked. For while we are in this tent, we groan and are burdened,
because we do not wish to be unclothed but to be clothed instead with our heavenly
dwelling, so that what is mortal may be swallowed up by life. Now the one who has
fashioned us for this very purpose is God, who has given us the Spirit as
a deposit, guaranteeing what is to come.

Therefore we are always confident and know that as long as we are at home in the
body we are away from the Lord. For we live by faith, not by sight. We are confident,
I say, and would prefer to be away from the body and at home with the Lord. So we
make it our goal to please him, whether we are at home in the body or away from it.
For we must all appear before the judgment seat of Christ, so that each of us may
receive what is due us for the things done while in the body, whether good or bad.

2 CORINTHIANS 5:1-10

When the apostle Paul wrote his letters to believers in the city of Corinth, he wrote
them to be an encouragement to them in their walk with God. And yet here we find
Paul speaking of believers having to someday fact the "judgment seat" of God. Does
that sound encouraging to you? It sounds terrifying to most modern ears.

Let me do a little thought experiment with you. Think back on the last time you
gathered with other believers for a time of corporate worship. It may have been on
a Sunday morning at New Life. It may have been during a retreat or a women's or
men's night out. Maybe it was a First Wednesday service, which always proves to be
a powerful time of prayer and praise. Whenever it was, I want you to picture yourself
there among other believers, your heart open to the activity of the Holy Spirit, your
arms perhaps extended overhead to God in adoration and submission and joy. Your
eyes may have been closed. You may have been feeling strong emotions—gratitude,
contentment, relief. You may hate your singing voice, yet there you were, belting out
spiritual songs to God.

Do you have that image firmly planted in mind?

Now, let me ask you a question: in that moment of unabashed praise, of total
and complete surrender to your heavenly Father, would you describe how you
felt as *terrified*?

That feeling never once crossed your mind, right?

You might have felt things like acceptance, or contentment, or humility, or peace. But terror? I highly doubt it. There is no *terror* to be found.

Here is the truth about the judgment seat you and I will someday face: it is a good-news story, through and through. Jesus has already paid the penalty for my sin and yours—past, present, future. *There is no additional penalty to be paid.*

Let me say that again: there is no additional penalty to be paid for the person who has been covered by grace in Christ.

When God gathers us before his throne at the judgment seat, he will be rewarding us for good deeds done, not punishing us for the bad. As is always the case in the presence of your Father, when we finally encounter him face to face our primary emotion will be *joy.*

A BLESSING FROM PAM

*May you come boldly before your Father today, releasing any fear
of being in his presence and instead relishing in his deep joy.*

Safe and Sound

The name of the Lord is a fortified tower;
the righteous run to it and are safe.

PROVERBS 18:10

As I write this, Ukraine has been under attack by its neighboring country Russia for many months. It has been devastating to watch the senseless violence, the unwarranted strikes, the thousands of grief-stricken people whose lives have been upended by the attacks. And while New Life has rallied along with scores of other churches to fund massive resource drops for the estimated 4.5 million refugees caused by this conflict, we've all felt helpless to do much else.

This week I saw news footage of an elderly Ukrainian woman that turned the tide on my helplessness. Cameras caught her walking along a typically busy street that had been emptied as missile strikes landed all around. She stopped in front of a wall that boasted a painted mural nearly a city block in length of the early church at Pentecost, when the Holy Spirit came to rest on believer's heads as flames of fire. In the mural there were hundreds of people, all worshiping God. The woman set down the sack she was carrying, lifted her arms to the heavens, and began to pray to God.

Bombs were falling as she did this. Russian troops were nearing her beloved city of Kyiv. Gunfire and whining air-raid sirens could be heard as the cameras were rolling. And yet there she stood, praising God.

When God reminds us through Solomon's words that he is a "fortified tower," he is speaking literally. Whatever battle is raging all around you today, your heavenly Father stands ready to receive you, to welcome you into safety, to offer you divine protection, to cover you as bullets fall.

A BLESSING FROM PAM

May you sense the impenetrable protection of your
heavenly Father's strong, safe arms today.

"You're Not Buying"

He who did not spare his own Son, but gave him up for us all—how will he not also, along with him, graciously give us all things?

ROMANS 8:32

When Pam and I were first married we noticed a trend unfold whenever we were out to eat with either set of our parents, which was that our dads never let us pay. "You're not buying," they'd say.

This dynamic was perpetuated over the years, and at some point I was probably making more money than either of those men were, and yet still they reached for the check. And every time they did, I saw manifested in their generosity the generous heart of God.

In his writings to the church in Rome, Paul confirmed that our God is a generous God. Referring to God, he wrote, "He who did not spare his own Son, but gave him up for us all—how will he not also, along with him, graciously give us all things?" (Romans 8:32). And while you and I sometimes wish that this "all things" included a new house and a new car and delicious meals out every night, in fact that "all things" includes something far better: eternity spent with God. What Paul is saying here is that because we have trusted God for salvation, we can also trust him for the growth that needs to occur in our lives for salvation to have its full effect in our lives.

It is God who can make that happen. It is God who will make that happen, as we continue to yield to him.

A BLESSING FROM PAM

When you are tempted to secure your own station in life, may you be reminded that it is God who provides all that we need for direction and good success.

Nothing Withheld

*When they reached the place God had told him about, Abraham built an altar there
and arranged the wood on it. He bound his son Isaac and laid him on the altar, on top
of the wood. Then he reached out his hand and took the knife to slay his son.*

GENESIS 22:9-10

It's one thing to say that we believe in God as our Source in life; it's quite another to activate those beliefs to the point of offering God things that really matter to us.

Abraham knew something about the nature of Yahweh God that simply wasn't true of the pagan gods so often worshiped in his culture. Those gods would have demanded child sacrifice and not intervened when Abraham complied. But he knew that this was not God's nature. He knew that God would make a way.

Whenever I read this account from Genesis, a lump forms in my throat. I know how the story ends: God doesn't allow Abraham to slay his son but instead provides a sacrificial ram in the thicket so that Isaac's life can be spared. Still, the thought of a father raising a knife above his own child and preparing to plunge that knife into the boy's chest ... it's more than I can take. I think of my son, Abram. Could I follow through with that plan, even to the point of death?

After Abraham slaughtered the ram God provided for the sacrifice, he named the makeshift altar The Lord Will Provide. Such a needed reminder. Whatever gains we have known, whatever losses we have sustained, whatever objects of affection we cling to still today, it is the wise believer who releases all back to God, saying with confidence, "the Lord will always provide."

A BLESSING FROM PAM

*May you willfully, joyfully offer up the entirety of your life
to your heavenly Father today, holding nothing back from him.*

Life in the Spirit

So I say, walk by the Spirit, and you will not gratify the desires of the flesh. For the flesh desires what is contrary to the Spirit, and the Spirit what is contrary to the flesh. They are in conflict with each other, so that you are not to do whatever you want. But if you are led by the Spirit, you are not under the law.

GALATIANS 5:16-18

After I preached on the Holy Spirit one Sunday, a man approached me and said, "Pastor Brady, do we need the Holy Spirit to go to heaven?"

I chuckled and said, "You need the Holy Spirit to go to Walmart!"

I was only partially kidding. We not only need the presence and power of the Holy Spirit to go to heaven, but also to accomplish *every aspect of daily life*. Why? Because left to our own inclinations, we will gratify the desires of the flesh.

I've told our church for years that people who walk by the flesh are always looking for a fight, while people who walk by the Spirit are always looking for *fruit*. That "fruit," according to Paul is love, joy, peace, patience, kindness, goodness, faithfulness, gentleness, and self-control, (see Galatians 5:22), and the only way to manifest it is to stay close to the Spirit from which it comes.

I cannot be your pastor without the presence and power of the Holy Spirit.

I cannot be Pam's husband or my kids' dad without the presence and power of the Holy Spirit.

Or I can't serve these roles *effectively*, anyway. And the same is true for you: you can only accomplish what God asks you to accomplish by the power of his Spirit living inside of you.

A BLESSING FROM PAM

May you listen carefully today for the Spirit's promptings, and may you find courage to act on each one.

Called to Closeness

Enter his gates with thanksgiving and his courts with praise; give thanks to him and praise his name. For the Lord is good and his love endures forever; his faithfulness continues through all generations.

PSALM 100:4-5

You know as well as I do that to live *with someone* is to get to know them quite well. Visitors never see the real you, the you that shows up when you're tired or hungry or irritated. We're on our best behavior when visitors stop by or stay for a night or two. But ask that visitor to move in, to become a resident in your home, and there's no longer a place to hide. You simply can't sustain the tidied up version of yourself or your home, and *the way things really are* eventually starts to peek through.

And yet it is this level of intimacy that God desires with us, for it is only when we are near him that we can become like him. It is only when we come close that we can be transformed.

The psalmist's exhortation in Psalm 100:4 is an invitation to intimacy. If you are allowed inside the gates, you are perceived to be friendly, not a threat. But to gain access into the *courts* is to be welcomed into the holy place—the living room, so to speak.

Here is where we commune with God, bringing all of our messes along. We come thankful that he has cleansed us. We come full of praise for the sacrifice of his Son. We come ready to be real with our heavenly Father. We come close, to be near God.

A BLESSING FROM PAM

The next time you're tempted to hide the truth of your inclinations or situations from God, may you instead turn from your running, face his full-on, and enter his courts with praise.

Merciful One

For the Lord your God is a merciful God; he will not abandon or destroy you or forget the covenant with your ancestors, which he confirmed to them by oath.

DEUTERONOMY 4:31

Just after God delivered his nation Israel from hundreds of years spent as slaves, he directed them across the Red Sea and now has them on track to reach the Promised Land. But still, the people get lost—not just for a day or two, but for a full *forty years*.

I have been a believer for forty years. It boggles my mind to think that for the same amount of time that I've been following Jesus, those Israelites wandered aimlessly through dry, dusty lands.

Eventually God looks down on his people and has mercy on them. Exodus 13:21-22 says that, "By day the Lord went ahead of them in a pillar of cloud to guide them on their way and by night in a pillar of fire to give them light, so that they could travel by day or night. Neither the pillar of cloud by day nor the pillar of fire by night left its place in front of the people."

Can you picture that throng of people, all of whom are desperate to get out of the situation they're in, being led by a natural phenomenon such as clouds or fire? Can you picture us being led in a similar way?

On your best day, God is in front of you, leading you, directing you, showing you how to walk in his ways.

On your worst day, the same is true.

No matter the condition of your life today, God longs to show you the way.

A BLESSING FROM PAM

When you feel aimless and lost, may you know that God has not left your side.
He is near, and his guidance is sure. Ask him for the direction you need today.

Fulfilled for Real

*The thief comes only to steal and kill and destroy; I have
come that they may have life, and have it to the full.*

JOHN 10:10

One Saturday during March Madness last year, I plopped down on the couch to catch a basketball game. Since I was watching live, I couldn't speed through the commercial breaks and therefore had to watch all the ads. I learned some things as I watched all those ads: I was living life unfulfilled.

I didn't know, for instance, that I was existing with a sub-standard home loan. I didn't know that I was making do with less than perfectly white teeth. I didn't know that my dog was discontented with her dog food. Actually, I don't have a dog anymore. But if I *did*, she'd be upset with me.

It's no secret that the key to effective advertising is stirring up discontent in the consumer's mind and heart. If I can make you believe that your windows are inefficient, your car is old, your clothes are out of style, or your ailment is stealing your fun, then I can get you to buy just about anything on planet Earth. Which is all well and good until the "solution" I've made you shell out hard-earned money is found out to be a fraud.

John 10:10 is oft-quoted but rarely understood. For the record, when Jesus says that he has come that we may have life and "have it to the full," he isn't exactly concerned with our mortgage rate or sparkling smile. He's exclusively concerned with the state of the eternal part of us, our *souls*. Why? Because he knows that as beings created in God's image, the only chance we have for fulfillment is when we find our fulfillment in him.

A BLESSING FROM PAM

In your quest for fulfillment today, may you set your gaze on Jesus, alone.

A New Old Command

"A new command I give you: Love one another.
As I have loved you, so you must love one another."

JOHN 13:34

This command to love wasn't exactly a new command. In Leviticus 19:18, we read, "Do not seek revenge or bear a grudge against anyone among your people, but *love your neighbor as yourself*. I am the Lord," (emphasis mine).

So, here in John 13:34, why was Jesus positioning the command as "new"? Because for his first-century disciples, the meaning behind them indeed was new. Those disciples were about to see something powerful take place that would cement their understanding of *love*. They were about to witness Jesus heading willfully to a cross, where he would die for the sake of their souls. They were about to see *love in action*, and the scene would redefine the concept forever.

I wonder if we recognize how activistic love must be in our lives, for it to be considered love at all. We "fall in love" with our spouse, but then a few years into our marriage we wonder where the spark has gone. We love our friends, but a handful of offenses later we're ready to bolt and never look back. We "love" everyone irrespective of preference ... as long as it's not an election year.

As people living on the other side of the cross, you and I must constantly view the call to "love others" through Jesus' perfect sacrifice. We have been so loved, and so we must love—unequivocally, unconditionally, unendingly. We must trust God to help us love our spouse, our children, our friends and neighbors, the world at large.

We must love as Jesus loved.

We can love as Jesus loved.

A BLESSING FROM PAM

Today, may you activate love, recognizing that nothing short of that will do.

One Source

You shall have no other gods before me.

EXODUS 20:3

When God gave Moses the Ten Commandments, the reason this first commandment was the first commandment is because the other nine could only be followed if the first one was upheld.

These words would have carried great weight for Moses and the entire nation of Israel because they all were living in a polytheistic culture. There was a god for *everything*: a god for war, a god for water, a god for crops. There were *thousands* of gods to worship. God wanted them to choose him.

Twenty years ago I sat in a stuffy restaurant eating bad borscht across from a Ukrainian pastor, a massive six-foot-five-inch man with a thick Russian accent. We were talking about our different ministries when he looked at me and said, "Pastor Brady, it must be very difficult to lead people in the United States."

I asked him why, and he said, "Because you have so much stuff."

At the time the people of Ukraine were emerging from their struggle for independence from the now-defunct Soviet Union and were nearly destitute as a people. "Let me tell you about our church here," he said, his eyes glistening with grateful tears. "We have but one Source. Just one. And that is as it should be."

I've remembered that conversation all these years and pray I never forget it. It is as it should be. Before we can take a single step in following God, we must first determine in our minds and hearts that we will put *nothing else in his place*. We will worship him uniquely as our one, true Source. We will have no other gods before him.

A BLESSING FROM PAM

May every other source of joy you know in life—your family, your friends, your work, your interests—pale by comparison to the joy you find in your heavenly Father.

Time to Go

*Then they gathered around him and asked him, "Lord, are you at this time
going to restore the kingdom to Israel?"*

*He said to them, "It is not for you to know the times or dates the Father has set
by his own authority. But you will receive power when the Holy Spirit comes on you;
and you will be my witnesses in Jerusalem, and in all Judea and Samaria,
and to the ends of the earth."*

ACTS 1:6-8

Something beautiful happens whenever a believer catches the vision of Acts 1:8, which says, But you will receive power when the Holy Spirit comes on you; and you will be my witnesses in Jerusalem, and in all Judea and Samaria, and tot he ends of the earth." That beautiful thing is that we refuse to stay still. We go.

We go to Mary's Home to pray with the single moms who live there and to help teach them life skills so that they can thrive.

We go to the local prisons we serve and listen to their stories and tell them they're loved by God.

We go to Alaska or Guatemala or Romania or Ukraine to refresh our ministry partners who live and work there and to remind them they're seen and loved.

We go to the row in front of us during the greeting portion of a weekly worship service and introduce ourselves and ask a few questions and eagerly anticipate if only for a moment being the light and love of Christ in that person's life.

We go not in our own strength but in the power of the Holy Spirit, to witness to God's goodness and grace.

A BLESSING FROM PAM

*Where will you be going today? May your path take you toward those in
need of a kind word, a cup of cold water, a moment of refreshment, a smile.*

Just the Thing We Need

And pray in the Spirit on all occasions with all kinds of prayers and requests.
With this in mind, be alert and always keep on praying for all the Lord's people.

EPHESIANS 6:18

For most of the month of January each year our staff and congregation convene in the World Prayer Center for morning and midday prayer, and while I absolutely love these gatherings, I can sometimes begrudge the energy they take.

During our most recent span of corporate prayer meetings, I was assigned Tuesday midday as the session I would lead. This would have been fine, except that Tuesday is my busiest day of work. Tuesday is when I meet with New Life's executive team, meet with our associate senior pastors, address staff issues, and finalize the main points of my weekend sermon. I was supposed to somehow magically shift gears from all that strategic and administrative stuff to *pray?*

After the second consecutive Tuesday leading the noon session, I got home from work and said to Pam, "You know how I was dreading that time slot for the prayer meetings? It has been an absolute gift to me."

And it had.

To come out of the most intense part of my week and step directly into a place of prayer had unbeknownst to me been just the thing I needed. The increased humility, perspective, boldness, clarity, wisdom, gentleness, confidence, direction, and peace I'd needed was found there before the throne of God.

We think we can't carve out time or energy to pray because we're occupied living life. In fact, we can't live life properly unless we're occupied with persistent prayer.

A BLESSING FROM PAM

May you bring your thoughts, your concerns, your questions, your obligations, and your desires to God today through prayer. And may you find him sufficient to every need.

A Certain Quietness of Soul

Rejoice in the Lord always. I will say it again: Rejoice! Let your gentleness be evident to all. The Lord is near. Do not be anxious about anything, but in every situation, by prayer and petition, with thanksgiving, present your requests to God. And the peace of God, which transcends all understanding, will guard your hearts and your minds in Christ Jesus.

PHILIPPIANS 4:4-7

Recently a pastor friend of mine texted me asking for prayer. He and his wife have three children under the age of five, and all three were sick—as in, things coming out of every orifice every hour of the day. It was Saturday night, and he was set to preach the following morning, not once but three separate times. "The bedrooms are contaminated," he wrote, "the bathrooms are toxic, and every towel we own is in the washing machine or in the trash."

We've all been there, in the chaos of a situation that has spiraled out of control.

And yet according to this passage in Philippians, we can exchange chaos for perfect peace.

Peace. Even the mention of that word has a calming effect.

Let me remind you today that whatever situation you're facing today, perfect peace awaits. You bring your needs to God and from a posture of humility articulate them, and he will hand you peace.

"God, I am hurting. And yet I trust you ..."

"God, you are so good to me. Even in this trial, I believe you are still good ..."

"God, I am so stressed that I can't see straight. I'm so grateful that you see clearly at all times ..."

Humbly make your needs known.

And today, you will know peace.

A BLESSING FROM PAM

May the Prince of Peace, Jesus, meet you right where you are today and baby-step you toward the quietness of soul you seek.

Making Life Work

Therefore, since we have been justified through faith, we have
peace with God through our Lord Jesus Christ, through whom we
have gained access by faith into this grace in which we now stand.

ROMANS 5:1-2

There's something exciting about being given access to something you really want, isn't there? It could be as simple as having a promo code work during an online shopping transaction, and yet there's that little feeling of elation: *It worked!*

Or what about when you find out that because of a booking error, you were getting bumped from economy to business class on a long flight?

How about when the host at the restaurant who just quoted you a thirty-minute wait comes and finds you and says, "Actually, we can seat you right now, if you're ready ..."

In Romans 5, the apostle Paul describes what is the greatest access granted in the history of time: access to God. And unlike every other access we gain in this world, *this* access is not temporal but eternal. And when this access works, *all of life works*.

It is only because of our access to God that our marriage works and that our parenting works and that our work lives work.

It is only because of our access to God that we can manifest things like love and joy and peace.

It is only because of our access to God that we can do anything worthwhile at all.

Whenever something is working in life, it is because we have gained access to the One through whom all goodness flows.

A BLESSING FROM PAM

May you rejoice today in the access you have gained
to God through faith in his Son, Jesus Christ.

Getting Along

After this I looked, and there before me was a great multitude that
no one could count, from every nation, tribe, people and language,
standing before the throne and before the Lamb ...

REVELATION 7:9

If you think about the things that are dividing our society these days, they all come down to diversity. *These* people don't agree with *those* people on which political candidate is better for the nation, or on what the definition of marriage should be, or on what our position as a country on war ought to look like, or on whether rich people should be allowed to get richer while poor people continue to stay poor.

It's a common misconception that when we get to heaven, somehow magically we'll be all alike. Revelation 7:9 begs to differ, explaining that there will be *wild* diversity there. People from every tribe, every nation, every language—all gathered in one place. And because heaven won't erase our differences, I don't bother with trying to erase them while here on earth.

In my view, the most spectacular aspect of heaven will be the diversity we experience there. Black people and white people and Asian people and Native American people will be worshiping one God as one people group. We all will be declaring *harmoniously* that Jesus is Lord.

If you're feeling a little protective of your preferences today, let me give you a prayer to pray. It's one you likely know by heart: "Your kingdom come, your will be done on earth as it is in heaven," (Matthew 6:10). Heaven will be filled with people totally unlike you. And filled with people totally unlike me. Wise believers start practicing now loving those they'll spend eternity with.

A BLESSING FROM PAM

May you set down your preferences
just for the moment and pick up love instead.

Into the Unknown

As the Philistine moved closer to attack him, David
ran quickly toward the battle line to meet him.

1 SAMUEL 17:48

Sixteen years ago I had a great job at a great church in the great state of Texas. The church was growing fast, and my job was secure, which is why I was shocked to receive a prompting from God that I would be leaving that place and heading west.

I tried to ignore the prompting for a while, but it kept resurfacing. "You're leaving, Brady. I have another job for you to do …"

The first time I met the congregation of New Life Church was the Sunday I introduced myself as the new senior pastor. I get what it's like to step out in faith, to go headlong into the unknown. Still, I wouldn't change a thing about how this journey unfolded. When it's of God, it's always good.

Whenever I think about the story of David and Goliath, I remind myself that David had never been in a battle before, and yet there he was racing not away from but *toward* the giant who was standing there taunting his God. David's willingness to say yes to God changed the course of an entire nation that day. Such is the power of following God.

Following Jesus is radical stuff. Are you radically following him? Let me give you one way to tell: When he asks you to do something, how quick is your affirmative response?

I want to be a God's yes-man. I really do. I want to spend the rest of my days utterly consumed by finding out where he's working and then joining him in that good work. You, too?

A BLESSING FROM PAM

May you be reminded today of God's faithfulness to lead us
only deeper into his protection, his provision, his peace.

Believing What We Believe

A man in the crowd answered, "Teacher, I brought you my son, who is possessed by a spirit that has robbed him of speech. Whenever it seizes him, it throws him to the ground. He foams at the mouth, gnashes his teeth and becomes rigid. I asked your disciples to drive out the spirit, but they could not."

"You unbelieving generation," Jesus replied, "how long shall I stay with you? How long shall I put up with you? Bring the boy to me."

So they brought him. When the spirit saw Jesus, it immediately threw the boy into a convulsion. He fell to the ground and rolled around, foaming at the mouth. Jesus asked the boy's father, "How long has he been like this?"

"From childhood," he answered. "It has often thrown him into the fire or water to kill him. But if you can do anything, take pity on us and help us."

"'If you can?'" said Jesus. "Everything is possible for one who believes."

Immediately the boy's father exclaimed, "I do believe; help me overcome my unbelief."

MARK 9:17-24

This scene perfectly reflects the entire emotional spectrum we experience as we deal with life in this broken world. The progression goes like this: we encounter the brokenness afresh; we see the devastation left in that brokenness's wake; we beg someone to do something but are left frustrated and flat; we finally make our way to Jesus, laying out our situation, blow by blow; we tell him we've "tried everything" but nothing has worked ... is there anything he might do?

You tell me, it's as if he says. *Am I at all able to help someone who is suffering unthinkable pain?*

We can sing songs about believing that Jesus is who he says he is and that he will do what he says he will do. But until we act on what we say we believe, we must question if we believe it at all.

A BLESSING FROM PAM

May you be inspired today and every day
to never set limits on what God can and will do.

The Bold Dailiness of Following God

Then he said to them all: "Whoever wants to be my disciple
must deny themselves and take up their cross daily and follow me."

LUKE 9:23

In our twenties and thirties, there was nothing that Pam and I wouldn't do for the sake of preserving intimacy with Jesus Christ. I think about wildly tempting opportunities we forsook because we sensed the quiet whisper of God saying, "No." I think about patterns we upended, even worthwhile "healthy" ones, all because something deep inside of each of us told us we'd be better going a different way. I think of the countless decisions we made as we raised Abram and Callie, all formed by what we believed God thought would be best. We built our family intentionally. We redirected our lives shamelessly. We ministered to people fearlessly. And it was all in the name of Christ.

There's a real temptation as we age to be content with "settling down"—with indulging in our own comforts and whims. What a colossal waste of a mature saint this is! Listen, it takes a long time to gather up spiritual wisdom and fortitude. The last thing we ought to do is to invest ourselves for twenty or thirty or forty years in gathering it up and then just ... coast ... for the rest of our lives. Nope. That's not for me. I'll take adventure with Jesus, please.

Here in Luke 9, Jesus reminds us that to follow him is to sacrifice greatly on his behalf. It is to keep at this faith thing daily, never abandoning the mission he's asked us to complete. It is to quit focusing on hoarding the good this life has to offer, instead obsessing over how to lose it for him.

A BLESSING FROM PAM

May you be compelled toward complete dedication
to your heavenly Father today.

Alive in Us

Do not quench the Spirit.

1 THESSALONIANS 5:19

One of my favorite songs these days is Micah Massey's song, "Spirit of God."

Spirit of God, fall on us
Fall on us
Oh, breath of God, breathe on us
Breathe on us

Your presence, your power, alive in us
Your glory descending, oh, flame of love

Every time we sing that song, I sense something cracking open in me, like God is renovating my heart and soul to accommodate more of him. By the song's end, I want to stand there perfectly still, lingering in that newfound space.

In the apostle Paul's letter to the church at Thessalonica, he offered up a set of final instructions to believers there about how to live successfully as righteous lovers of God. He told them to hold their leaders in high regard and to live at peace with each other and to be patient with everyone because people can be annoying and to encourage those who were disheartened because life is always tough. And then he said this: "Do not quench the Spirit," (1 Thessalonians 5:19). In other words, *don't shut him down.*

I love this idea. Don't you and I want the *full expression* of God's Spirit to shine through us? Don't we need the full expression of God's Spirit to shine through us?

How I pray your answer is yes to both.

Yes and yes, New Life, yes and yes. Fall, Spirit. Breathe, Spirit. Come.

A BLESSING FROM PAM

May you be encouraged today to give God's Spirit complete access
to your thoughts, your words, and your actions.

Mutual Submission

Wives, submit yourselves to your own husbands ...
Husbands, love your wives ...

EPHESIANS 5:22, 25

If you are married and your marriage is struggling today, I have good news for you. In fact, if you will do what I'm about to ask you to do, you will be among the full 99 percent of people who have also taken this same step and literally saved their marriages. I'm not exaggerating here. Ninety-nine percent of the time, when couples who have sought my counsel because their marriage was in a bad way have agreed to do what I'm about to ask you to do, divorce has been taken off the table as an option for them ... *permanently.*

If your marriage is in trouble, stop fixating on all that your spouse has done or continues to do to wreck the relationship. Instead—and I realize this is a huge ask—focus only on *your* contribution to the problems you're facing. Fixate only on what *you've done wrong.*

Practice saying these words aloud: "My marriage is in a bad place, and I take full responsibility for that."

If you are married, you are in a covenant relationship before God with your spouse. The moment you said "I do," you gave up all personal rights. The two of you became one! This means that your spouse's problem is your problem, and your problem is also your spouse's. No sense parsing who's at fault for which specific piece. *Own the whole deal.* I'm asking you to own it all. Take full responsibility for all that has gone on, and you will set your marriage back on track.

A BLESSING FROM PAM

May you know the utter relief of unity today as you consider perhaps for the first time that frustration or anger pointed at your spouse is in fact frustration or anger pointed at you.

Pressing On and Moving Ahead

The end of a matter is better than its beginning, and patience
is better than pride. Do not be quickly provoked in
your spirit, for anger resides in the lap of fools.

ECCLESIASTES 7:8-9

A woman in our congregation and I were having a conversation once when she said to me, "You know, Pastor Brady, I wish you had grown up in the America I grew up in."

She'd grown up in the early 1950s and explained with a twinkle of nostalgia that she sure did miss the days of "noble family values" and "far less violence" and all the good times of "sock hops and diners and small-town life at its best."

"Well," I said, "life in this country wasn't quite so idyllic for everyone. Black people couldn't use the same water fountains or attend the same schools as white people back then. Women were marginalized in the workplace. Young children were dying of diseases that we now can prevent. I'm not saying nothing good came out of those decades, but it certainly wasn't *all* good during those days."

She looked at me like I'd just run over her new puppy with my pickup truck.

In Ecclesiastes 7:8-9, when Solomon says, "the end of a matter is better than its beginning," he's acknowledging that the best times aren't behind us, but in front of us.

Think about it: As Christ's followers, as we look upon the future that has yet to unfold, should we approach it with anger or hope?

We should approach the future with hope because the best is yet to be.

A BLESSING FROM PAM

May you rest in the knowledge that God's coming kingdom is marked
not by chaos but by order, not by divisiveness but by unity, not by disease
but by healthfulness, not by despondency but by joy.

Peace as Fair Play

Let the peace of Christ rule in your hearts ...

COLOSSIANS 3:15

If you grew up playing sports—baseball, maybe, or basketball or hockey—then you know that one of the most useful roles involved is the umpire or referee. Refs are there for a reason; they're there to call infractions as play ensues. They're sorely needed because players have a tendency to get out of bounds, to break the rules, to go places they're not supposed to go. And so whenever one of these things happens during the course of play, the ref is the one who calls foul.

In his letter to the Colossian church, the apostle Paul wrote guidelines for how to live as those who had been "raised with Christ," (Col. 3:1), which just meant *saved by grace*. It might be acceptable when you're still going against God's will and ways to manifest things like bitterness and quarrelsomeness and rage, but once you go God's way, new boundary lines are immediately drawn. And one of the specific lines Paul draws attention to is the boundary line of peace.

If you're a believer, then I want to give you a phrase to carry with you for the rest of your days. You'll remember this phrase from time to time and I hope will be convicted to play by the rules. Here it is: *peace is always fair play*.

Isn't that good? So many things are situationally contingent, but here's something that is always wise: you can *always*, *always* choose to be a person of peace and know that you're getting it right.

A BLESSING FROM PAM

May you be ruled today only by the rule of peace.

Plenty

Jesus then took the loaves, gave thanks, and distributed to those who were seated as much as they wanted. He did the same with the fish. When they had all had enough to eat, he said to his disciples, "Gather the pieces that are left over. Let nothing be wasted." So they gathered them and filled twelve baskets with the pieces of the five barley loaves left over by those who had eaten.

JOHN 6:11-13

This well-known story begins with a great crowd of people pressing in on Jesus to hear what he has to say. There is eagerness there—to listen, to learn, to be healed. Seeing the throng, Jesus turns to his disciples and asks them how they're going to feed so many people. Philip answers first: "It would take more than half a year's wages to buy enough bread for each one to have a bite!" (John 6:7).

A boy with five small loaves of bread and two small fish is spotted. "Have people sit down," Jesus says, (v. 10). Then he took the food and gave thanks before distributing it to the crowd.

After everyone had eaten, Jesus told the disciples to walk around with baskets, filling them with the left-overs. From the equivalent of a sack lunch. After thousands had eaten themselves full.

"I am the bread of life," Jesus would say of himself, a few verses later, (John 6:48). He's nourishment that gives and gives and gives. Support that sustains and sustains and sustains. Strength for every leg of the journey to come.

Regardless of the hunger you're experiencing today—for peace in your marriage, for unity with your kids, for relief in your finances, for impact in your world—Jesus stands ready to feed you, ready to supernaturally fill you up.

A BLESSING FROM PAM

May you feast on the bread of heaven today,
and may you be satisfied as never before.

The Triumph of the Cross

When you were dead in your sins and in the uncircumcision of your flesh,
God made you alive with Christ.

COLOSSIANS 2:13

I met a man at New Life who at age nineteen climbed into a car with a group of guys to make a beer run. En route, he realized those guys planned to rob the liquor store. He was in over his head, and he knew it. But what was he supposed to do?

The driver pulled into the parking lot of the store and handed this young man a gun. The foursome stormed through the door, and the young man held up the cashier as the other three grabbed bottles of booze. When the cashier drew a gun of his own, the young man panicked and pulled the trigger, killing the cashier. "I'd never had a speeding ticket," he told me that day at church, "and yet now I'd killed a man."

After being tried and convicted, he'd spend the next twenty years in a Mississippi state penitentiary. Despite his life sentence, the governor of Mississippi had taken a liking to this kid and decided to pardon him at age thirty-nine.

He'd spent every day of those twenty years repenting of his sin before God. And by God's grace, he'd been freed from his guilt. He'd been declared innocent despite the wrongs done.

When the apostle Paul wrote to the Colossian church, he wanted to be sure they knew that despite their sin and pain and death, through faith in Jesus Christ they could be made alive once more in him.

This is the hope of the gospel. We were *dead* as sinners separated from God but now are *alive* by the power of Christ.

A BLESSING FROM PAM

May you walk in confidence today, knowing that if you are in Christ Jesus,
you have been freed from your burden of guilt.

JUNE

"As you walk with God, remember that he designed you and called you into being. He knows how your mind works and what touches your heart. He knows what excites you and what moves you. He knows what will help you to grow."

- Pastor Brady Boyd -

God with Us

And surely I am with you always,
to the very end of the age.

MATTHEW 28:20

We looked previously at the Great Commission, the set of instructions Jesus left for his followers regarding what their mission in the world was to be, but I'd like to revisit that text again to draw our attention to how it ends.

The full passage appears in Matthew 28 and says this: "All authority in heaven and on earth has been given to me. Therefore go and make disciples of all nations, baptizing them in the name of the Father and of the Son and of the Holy Spirit, and teaching them to obey everything I have commanded you. And surely I am with you always, to the very end of the age," (vv. 18b-20).

To those disciples, this news was a relief. They had lost their families and their careers. They'd lost their homes and their livelihood. They'd been driven far and wide, and yet they hadn't gone alone. Jesus had stayed close. They'd seen their peers boiled in oil, brutally beaten, sawed in two, and decapitated for loving God, and yet they hadn't faced those travesties alone. Jesus had stayed close.

One of my favorite spiritual themes is that of a loving God persisting with his people, staying close to them even when they insisted on going their own way. His faithfulness was always sure for them, and it remains sure for us too.

If you are disillusioned today, rest assured that God is near. Jesus is with you. You don't face that struggle alone. He has always been with you. He will always be with you. In a world where nothing is certain, you can be certain that God is here.

A BLESSING FROM PAM

May you be comforted by the reliable presence of your Father today,
who has promised never to forsake you, never to leave.

The War for Your Attention

You will keep in perfect peace those whose minds
are steadfast, because they trust in you.

ISAIAH 26:3

In our harried day-to-day lives, it's no exaggeration to say that you and I are at war. It's a war, and the spoils are our souls. And yet tiny disciplines can yield the biggest of results.

I'm reminded I'm at war when my family finally sits down for dinner—to pray, to eat, to relax—and someone's phone rings. Or when I get settled on the back deck for half an hour of solitude with God and my kids choose *then* to be chatty. Or when I set aside a day for hiking and communing with God and a freak snowstorm blows into town. All these things have happened to me, and they'll happen again and again. Why? Because we're at *war*. And the enemy hates to lose.

I begin to win the war when I silence the phone and keep my family's dinnertime conversation afloat; when I embrace my kids there on the back deck, tend to their immediate needs, and then tell them I'll be with them in twenty minutes or so; when instead of cursing that freak snowstorm, I watch with awe as it blows through.

How do you begin to win the war? How *will* you win this week? To refuse to go on the offense is to hand swift victory to the other side. I pray you won't give up the fight. I pray you'll carve out time each day to commune with God and in so doing fix your mind on him.

A BLESSING FROM PAM

Today, may you joyfully, intentionally, and continuously
train your wholehearted attention on God.

Reflexive Yes

The Lord had said to Abram, "Go from your country, your people and
your father's household to the land I will show you."

GENESIS 12:1

Abram knew what God was after, when God told him he'd be leaving home. All Abram had to do was survey the horizon in any direction to see that danger loomed, that violence would be his certain fate. He would need to move away from his household, his people, his country—all things that represented safety, predictability, peace—and move toward the opposite reality, a reality he did not want. And yet immediately after Abram received this word from the Lord, his response was a heartfelt yes. Genesis 12:4 says, "So Abram went, as the Lord had told him."

God said go, so Abram went—that's about as complicated as that exchange was.

I wonder in our daily lives if we are reflexive with our yeses as Abram was.

God tells us to approach someone we don't know, and we hem and haw.

God tells us to help someone in need, and we find something else to do.

God tells us to yield to the preferences of our spouse, and we pretend that we didn't hear.

If we want to do anything significant for God, we must be willing to leave the safe, comfortable place we're in and strike out into the wild unknown. Unknown people. Unknown cultures. Unknown situations. Unknown serving opportunities. Unknown investments toward unknown futures with results that are uncertain at best.

Sounds scary, right? The alternative is more frightful still: a blah existence that requires no faith, no trust, no sacrifice, no belief, and no zeal.

Yes is where real living begins.

A reflexive yes starts that life now.

A BLESSING FROM PAM

May you courageously and swiftly offer God your yes today,
regardless of what he asks you to do.

Neighborliness for the Win

Peter replied, "Repent and be baptized, every one of you, in the name of
Jesus Christ for the forgiveness of your sins. And you will receive the gift of the Holy Spirit."

ACTS 2:38

During our last baptism Sunday a single mom and her three children were among those who were baptized, and when I heard how she'd come to New Life and then to faith in Jesus Christ, I was refreshed in my belief that God is still on the move.

The single mom was a longstanding, self-avowed atheist who lived next door to a New Lifer. And while she wanted nothing to do with the congregant's lifestyle or church or God, she *did* appreciate the regular offers of practical help with meals.

The New Lifer told me that the grand, sweeping, wildly spiritual things she did in trying to minister to this neighbor centered on—and I quote—"just being nice."

Niceness? That's it? Niceness can win a wayward soul?

"Well, that, and prayer," she admitted. "I've also been praying for her."

As time elapsed, the single mom began to trust her neighbor with some of the tougher truths of her past. And when that neighbor simply received the truth instead of judging or shutting her out, the two were able to have deeper conversations—even spiritual ones, over time.

Eventually she agreed to visit New Life Church, and then God's Spirit took it from there.

But it all started with a nice word, a nice gesture, another niceness after that. It's enough, isn't it. In an increasingly cynical, critical, caustic world, sometimes it's absolutely enough.

A BLESSING FROM PAM

Today may you not underestimate the power of a kind word
or gesture in compelling people toward salvation in Christ.

Divine Filling

Now the earth was formless and empty, darkness was over the surface of the deep,
and the Spirit of God was hovering over the waters.

GENESIS 1:2

When the news regarding the pandemic was at its bleakest, I revisited the creation story and was reminded that before God began populating the earth, the earth was described as "formless and void."

You can ascribe a lot of adjectives to Covid era, but you'd be hard-pressed to find a stronger pair than that one: *formless and void*.

In the Genesis account, that formlessness, that emptiness, was used to provide contrast to all that was about to unfold. The world was about to receive light, oceans, land in which plants could grow. There would be trees thick with fruit, stars to punctuate the night sky, winged birds taking flight, wild animals to howl at the brand-new moon.

I sat with those images, those empty-to-full transitions, and I began to pray the same over our church, and over our world. "Father, all we see right now is emptiness: empty buildings, empty roads, empty calendars, empty shelves at the store. And yet here you are, right where you've always been, the fullness of your presence still at hand."

I asked God to help every New Lifer to sense his presence in fresh and significant ways. And I prayed that as we reconnected with that fullness, that fullness would overshadow the emptiness we were tempted to feel.

God answered those prayers. Our church didn't die a Covid death; in fact, New Life thrived. There is no emptiness that God can't fill. There is no void that he won't consume. He pours into every crack and crevice his presence and power.

It is all the filling we need.

A BLESSING FROM PAM

Today may you be filled to overflowing with God's goodness,
his gentleness, his provision, his protection, and his peace.

Clothed in Humility

All of you, clothe yourselves with humility toward one another, because,
"God opposes the proud but shows favor tot he humble." Humble yourselves,
therefore, under God's mighty hand, that he may lift you up in due time.

1 PETER 5:5B-6

To "clothe" ourselves with humility is to literally "put on" a posture that's ready to give, ready to sacrifice, ready to help. It's to show up in our various relational interactions—both with God and with people we meet—prepared not to observe from the sidelines, but rather to jump in with both feet and serve.

In our hyper-material culture, it can be tempting to fixate on the clothes we wear each day. Are we on point, trend-wise? Are we keeping up? Are we showing that we're somehow *cool* because we have the right brand of shoes? If you like fashion, fine. If you keep up with it, fine. But let me say this: When God is looking for someone who will go help someone who is poor or to go buy some food for someone who is hungry or to go sit with someone who is lonely, he's not looking at our footwear to decide who to pick. You know what he's looking for? A humble heart—that's it.

A humble heart communicates to God that we are ready to do whatever he asks us to do. No matter how inconvenienced we are, no matter how dirty we'll get, no matter what other things have to fall away so that we can prioritize our availability to him. Humility says, "I'm in. Whatever you want, God, I'm in."

A BLESSING FROM PAM

May you be known for your humility—today and every day.

Beware the Bitter Root

*See to it that no one falls short of the grace of God and that no bitter
root grows up to cause trouble and defile many.*

HEBREWS 12:15

A few years ago I was going through a rough patch relationally with another pastor,
and over the course of several months I noticed that whatever free time I had I'd
use up by imagining conversations with this person.

In his book *Social Intelligence*, author Daniel Goleman said that "rehashing our
social lives may rate as the brain's favorite downtime activity," which tells me I'm
far from alone in this regard. We fondle our social relationships, turning them over
in our minds. We revisit memories, we plot future exchanges, we wish for do-overs
where we come across witty and wise. And while there is nothing inherently wrong
with this practice, it sure does siphon unassigned time.

One morning in my office, when I had headed over to my credenza for a cup of
fresh coffee, I sensed God saying, *You know, you're giving a lot of mental space to
this, even though the conversations you're envisioning are never going to transpire.*

I kind of scoffed over the rebuke, even as I knew that God was right. I needed to
start minding my mind.

Later, I talked to the entire staff about what had happened, explaining that spinning
our wheels over virtual conversations only serves to stir us up, while bringing our
challenges to God calms us down and puts our anxious thoughts to rest. It was
true then, and it's true still today: the sense of peace we seek is found only in the
presence of God.

A BLESSING FROM PAM

*May you come quickly into God's presence with every frustration, failure, and fear.
Time with him will keep bitterness at bay and will reset your perspective on things.*

Miracles in Our "Mist"

For no matter how many promises God has made, they are "Yes" in Christ.
And so through him the "Amen" is spoken by us to the glory of God.

2 CORINTHIANS 1:20

Earlier this spring I woke one morning to a heavy layer of mist covering the entire city, which is unusual for the high-desert climate of Colorado Springs. But as the hour ticked by, the weather pattern shifted, and rays of sunshine began to warm the clouds, the mist, the earth. Over a period of about twenty minutes, what had been shrouded in gray somberness now glistened, awash in a vibrant glow.

Reflexively I thought about you, about New Life Church. I thought about all that we've been through together: a scandal, a shooting, a terrible economic recession, a pandemic, war upon war. And I thought about how each time, God has been faithful to lift the fog that clouded our sight and give us clarity and vision once more.

This passage from the apostle Paul to the Corinthian church is every bit as energizing to me now as it probably was to them. Through the finished work of Jesus, God's promises are yes and *amen*. We don't have to worry that the fog has descended, or whether the fog of circumstance ever will lift. In Jesus, we will see clearly one day— either here or in the kingdom to come.

Until then, we have the privilege of joining God in that redemptive work, trusting his provision, his promises, his power. Each time we see heaven breaking into earth, that momentary lifting of the clouds, of the mist, we are reminded that the day is coming—it will come!—when our sight will be obscured no more.

A BLESSING FROM PAM

May you know today that even in the clouds, the light of God shines brightly.
Even through the fog, he still sees you.

Healthy, Messy, Good

I appeal to you, brothers and sisters, in the name of our Lord Jesus Christ,
that all of you agree with one another in what you say and that there be no divisions
among you, but that you be perfectly united in mind and thought.

1 CORINTHIANS 1:10

I travel around to other churches to preach from time to time, and whenever I'm asked by people who have never been to Colorado Springs what New Life Church is like, three adjectives tend to rise to the surface for me: "We're *healthy*," I say. "We're *messy*. We're *good*."

I've always thought that the best churches should be kind of like the best families; we are a family, after all. And in a family, in case you haven't noticed, while things may not always be nice and neat, they can and should be healthy and safe. That's what I'm conveying with those three words: yeah, we're a messy bunch—literally and emotionally, too. But we're healthy. We're forgiving. We're loving. We're hopeful. We're servants. We're worshipers. We're absolutely *crazy* about Jesus Christ. And together, that makes us good.

Watch for your reflexive assessments of our church as you make your way through this year. Are you expecting perfection from an imperfect bunch? Are you frustrated by messes you find? Listen, I long for the glory of our glorified body as much as the next guy, but that just isn't our reality quite yet. Let's set our sights on functional. On caring. On devoted. On trusting. On kind. And let's seek to be those things for each other, unified in our goodness, in our messiness, in our health.

A BLESSING FROM PAM

Today may you smile on the perfectly imperfect body of believers
called New Life—your family, your friends, your home.

Freely, Serve

The rich rule over the poor, and the
borrower is slave to the lender.

PROVERBS 22:7

For many years, until we as a church started to make significant strides toward eradicating our debt, we were paying $150,000 per month to service the money we owed. Can you imagine writing a check for that amount every thirty days just to cover the minimum payment plus fees on outstanding debt? I can imagine it. And it's devastating every time.

Nearly every month that that check would go out, I'd sit there thinking, *Just imagine what we could do with that $150,000 in our community! We could buy a house for a single mom. We could buy several cars for people in need. We could get entire families off the streets of our city. We could gift life-saving medical interventions over at Children's Hospital to parents who are strapped for cash.*

On and on the thoughts flowed, but each month, I'd have to say no. No to this dream. No to that dream. No to such expensive whims. We had debt to service, after all. We had a slave owner to pay.

This all begs the question: what dreams are you having to defer right now because you've enslaved yourself to a bank? Sure, your numbers might look different than New Life's—*please* tell me that they do. But that feeling of wishing you could act on divine promptings from God ... can you relate to that sensation at all?

You will never serve the Lord with greater freedom or joy than when you're simultaneously not servicing debt. Test out that theory for yourself, and see if it isn't true.

A BLESSING FROM PAM

May you find courage and boldness to take one step toward financial freedom today: one less dollar spent, one more dollar paying down debt, one more necessary conversation had.

Civilians Acting Civilly

I urge, then, first of all, that petitions, prayers, intercession and thanksgiving
be made for all people—for kings and all those in authority, that we may live peaceful
and quiet lives in all godliness and holiness. This is good, and pleases God our Savior.

1 TIMOTHY 2:1-3

Especially during an election year, I'm always floored by how vitriolic conversations surrounding politics can become. People I've known for years to be meek, mild, and measured in their speech suddenly become name-calling mockers of the other side. Gentle lovers of Jesus one day; angry antagonists the next. This isn't as it should be.

A few reminders, for the next time you're tempted to let partisanship rule the day:

· As the people of God, we are citizens of heaven, but we also are citizens of a democratic republic, where government plays a critical role. We must use our *vote* to elect the people we wish to fill these roles and use our *voice* to encourage those who lead.

· As the people of God, we are called to submit. Governing authorities may prove to be hypocritical or even incompetent from time to time, but the positions they hold must be respected still. Here's an easy one to try: practice submitting to the roles, not the people filling those roles.

· As the people of God, we are called to pray. When we fret and fume over our leaders, we signal to the watching world that we are totally out of touch with the power that resides in us all. In Christ, we have the same Spirit living inside of us that raised Jesus from the dead. May we be people who pray instead of provoke, who press in instead of act out.

A BLESSING FROM PAM

May you honor those whom God has placed in authority over
our country today—in thought, in word, in deed, and in prayer.

The Mind of Christ

*"Who has known the mind of the Lord
so as to instruct him?" But we have the mind of Christ.*

1 CORINTHIANS 2:16

In his letter to the Corinthian church, the apostle Paul ends a litany of instructions on how to live effectively in this world by walking by the Spirit of God. This is a magnificent passage of Scripture, so let me give it to you whole. After acknowledging that Paul had not come to ministry to believers in Corinth using impressive language or worldly wisdom but instead had come trembling, in humility and in fear, here is what he says:

"We do, however, speak a message of wisdom among the mature, but not the wisdom of this age or of the rulers of this age, who are coming to nothing. No, we declare God's wisdom, a mystery that has been hidden and that God destined for our glory before time began. None of the rulers of this age understood it, for if they had, they would not have crucified the Lord of glory. However, as it is written: 'What no eye has seen, what no ear has heard, and what no human mind has conceived'—the things God has prepared for those who love him—these are the things God has revealed to us by his Spirit.

"The Spirit searches all things, even the deep things of God. For who knows a person's thoughts except their own spirit within them? In the same way no one knows the thoughts of God except the Spirit of God. What we have received is not the spirit of the world, but the Spirit who is from God, so that we may understand what God has freely given us. This is what we speak, not in words taught us by human wisdom but in words taught by the Spirit, explaining spiritual realities with Spirit-taught words. The person without the Spirit does not accept the things that come from the Spirit of God but considers them foolishness, and cannot understand them because they are discerned only through the Spirit. The person with the Spirit makes judgments about all things, but such a person is not subject to merely human judgments, for, 'Who has known the mind of the Lord so as to instruct him?' But we have the mind of Christ," (1 Corinthians 2:6-16).

I want to say something to you that is absolutely the truth, even as it might sting a bit: you are not that smart. You are not that powerful. You are not that creative. And you know what? Neither am I. True, education is important to our growth.

What we learn to acquire a skill or improve a talent or steward a spiritual gift is critical to our effectiveness in our world. For this reason, please don't check your brain at the door as you gain intimacy in your relationship with Christ. But at the end of all that knowledge, never forget that the entirety of the gains you've made would fill little more than a single droplet of water compared with the vast oceans of wisdom God owns. If your brainpower were enough to save you, then you'd have no use for God.

But it isn't enough. It will never be enough. You and I will always, always need God.

I say this because we simply must remember as we make our way through this life that our only hope is accessing more and more of the mind of Christ. How else are we to opt for things like humility and selflessness? How else are we to seek to serve? How else are we to love in the face of oppression? How else are we to lay down our weapons and choose to pray?

Long for the mind of Christ. Ask for the mind of Christ. Praise God for the mind of Christ, for it is by the mind of Christ that we live.

A BLESSING FROM PAM

May you see all of life through the lens of God's vast wisdom today,
remembering that he is over it all.

Glory to God in All Things

So whether you eat or drink or whatever you do,
do it all for the glory of God.

1 CORINTHIANS 10:31

I once heard a story of a monk who, in the course of everyday life, periodically rang what's called a "mindfulness bell." People nearby who heard the bell would stop what they were doing and take three silent, mindful breaths. Then they would continue their work, awakened ever so slightly by the simple act of pausing, of breathing, of practicing mindfulness.

I love this idea. And it's more practical than we may first think. I vote for ringing a mindfulness bell throughout our days, whether we have an actual bell or not. Maybe the "bell" is the instant your feet hit the floor in the morning. (That's the "bell" in my life.) Or maybe it's each time you slip behind the wheel of your car. Maybe you set a bell chime as your ring tone, and thus it sounds each time someone calls.

The "bell" could be sitting down to a meal or kissing your spouse at the end of the day or every time you stop to pray.
With a little creative thought, you and I can come up with some reminder to
focus our thoughts,
to mind our minds,
to choose to rest in God.

The great Coach Vince Lombardi once said, "Winning is a habit," an idea that transcends the world of sports. We practice taking every thought captive because minor habits really do wind up equaling major wins in the end.

A BLESSING FROM PAM

May you do all to God's glory today!

God Believes in Homeschooling

Search me, God, and know my heart; test me and know my anxious thoughts.
See if there is any offensive way in me, and lead me in the way everlasting.

PSALM 139:23-24

I always catch people off-guard when I talk about God being in favor of homeschooling. Although, since the pandemic, you might say that we all became homeschoolers in a jiffy. Here's what I mean by the assertion, pandemic coping skills notwithstanding: God longs to sit with each of us individually and teach us about himself. Think of a homeschooling family: generally a parent sits with a student or two and imparts wisdom in a way that the specific child or children can understand. Similarly, God desires unhurried time with each of his children, conveying *who he is* in ways that he or she can grasp. God isn't distant. He isn't looking to shout at us from on high. No, he's personal. He's intimate. He's interested in us.

As you walk with God, remember that he designed you and crafted you and called you into being. He knows how your mind works. He knows what touches your heart. He knows what worries you and what excites you. He knows the things that will help you grow. He knows whether you're a visual or auditory learner. He knows whether you're into technology or nature or both. He knows the kind of music that moves you. He knows the words that can make your soul soar.

I'm going to ask you to do something pretty radical today, which is to let yourself be homeschooled by God. Come to him at some point today and ask him to teach you, as a patient teacher explains a math problem to a child. Ask him about himself. Ask him about how he made you. Ask him questions whose answers he alone possesses. Ask him to reveal himself, and he will.

A BLESSING FROM PAM

May you sense the patience and delight of your loving
heavenly Father today, as you sit and talk with him.

The Seat of the Offense

For the sake of your name, LORD, forgive
my iniquity, though it is great.

PSALM 25:11

Have you ever been honest enough during a time of prayer to tell God you were discontented in him?

I have a theory, which is that whenever you and I find ourselves offended with one another, the root of that offense can be traced back to discontentment with God.

You lose out on a promotion to a (less spectacular) colleague and are thus offended with your boss.

Your teenager fails to clean up his room for the millionth time, and you feel offended by the slight.

A friend reacts negatively to a text you sent her, and the correction feels offensive and harsh.

Day by day we have countless reasons to be offended by what people thoughtlessly say and do. But how do those horizontal petty annoyances relate to our vertical posture toward God?

When we consider the sacrifice that Jesus made on our behalf—the just for the unjust, or the "righteous for the unrighteous," as 1 Peter 3:18 says—we must remember that in willingly dying for our sins, (past, present, and future), he literally took on those sins. If Jesus was delivered for our offenses, taking them on in bodily form himself, then why on earth would we ever take them back? Wouldn't we let them all die with him?

Here is the opportunity for you and me both: the next time we are tempted to feel offended by someone or something, may we run into the presence of God and thank him for the gift of his Son. May we confess our momentary discontentment in his vast provision and ask him to help us begin again.

A BLESSING FROM PAM

Today, take heart in Jesus' perfect sacrifice, which has absorbed every offense you have ever felt before and every offense you'll feel again.

Sin at the Door

*"But if you do not do what is right, sin is crouching at
your door; it desires to have you, but you must rule over it."*

GENESIS 4:7B

In this story from Genesis, we learn in the preceding verses that Adam and Eve have just given birth to their first son, Cain. Soon thereafter she'd birth a second son—Abel, keeper of flocks.

As the story unfolds, we find Cain tending his soil while Abel tends his flocks. Eventually Cain brings his offering to the Lord, but it wasn't the best of the best. Abel brought the best of the best, and God looked with favor on him. This infuriated Cain.

God took in Cain and said, "Why are you angry? Why is your face downcast? If you do what is right, will you not be accepted? But if you do not do what is right, sin is crouching at your door; it desires to have you, but you must rule over it," (vv. 6-7). God was telling Cain to simply bring his first fruits as his offering, and all would go well for him. "*That* offering, I will accept," God was saying. "*That* offering, I will bless."

If you are indulging a sin streak and therefore *actively displeasing* God, be forewarned: sin is all around you, and it's crouching at your door. It wants to own you. It wants to master you. It wants to take a wrecking ball to your world.

But just as was the case with Cain, it doesn't have to win the day. Repent of your sin. Claim the forgiveness that God says is yours in 1 John 1:9. Begin anew today. Make things right with your heavenly Father, who longs to lift your countenance once again.

A BLESSING FROM PAM

May you be freed from sin today.
May you dance in your freedom today.

The Fruit of Repentance

*"The time has come," he [Jesus] said. "The kingdom of God
has come near. Repent and believe the good news!"*

MARK 1:15

Let me start by saying that Jesus did not come to correct our behavior.

Let that sink in for a moment.

He did not come to correct your behavior; behavior modification was not his ultimate aim.

In the same breath let me say that this does not mean that you and I should throw all caution to the wind and just stir up a wild sin-storm every day. You may have heard what the apostle Paul had to say along these lines: "What shall we say, then? Shall we go on sinning so that grace may increase? By no means! We are those who have died to sin; how can we live in it any longer?" (Romans 6:1-2)

The reason our behavior changes as we gain increased intimacy with Jesus isn't because the goal was behavior modification but simply because we don't *want* to sin.

Talk with any devoted Jesus follower, and I guarantee you'll hear the same story time and again: they are sinning less today than they did before because their heart, quite simply, has changed. And the same will be true for you. So yes, while God asked Cain to make some changes, lest sin overtake him and wreck his life, he also conveys to every human being that they are seen and known and loved—just as they are, no change required.

And as we let those messages of acceptance and kindness and grace seep into the crevices of our hearts, we will begin living in that identity more than the identity that was known for its sin.

A BLESSING FROM PAM

*May the good news of the gospel compel you to go God's way today.
And may that same decision be easier tomorrow, and the day after that.*

On Purpose

"Come, follow me," Jesus said,
"and I will send you out to fish for people."

MATTHEW 4:19

With few exceptions, people live ordinary lives. We get up in the morning. We have a cup of coffee. If we have kids, we might help them get ready for school or drive carpool a few days a week. We work. We manage household chores. We have meetings and appointments. We have bills to pay. We plan for future trips. We are forever running to the grocery store.

We're all doing about as much as we can, and yet how many of us are satisfied—I mean *truly* satisfied, day after day?

During the early days of Jesus' earthly ministry, he walked along the Sea of Galilee and spotted two brothers casting their nets into the water. They were working hard, doing their job, seeing if the fish were going to bite that day. Jesus approached them. He didn't tell them to quit doing what they'd been doing all their lives. Instead, he invited them to do the same thing with an altogether different purpose:

After we say yes to Jesus, most likely we reenter the very same life we had on the day *before* we said to him. We'll probably have the same job. We'll probably have the same hobbies and neighbors and friends. What will be different is our sense of purpose. Now, we're fishing for people.

I'll tell you what brings joy to my rather ordinary life each day: it's knowing that at any moment Jesus could use me to join his redemptive work. It's the *supernatural possibilities* in our natural reality that make the mundane remarkable for us.

A BLESSING FROM PAM

May you see the ins and outs of your responsibilities today as conduits for the grace of God to flow through you to others, to bring something remarkable to life.

A Word When You're Lonely

Trust in him at all times, you people; pour out
your hearts to him, for God is our refuge.

PSALM 62:8

According to the Worldometer, the current world population at this writing is 7,945,031,463—nearly *eight billion* people and counting. No wonder traffic is increasing on I-25—am I right?

Eight billion people, and yet never before has there been a time when people have been lonelier than they are right now. We are the loneliest set of consecutive generations ever to live, despite eight billion reasons to connect.

Oh, sure: we're digitally connected. We have Instagram accounts and Facebook friends and Snapchat followers galore. But what we've gained in technological connectivity I fear we've lost in our "humanness" score.

We're living digitally connected but relationally all alone.

If I'm writing to you right now, let me give you two words of encouragement: first, come to your heavenly Father, and pour out your heart to him. Trust him to be your good, safe refuge, the One who connects instantly to your soul.

And second, get in front of a real, live human today. Sit with someone. Talk with someone. Tell the truth to someone you trust.

You're not meant to do life all alone, my friend.

You don't have to do life alone.

A BLESSING FROM PAM

May you be enveloped in divine care today,
and may you spread that love around.

When Things Don't Quite Work Out

When John, who was in prison, heard about the deeds of the Messiah, he
sent his disciples to ask him, "Are you the one who is to come, or should
we expect someone else?" Jesus replied, "Go back and report to John
what you hear and see. The blind receive sight, the lame walk, those
who have leprosy are cleansed, the deaf hear, the dead are
raised, and the good news is proclaimed to the poor."

MATTHEW 11:2-5

Here's a story about John the Baptist, the cousin to Jesus, the predecessor to Jesus, the guy many mistook for Jesus, even as he was simply trying to pave the way for Christ. John the Baptist got his name because of having baptized hundreds of people in the Jordan River, long before Jesus showed up on the scene. John the Baptist accumulated a gigantic following of people and in those days was a big, big deal.

But then Jesus showed up.
And he asked John to baptize him.
And then he kind of stole the show.
Jesus.
Everything was now about him.

To make matters worse, after mustering the courage to confront an evil ruler, John the Baptist was arrested, thrown in prison, and martyred for his faith. That evil ruler was having a party and wanted to give his step-daughter a birthday surprise. He asked her what she wanted, and guess what she said? She wanted John the Baptist's head on a platter. Astoundingly, the ruler complied.

Before he was beheaded, John the Baptist sent word to one of his disciples from prison to find out how Jesus was doing ... and to find out *who he was*. And in the passage above, we find Jesus' reply.

There was frustration buried in John's query. Here he was headed to a bloody beheading, while Jesus was enjoying celestial glory as the New Guy, the Big Guy, the One. And what did Jesus offer, by way of consolation? "Tell him the blind are seeing. The lame are walking. The lepers are being cleansed. The deaf can now hear. The dead have been raised. The poor are being given good news."

I don't know what you would put on the list of things that are "not quite working out for you" today. Your marriage, maybe? Your visions of healthy interactions with your teenage kids? Your ability to afford the quality of life you desire? Your physical strength? Your desire not to drink?

Here is what I know: God's redemptive plan is unfolding in the earth, and we can let that be enough for us. People are coming to faith in Jesus. People are relating to him through baptism. People are leaving a lifetime of sin to pursue God's will and ways. And between now and when you and I enter our future reality, where there is no suffering, no disease, and no pain, we can praise God for his immense longsuffering as he brings more and more into his fold.

Who does Jesus think he is? He thinks he is the perfect sacrifice affording us access to God, both now and for all of eternity. He thinks that ought to be enough for us. He does. It should. He is.

A BLESSING FROM PAM

May you reconnect today with God's earnest desire to lift
every burden you presently face and wipe every tear from your eye.

In the Likeness of God

When God created mankind, he made them in the likeness of God.
He created them male and female and blessed them. And
he named them "Mankind" when they were created.

GENESIS 5:1B-2

You were created in the likeness of God.

Does that fact boggle your brain?

Try saying it aloud: "I was created in the likeness of God."

Me. With all my foibles and failings. With all the dumb stuff I've said along the way. With all the dumb stuff I've *done* along the way. With my bad attitudes and worse-still moods. With my selfish streaks and persistent sin.

And what about you? You! Created in the likeness of God. You, with all your you-ness! This ought to take your breath away.

This says nothing of the people around us; *they* bear the image of God? That crazy uncle you try to hide away at family reunions? That friend of your son's who says the most obnoxious things? That boss who can't control his temper? That neighbor who has the audacity to vote for *them*?

They were created in the likeness of God?

(Are we absolutely *sure* about that?)

Look around. Seriously: do it. Do you see what I see? The likeness of God on every countenance. A whisper of divinity in every voice. That hint of goodness peeking out from every gaze. The sense that there's depth we have yet to unearth.

I will make you a promise here and now: You will never regret treating another individual with the honor, dignity, attention, and care that you would offer to Jesus himself.

This is God's call on your life and mine: *be gentle with them … they're mine.*

A BLESSING FROM PAM

May you see every person you encounter today through the lens of
God's image having been imprinted on them, his divinity, his beauty, his grace.

True Surrender

You're in charge! You can do anything you want!
You're ablaze in beauty! Yes. Yes. Yes.

MATTHEW 6:13 MSG

When the late Eugene Peterson was a pastor in suburban Baltimore, he saw many people leave drug addiction and prostitution to go God's way with their lives, and while this radical transformation was worth celebrating, Eugene noticed that discipling them was tough. They wanted to thrive in their newfound faith but had no familiarity with the Bible. What's more, all the available versions of the Scriptures were difficult for them to grasp. They needed a bridge to these biblical concepts. And so Eugene picked up his pen.

Whenever I think of those converts who left one way of life for another, I think about how they gave "charge" over their lives to a whole new force. When you're addicted to drugs, drugs are in charge of you. When you're turning tricks every night to make ends meet, a pimp is in charge of you. Whatever we're doing in life and whoever those efforts are for, someone or something is in charge of us. We're given over fully at all times.

True surrender says this: "Lord Jesus, you're in charge. You can do anything you want."

Don't you wonder what it would be like to pray that prayer each day? "Lord Jesus, you're in charge. You can do anything you want." I just wonder what types of opportunities we'd see, if we made a practice of praying that prayer.

A BLESSING FROM PAM

May you be drawn into the greatest possible adventure today,
that of going where Jesus already is.

How to be a Friend

*"Greater love has no one than this: to lay
down one's life for one's friends."*

JOHN 15:13

"Greater love has no one than this," Jesus said in John 15:13, "to lay down one's life for one's friends."

Jesus was about to make the ultimate sacrifice on behalf of his friends—a powerful example for you and me both. We may never be asked to sacrifice on that level for our friends, but Jesus' action here does beg the question of us of whether we're *willing to sacrifice at all*.

Are you a friend to people in need? Do you rally the courage to speak the truth to them? Are you willing to sacrifice your time, your money, your resources, your attention, so that their lives can be improved?

It's easy to say we're good friends. Much tougher is *being* good friends as Jesus would have defined the term.

A BLESSING FROM PAM

*May you be on the receiving end of a friend's kindness today,
and may you extend that kindness to someone you know.*

Abounding in Love

The LORD is compassionate and gracious,
slow to anger, abounding in love.

PSALM 103:8

When I was a freshman in high school, my all-boys English class was Mrs. White's worst nightmare. Not only did we want nothing to do with grammar and literature, but our classroom was positioned next door to the cafeteria, and our class met just before lunch.

Mrs. White never cracked a smile, laughed, or spoke a single word of encouragement. She was just livid—all the time.

As I grew up, I had a tough time seeing God as anything different from Mrs. White. Whenever I thought about God, I pictured Mrs. White, but up in heaven somewhere. I envisioned an old, crotchety, rage-filled taskmaster who was less than thrilled to be stuck with me. When I thought about how God must feel toward me, the word *disappointed* was always top of mind.

I was twenty-two when I really and truly surrendered my life to the Lord. Maybe I'd come across Psalm 103 sometime before then, but the first time I remember the words to that psalm sinking deep into my soul was then. I got to the part about God being "compassionate and gracious, slow to anger, abounding in love," (v. 8), and I audibly exhaled. What relief I found in those words. Could it be true that God wasn't at all mad at me?

This is a worthwhile starting point, if you're convinced God is mad at you: he is thinking of you, and his thoughts are filled with love. He is not angry toward you. He created you and adores you. He longs to be in pure, unbroken, unhurried fellowship with you. He is for you. He is with you. His posture toward you is *grace*.

A BLESSING FROM PAM

Today may you reject all notions of God
that do not align with this fact: God is love.

A Worthwhile Belief

Each of you should give what you have decided in your heart to give, not reluctantly or under compulsion, for God loves a cheerful giver.

2 CORINTHIANS 9:7

This verse from the apostle Paul's letter to the Corinthian church is a fascinating one; after all, why does God care what our attitude is when we give to his efforts here on earth? What difference does it make to him if we give when we're feeling irritated or elated or guilty or generous or stingy or celebratory—so long as we *give?*

The answer has to do with the reason we give to begin with.

When we honor the Sabbath, it's not God who benefits, but us. We remind ourselves that God can do more in and through our lives in six full days than we can in seven on our own.

When we tithe to the Church, it's not God who benefits, but us. We remind ourselves that God can do more with 90 percent of our income than we can with 100 percent on our own.

When we surrender our skills and talents and gifts to God, it's not God who benefits, but us. We remind ourselves that God can accomplish in and through us *that which we cannot do by ourselves.*

Here's what cheerfulness in the disposition of the giver says to God: "I am offering this time or money or talent from a place of joy, from a place of contentment, from a place of full and complete trust that there is nothing more important to me in this moment than your divine activity in and through my life."

What a beautiful thing to say to God.

What a worthwhile thing to believe.

A BLESSING FROM PAM

Give to the Lord today. Whether time, money, or talent, give cheerfully. Give wholeheartedly. Give, trusting that you will be the one who is blessed by the faithful act.

Come Back to God

Then God blessed the seventh day and made it holy, because on
it he rested from all the work of creating that he had done.

GENESIS 2:3

I've had the opportunity to visit Jerusalem, and nothing is better than being there on a Friday afternoon. From sundown on Friday until sundown on Saturday, residents there honor the Sabbath—the *Shabbat*, as they call it. And if you're in town during the Sabbath, there is one phrase you'll hear time and again: "Shabbat shalom."

It's a greeting, a way of wishing peace to each other as they begin their Sabbath celebration. But it's more than that. To wish someone "Shabbat shalom" is to exhort that person to come back to God, to his completeness, to his original order, to his rest. It's quite an invitation, don't you think?

Whenever my family honors the Sabbath and unplugs from the hum of everyday life, I love the idea that I'm reminding my own soul and the souls of anyone who may be aware of our practice that it is possible to return to God's rest. At least once a week, by simply doing what God has asked us to do, we can return to the sense of completeness that we chase on the other six days.

By our action—or inaction, in this case—we can communicate to the watching world that we understand a fundamental truth, which is that the rest we long for cannot be found at the movies, or on a Netflix binge, or at the bottom of a bottle or wine, or in front of the big game, or even at the end of the greatest novel ever written. The rest we long for is found only in God.

Our rest is found only in him.

A BLESSING FROM PAM

May you enjoy the deepest of exhales today
as you rest—fully rest—in God.

Spiritual Daughters and Sons

I have no greater joy than to hear that my
children are walking in the truth.

3 JOHN 1:4

For the past three decades, one of the key measures of success in my life has centered not just on how well I was raising my actual daughter and son but on whether I was raising *spiritual* children as well. Like the apostle John, who wrote the verse above, was I pouring into younger believers, helping them grow in their walk with Christ? Was I training young women and men in righteousness, showing them how to go God's way in their lives? Was I spurring on the next generation to "love and good deeds" (see Hebrews 10:24) so that they could then multiply too?

It's tempting to think at a certain age and stage of life that the literal parent/child relationship is the only parenting task expected of us, but as believers, we must think twice. Our entire mission as lovers of Jesus is to also *spiritually* reproduce.

A BLESSING FROM PAM

May you speak the encouraging word, ask the penetrating question, correct the errant thinking, or act on the noble impulse with a newer, younger believer today.

The Worth of a Friend's Wound

Wounds from a friend can be trusted, but
an enemy multiplies kisses.

PROVERBS 27:6

A few years ago, after nearly five decades of peaceful coexistence with my gall bladder, sadly, one of us had to go—and thankfully it wasn't me. Upon realizing (courtesy of my doc) that this organ needed to be removed, I was informed that that removal would require surgery. During the one meeting I'd had with the surgeon, I'd asked him how many of these surgeries he did in a given year. He'd said, "Oh, about a hundred and fifty."

"What's your success rate?" I then asked, to which he said, "I get them all out."

"How do your patients do afterward?" I continued.

"Haven't lost one yet," came the reply.

I could tell I liked this guy. He knew practically what has taken me half a lifetime to sort out on the relational front: to get something toxic out, a wound must be created.

This is the image we're to have in mind as we read Solomon's words in Proverbs 27:6. If we want the bad stuff rooted out of our lives, we're to have to open ourselves us, just as I was laid bare there on the operating table. We're going to have to allow someone we've decided to trust to get the junk out so that we can live life stronger and healthier than we were before.

If you have found a friend, you have found a rare treasure indeed. Let that person in. Hand that person the scalpel. Allow that person to make the cut. Trust that you'll be okay.

A BLESSING FROM PAM

May you choose to entrust yourself to the care of a friend today,
knowing that his or her assessment of you is worth something valuable, trusting
that the wound you sustain might very well be the key to your future growth.

Divorce Court or the Kitchen Table

*"In your anger do not sin:" Do not let the
sun go down while you are still angry.*

EPHESIANS 4:26

Pam and I figured out early in our relationship that if we were faithful to keeping short accounts with each other, we could avoid major blow-ups later on.

It sounds simple, doesn't it?

In actuality, it is.

The apostle Paul's counsel to believers in Ephesus is applicable to us still today: we are fools to let anger between our spouse and us simmer instead of addressing it right here, right now. We think it's a benign thing, this idea of going to bed in the middle of a fight. *Things will be better in the morning,* we say to ourselves. *I'll have a clearer head after some rest.*

I'm not saying that every problem can be solved in the space of a day. What *can* be solved is your anger. You can soften, you can come closer, you can remind your spouse that you're on the same team.

If there is tension in your home, take the edge off before going to bed. Ask your spouse for three minutes to talk. Sit down across from each other. Look into his or her eyes. Exhale. Gather yourself. Speak kindly and without amping up. Say, "I know we have things to work through, but I want to acknowledge that I'm on your side, that I'm for you, that I'm for us, and that I'm committed to doing whatever work is necessary for us to move forward in confidence and peace."

Don't let the sun go down on your anger. Let it set on gentleness instead.

A BLESSING FROM PAM

*May you be the picture of resolve, of faithfulness,
and of peace in your home, in your marriage, today.*

Built in Drops, Lost in Buckets

A gossip betrays a confidence; so
avoid anyone who talks too much.

PROVERBS 20:19

When Pam and I were a young married couple, we attended a small group led by Pastor Garvin and his wife Kim McCarrell in West Texas, where we all lived at the time. Now, I know I just told you that Pam and I have rarely gotten upset with each other across the three-plus decades we've been married, but full disclosure demands that I 'fess up about the one season of our marriage that defied that trend. It was in West Texas, in those early days of our marriage, when things were about as bad as they've ever been. We weren't contemplating divorce, but we also weren't getting along. My priorities were way out of whack, and the effect on us both was making us short-tempered, easily irritated, and just plain annoyed with life.

We would go to small group each week and not knowing that faking it was an option say, "We're struggling. We're still struggling. We're being petty and immature. We need to grow in this area. We need to just *grow up* ..."

And then we'd both lay out all the sordid details for Kim and Garvin and the rest to hear.

Week after week we'd do this, confessing to God and to each other and to our group all the ways we'd failed. Kim and Garvin would pray for us, they would encourage us, and they would be honest about what a healthy marriage required. I look back on those experiences and shake my head over God's goodness. He gave us a safe, life-giving place where we could express our brokenness so that we didn't have to go it alone. He gave us safe, life-giving people who listened and did not condemn.

Fast-forward many years later, and Pastor Garvin was on our staff at New Life, serving as executive pastor to our team. During his years at that post, he was my closest associate on staff. And more than anyone else, Garvin was the one who would approach me after a given meeting and say, "Brady, you came on a little strong in there ... everything okay?"

Or, "Brady, you handled that really well. Just wanted to tell you so."

Or, "Brady, I know you're tired and maybe a little angry, but that person didn't deserve to be treated that way."

Guess how often I received Garvin's input? One hundred percent of the time. Garvin had earned my trust decades prior, and now I'd go with him *anywhere*.

There's an old saying that goes like this: trust is built in drops and lost in buckets. I love that quote because I have *lived* that quote. We build trust with each other day by day as we steward each other's stories well, and as we listen patiently to each other's pain, and as we pray earnestly for each other's growth, and as we tell the truth to each other without fear. It's also true that that trust can be lost—through gossip, through slander, through carelessness, through envy, through spite—but we don't have to cave to all that. I have a firm conviction that we all can be like Garvin: careful, thoughtful, kind.

Here's a starting point: the next time you discover a vulnerability in a friend's life, a weak spot they've divulged to you, a little bad information about an otherwise really good person, be mindful of how you respond. Choose to hold the confidence. Avoid the temptation to judge. Speak a truthful word of encouragement. Sit with your friend in the pain. Then, as time marches on, keep stewarding the gift of their honesty, of their vulnerability, of what's real. Walk with them through it. Hold space for their truth. Make room for their growth. Love well.

A BLESSING FROM PAM

May you be a safe space for someone today.
And may you find a safe space of your own.

JULY

"God will be worshiped. The only question is whether we'll be among those worshiping him … among those who worship him, alone."

- Pastor Brady Boyd -

Coming to Our Senses

When he came to his senses, he said, "How many of my father's hired servants have food to spare, and here I am starving to death! I will set out and go back to my father and say to him: Father, I have sinned against heaven and against you. I am no longer worthy to be called your son; make me like one of your hired servants."

So he got up and went to his father. But while he was still a long way off, his father saw him and was filled with compassion for him; he ran to his son, threw his arms around him and kissed him.

LUKE 15:17-20

The prodigal son thought he had a great plan: He'd demand his inheritance money early from his father, and he'd go live it up in a foreign land, throwing caution to the wind. What could possibly go wrong?

After he'd blown through his money and was looking up from the bottom of a pit, he realized he'd miscalculated a bit.

Not long ago, Pastor Tim and I were talking about wisdom. I said, "You know, it's funny. As we get older, our parents get smarter."

This is what happened to the prodigal son. He chased down his own path, defying the plans his father had had in place, and wound up staring at a dead end.

My favorite line in this parable is the phrase, "When he came to his senses ..."

It's likely that you've made some mistakes along the way. I sure have. Here's what I want us to know: the Father still welcomes us home. All we need to do is to *come to our senses*, to come to our senses and start making our way home.

A BLESSING FROM PAM

May you rest confidently in your heavenly Father's commitment that upon seeing you make your way back into his sight, he'll come eagerly running toward you.

What True Christ-Followers Do

"I tell you," he replied,
"if they keep quiet, the stones will cry out."

LUKE 19:40

If I had to name one thing that points to a person being a follower of Jesus, I wouldn't look to whether they attend church regularly, or to how much they tithe, or to how many Bible verses they know. I would look to whether they wholeheartedly worship God.

In this passage from Luke, Jesus is entering the city of Jerusalem, where he will face his final days before his crucifixion on a Roman cross. As he nears, his disciples cheer and shout praises: "Blessed is the king who comes in the name of the Lord!" they say. "Peace in heaven and glory in the highest!" (Luke 19:38).

Among the throng were many Pharisees, who found these outbursts ridiculous. "Teacher, rebuke your disciples!" they shouted to Jesus, (v. 39), to which Jesus said, "I tell you ... if they keep quiet, the stones will cry out," (v. 40).

If I find someone who is passionately, earnestly, devotedly, insistently worshiping God, I know that nothing else is getting worshiped in their life.

If you are passionately, wholeheartedly worshiping the one, true God, then you are worshiping him, alone.

God will gather worship for himself—there's absolutely no question about that.

The only question here is whether you'll be among those worshiping—among those worshiping him, alone.

A BLESSING FROM PAM

May you resolve in your mind and in your heart that you will direct both exclusive attention and exclusive affection toward your heavenly Father today.

On Being Led Well

The Lord is my shepherd,
I lack nothing.

PSALM 23:1

I've loved the twenty-third psalm for decades now, and my favorite part of the entire passage is the first sentence: "The Lord is my shepherd, I lack nothing."

Embedded in these words is a decision, the decision to seek guidance in life. Think of it: the only way you'd need a shepherd is if you were a sheep. In saying, "The Lord is my shepherd," the psalmist is admitting his status as sheep. He's saying, "I'm dependent as a person, and my dependence is directed toward you."

This begs a few questions of us:

Will we acknowledge our need for a shepherd?
Will we admit our status as sheep?
Will we downgrade all other dependencies and look to God and God, alone?

The first step to following Jesus is complete surrender. It is saying, "I need the leadership only you can provide."

A BLESSING FROM PAM

May you celebrate your dependence on God today.
Your Good Shepherd loves his sheep!

All That's Left is to Rest

*He makes me lie down in green pastures, he leads me
beside quiet waters. He refreshes my soul.*

PSALM 23:2-3A

Every time I fly back to Colorado Springs, I notice two things: first, our landscape is brown. Really brown. Second, wherever there's water, things are nice and green. From about ten thousand feet, you can tell who waters their grass and who doesn't. Where sprinklers have been active, lawns look thick and lush.

Similarly, in the psalmist's ancient land, the terrain was dry, dusty, and brown. It was tough to find green pastures because water was hard to find. And yet this was the shepherd's responsibility: watering his sheep day by day, lest they die.

After admitting that we need a shepherd, we then put our complete trust in him.

He is the one who provides grass to graze on, water to slurp up, refreshment for our souls.

He knows what we need, and he supplies it.

He cares for us like no one else can.

If you've ever seen a flock of sheep after they've eaten and drunk to their hearts' content, then you know that what they do next is to fold their legs and lie down. They are hydrated. They are full. They feel protected. All that's left is for them to rest.

If only you and I could catch this vision for our lives! In God, we receive complete provision. All that's left is for us to *rest*.

A BLESSING FROM PAM

*May you cast every last burden on your Father today,
knowing that he deeply cares for you.*

Guided Toward Good

He guides me along the right
paths for his name's sake.

PSALM 23:3B

One of my favorite things to do in Colorado is to go hiking, and one of my favorite things about hiking in our state is that trails are clearly laid out. If you follow a trail map, it is all but impossible to get lost. What this means for me is that I can focus on enjoying the beauty of the journey instead of living in perpetual fear that I won't be able to find my way home.

When David wrote this psalm, I believe a major point he wanted us to catch was that walking with God is a lot like my experience walking a trail in our state-park system: as long as we follow the signs pointing to God's will, God's ways, we can keep from getting lost.

This idea is revelatory for many believers, who think that walking with God is more akin to teetering on a tight rope strung over a terrifying canyon below. They errantly believe that one false move, and they'll plummet to their death, that a puff of stiff wind, and they're gone. It couldn't be further from the truth.

There is a reason our spiritual experience is described here as a "path." Paths are often marked and are easy to follow. Paths are made for walking, for strolling, for enjoying the day. And also: while paths may bend and meander, they rarely include harrowing drops.

Listen, if you want to follow the "right paths" for God's sake, then you will follow those paths every time. God is not hiding his righteous path from you. That path is always clearly laid out.

A BLESSING FROM PAM

May you long to stay
on the path of right living today.

Fear No Evil

Even though I walk through the darkest valley, I will fear no evil,
for you are with me; your rod and your staff, they comfort me.

PSALM 23:4

Every time we move to a different house, I go through the same reorientation period. I'll get up in the middle of the night to get something to drink or to go to the bathroom and will bump into walls or cut a corner too closely. I'd turn on the light, but I never want to wake Pam, and so I fumble and bumble around like an idiot who hasn't yet learned his own home.

This is how the darkness always makes us feel, I think: vulnerable, lost, and alone. And when we feel this way, we can start making agreements that simply aren't true: *This darkness will never lift. It will never be light again. This is how things will always be. I'll never feel safe again.*

The best part of verse 4 in this psalm is the psalmist's acknowledgment that the darkness we walk through is a *valley*. The reason part of the topography is considered a "valley" is simply because it is a low point between two points that are high. In the phrasing of darkness as a valley, the psalmist is reminding us not to pitch our tent in the darkness, because the darkness will soon be light.

That valley of debt?

That valley of marital strife?

That valley of confusion in your child's mind?

It's a low point that you are *walking through*; that valley is not your new home.

In this life, there will be darkness, but the sun will rise again. There will be joy. There will be celebration. There will be dancing. There will be peace.

A BLESSING FROM PAM

May you trust in the darkness what you believed in the light,
that God is at hand, and that he's leading you on.

Chosen and Equipped

You prepare a table before me in the presence of my enemies.
You anoint my head with oil; my cup overflows.

PSALM 23:5

A few weeks into my tenure at New Life I asked God why he had chosen me to be pastor here. The transition had garnered a lot of media attention, and I felt like I'd started living in a glass bowl. *Couldn't you have picked someone a little more qualified for the job?* I'd say to God. *Someone sharper, more educated, more capable of saying the word "oil" correctly?*

God reminded me that he saw more in me than I saw in myself.

God always sees more in us than what we see in ourselves.

When David wrote this psalm, he must have been thinking back on when the prophet Samuel visited his house in search of a new king. David's dad, Jesse, had paraded out all of David's brothers, thinking that surely one of them would be "the one," but at the end of that lineup, Samuel just shook his head. "Don't you have any other sons?" he asked Jesse, to which Jesse said, "Well, just David ..."

David was brought in from the fields, and as soon as Samuel saw him, he knew. He knew that David would be king.

David wasn't the obvious choice, but in God's eyes, he was *it*. That day, David was anointed with oil as the nation's future king, and his life would never be the same.

Let me ask you a question. Do you know what your assignment is, the assignment God has given you to do?

God is looking for someone just like you to complete a very specific task, and all that is required is your earnest yes ... your weakness for him to make strong.

A BLESSING FROM PAM

May God make clear his assignment for you today.
And may you joyfully and fearlessly say yes.

What Follows

Surely your goodness and love will follow me all the days of my life,
and I will dwell in the house of the Lord forever.

PSALM 23:6

What is following you these days?

Do you feel followed by chronic pain? Do you feel eyed by creditors wanting to be paid? Do you feel trailed by the wounds of a friend? Do you feel stalked by a quota you can't seem to hit?

On our worst days, this is exactly how life feels, isn't it? We feel like there's nowhere we can go to escape our fears and frustrations. We feel like there's simply no place to hide.

Psalm 23:6 opens with a powerful word: "Surely."

In Scripture, whenever you see the word *surely,* you should prepare to receive a guarantee. God is about to promise something here, something you and I can take to the bank.

The promise is this: regardless of the circumstance that seem to be trailing you, God's love and goodness are following you, too.

Whenever you come to the end of a difficult day, take a look behind you. You'll find God's love and goodness there. Whenever you come to the end of a challenging conversation, take a look behind you. You'll find God's love and goodness there. Whenever you come to the end of a string of negative thoughts, take a look behind you. You'll find God's love and goodness there.

As followers of Jesus, we're not only pursuing him; he's actively pursuing us too. The Father's goodness is chasing after us; the Father's love keeps us in its sight.

The entire gospel can be summed up in this singular promise: God's goodness and love pursue us.

A BLESSING FROM PAM

May you be upheld by God's goodness and love throughout today.
May these be anchors in any storm that you face.

The Pursuing God

The LORD your God is with you, the Mighty Warrior who saves. He will take great delight in you; in his love he will no longer rebuke you, but will rejoice over you with singing.

ZEPHANIAH 3:17

Since we're on the topic of God pursuing his people, it seemed fitting to recount the story of Francis Thompson, drug addict and poet extraordinaire.

Francis was raised in a good Catholic home by loving parents who sent their son off to university in London with expectations that he'd hone his poetic gift. But less than two years later, Francis was strung out on opium, homeless and living on the streets.

One day, in a burst of energy, Francis jotted down the words to a poem he'd written and mailed it to a publishing contact he'd found in a magazine. "I know you will hate this," Francis wrote on the accompanying note, "so here's an address where you can send it right back."

But the publisher didn't hate it. He loved it. He wrote back, asking Francis if he could publish his poem, but the post office couldn't find Francis, seeing as the man had no permanent address.

So, the publisher risked publishing the poem without permission, hoping that Francis would see it and reach out again. When Francis did, a meeting was scheduled, and as soon as the publisher realized that this poetic genius was a drug-addicted vagrant, he jumped in to help Francis get his life back on track.

That poem was titled, "The Hound of Heaven," referring to God's unyielding pursuit of us.

"I fled Him, down the nights and down the days," he wrote. "I fled Him, down the arches of the years; I fled Him, down the labyrinthine ways / Of my own mind; and in the mist of tears / I hid from Him, and under running laughter."

The end of the poem testifies that God won that footrace between Francis Thompson and him. God pursues that which is important to him. He pursues and pursues and pursues.

A BLESSING FROM PAM

May you be caught by God today. Willingly, joyously caught.

Amazing Grace

Out of his fullness we have all received grace
in place of grace already given.

JOHN 1:16

Recently I watched a documentary produced by the prolific journalist and filmmaker Bill Moyers titled, *Amazing Grace*. In it he worked to explain the origin and societal impact of John Newton's famous hymn, which has been recorded twenty times more than any other hymn in history. He interviewed prisoners, celebrities, people from all walks of life, and overwhelmingly people said that the reason the song was so beloved centered on the words to the song's third verse. Here's what that verse says:

> *Through many dangers, toils, and snares*
> *I have already come*
> *'Tis grace has brought me safe thus far*
> *And grace will lead me home*

I love the gist of that verse. I was saved by grace. I am kept by grace. And I will be with God in heaven someday—all because of grace. I've been in dangerous situations of my own making, snares that I wish I'd never fallen prey to, and yet grace, grace, God's grace ... I made it through because of grace.

I wonder if you feel this way too. You have probably done things you wish you hadn't done. You have probably found your fair share of trouble in this life. You have probably embarrassed yourself and your family from time to time. You probably carry a few regrets.

Guess what? You're not alone.

The hope of the gospel is this: despite our foibles and failures—and we have plenty, I'm sure—grace is there waiting to kindly lead us home.

A BLESSING FROM PAM

May you be freshly grateful for God's grace today, his unrivaled, unparalleled gift.

Slow to be Provoked

Do not be quickly provoked in your spirit, for
anger resides in the lap of fools.

ECCLESIASTES 7:9

When my dad was sixty-one, he was diagnosed with stage four colon cancer and given two years to live. Soon after, a trusted friend reached out and said, "Brady, there is an all-natural treatment that is healing people of this exact cancer. It will absolutely help your dad."

Pam and I spent the several thousand dollars to obtain this special medicine, and my dad followed the prescribed regimen precisely as he'd been told.

It didn't help at all.

For some time after my dad died, every time I'd hear that friend's name, I'd get aggravated inside. One night at an elders' meeting of the church where I worked at the time, that name was spoken, and I erupted. I don't even remember what I said; I only remember what one of the elders said to me: "Brady, why are you so offended by him? What did he ever do to you?"

And that's when it hit me. I'd opened a door in my heart to anger, and it had come in and made itself at home.

I claimed God's forgiveness and repented of my anger that day. "This is a good man," I told God, "a godly man. He meant to harm. He was actually trying to help ..."

When our expectations go unmet, it's tempting to get angry with people. But in this verse, we're cautioned against this approach. I know it seems impossible in the moment, but never forget that by God's grace, we can be people who are *slow* to be provoked. We can close the door on anger, refusing to let it come into our hearts.

A BLESSING FROM PAM

May you be quicker to bring peace than to provoke anger today.
May you be a person of peace.

Willing

*"I am the Lord's servant," Mary answered. "May your word to
me be fulfilled." Then the angel left her.*

LUKE 1:38

A young, poor, Jewish teenager—a girl living in the middle of nowhere in Israel—
came to her family and to the man to whom she was engaged one day and said
to them, "An angel just appeared to me. He said that I would conceive a son, the
Messiah that for three thousand years our nation has been hoping would come.
Evidently, I am going to carry that Messiah in my womb. I am going to give birth to
him, and he will be named Jesus, and he will be great, and he will reign over all of
us forever, and his kingdom will never end. He is actually the Son of the Most High.
Oh, and I'm not supposed to be afraid. All of this means I've found favor with God."

Out of curiosity, if you'd been on the receiving end of that update from Mary, how
would you have responded?

Furthermore, if you'd been Mary herself, what would you have said to the angel
that day?

If the means by which Jesus entered our earthly reality boggles your mind, take
heart. *It's supposed to.* We aren't meant to grasp all that God says and does. We
aren't meant to always track with him.

Here's something we are meant to do: follow the example of Mary.

After the angel laid out for Mary all that would occur, she pushed past her fear
and insecurity and said simply, "I am the Lord's servant. May your word to me be
fulfilled," (Luke 1:38).

This is our heritage: *I am willing, Lord. I'm here not to be served, but to serve.*

This is who we're called to be.

A BLESSING FROM PAM

*May your response to God's every invitation to join him
in his work be the same as Mary's was on that day.*

Your Messiah has Come

After he said this, he was taken up before their very eyes,
and a cloud hid him from their sight.

ACTS 1:9

In the movies, whenever a Roman emperor wants to showcase his power, he ascends a series of steps and takes a seat on his throne. From the throne he can rule and reign over the people. From the throne he's in total control.

In this verse from Acts, we see Jesus similarly assuming his throne. By way of context, Jesus has already been crucified and resurrected and is now outside the city gates of Jerusalem having a conversation with his disciples. It's worth noting that when the nation Israel, which included all the forefathers of those disciples, was freed from Egyptian bondage, God appeared to them as a cloud by day and a pillar of fire by night. Here, Jesus is taken by cloud to his throne; soon after, the disciples would head to the Upper Room and wait on the Holy Spirit to arrive, appearing, according to Acts 2:3-4, as "tongues of fire."

The disciples surely understood the imagery here: their story was being completed, right before their eyes. Their long-awaited Messiah had come and secured eternal victory for anyone who would call on his name. Their emperor, in other words, was headed for his throne.

Our Messiah isn't floating around in some unknowable space, having left us to fend for ourselves. No, he came to us, becoming one just like us, and went to the cross on our behalf. He lived separate from sin and then returned to his Father, where he now intercedes intimately on our behalf.

He didn't retreat.

He *won*.

We now have victory in his name.

A BLESSING FROM PAM

May you be captivated today with the thought that God is victoriously seated on his throne.
No scheme of Satan's need overwhelm you. No scheme of man's need lead you astray.

How to Enjoy the Presence of God

I undertook great projects: I built houses for myself and planted vineyards. I made gardens and parks and planted all kinds of fruit trees in them. I made reservoirs to water groves of flourishing trees. I bought male and female slaves and had other slaves who were born in my house. I also owned more flocks than anyone in Jerusalem before me. I amassed silver and gold for myself, and the treasure of kings and provinces. I acquired male and female singers, and a harem as well—the delights of a man's heart.

ECCLESIASTES 2:4-8

Solomon was an old man when he penned these words, and I get the feeling that he was reflecting on his life, on his longings over time, on his legacy that would trail him, and wondering what it all meant. Surely he would have been familiar with the creation account, having grown up going to the temple to hear the priest tell and retell Moses' story. He would have heard all about the Garden of Eden and about Adam and Eve being placed there to steward God's masterpiece well. He would have learned of God having walked with the crown of his creation in the cool of the day.

Something about Solomon's focus on the natural world he owned makes me wonder if he longed to return to that original garden, to a level of intimacy with the Lover of his soul.

It's easy to come down hard on Solomon, even as the dynamic he'd come face to face with is the same one that threatens us still: If we center our lives on satisfying our desires—"the delights of a man's heart," as Solomon put it—God's presence cannot be found.

It's only when God creates the garden that he is present to walk with us day by day.

A BLESSING FROM PAM

May you pause today to ask God where he's building, and may you join him in that divine work.

How are You Doing?

Test me, LORD, and try me, examine my heart and my mind; for I have always been mindful of your unfailing love and have lived in reliance on your faithfulness.

PSALM 26:2-3

I had lunch with a guy many years ago, and while we didn't know each other well, something he asked me almost in passing has stuck with me all this time. It was a random question that awakened me and even troubled me a bit. The question was, "How are you doing?"

Seems like a harmless question, right?

The Holy Spirit had an agenda with that question that even the asker wasn't aware of.

We had just come off of Easter weekend, which as you probably know is a huge deal around New Life. In all honesty, I was doing great. It had been wonderful seeing so many fresh faces. I'd loved the services, the worship team's contribution, and all that God had done in our midst.

But evidently the Holy Spirit didn't want just a rundown of the weekend. He wanted to know *how I was*. He had shown up to ask me some "Psalm 26" kinds of questions. Questions like, how was my heart? What was captivating my thoughts? Was I living each moment mindful of God's unfailing love? Was I *actually* relying on his faithfulness?

Ever since that lunch appointment, I've been asked in passing "how I'm doing" a thousand times. Ten thousand times, perhaps. And it's not uncommon for that simple, almost rhetorical question to prompt a deeper discussion between God and me. How *am* I doing? I ask myself. In the ways that really count, I mean, how are things going for me?

In the spirit of a little self-reflection, allow me to ask this of you: How are you doing today? How are you *really* doing? With the words of Psalm 26 fresh on your mind, how would you say that you are?

A BLESSING FROM PAM

May you risk being honest with yourself and with God as you assess how you're doing today.

He Will Provide

*"Therefore I tell you, do not worry about your life, what you will eat or drink;
or about your body, what you will wear. Is not life more than food, and the
body more than clothes? Look at the birds of the air; they do not sow or reap
or store away in barns, and yet your heavenly Father feeds them.
Are you not much more valuable than they?"*

MATTHEW 6:25-26

One night years ago when I was traveling, my iPad alerted me that Callie, fourteen at
the time, was Facetiming me. I was instantly suspicious.

"How's your trip going, Dad?" Callie asked, to which I said, "Good. What do you want?"

She laughed nervously.

"Well, Dad, I found this husky that we can adopt ..."

"Awesome," I said without emotion. "Can we talk about this when I get home?"

"The thing is, Dad ... um ... the dog is already here. I was just wondering if I could keep it."

Days later, we talked about how nice children don't manipulate their fathers and about
how Callie was going to be responsible for 100 percent of the dog's care. I just forgot to
mention where she should brush her new dog. The first time I worked in my flower beds
after that little grooming session, I had husky hair all over me. *At least it's not in the
house,* I muttered, as I picked a piece off my tongue.

To my shock, I then noticed six birds darting in and out of the flower beds surrounding
the front porch, the beds that were covered in husky hair. I couldn't help but grin.
*Those little guys have probably been praying for husky hair, so that they could get
their nests ready for spring,* I thought.

I imagined the whole series of events being orchestrated by God, just to send those
fearless flyers some love. What I'd seen as an aggravation those birds had seen as
provision. God always, always provides.

A BLESSING FROM PAM

May you totally relax today, believing fully that your Father will provide for you.

The Dailyness of Daily Bread

Give us today our daily bread.

MATTHEW 6:11

I'm not sure how you feel about Costco, but personally I'm a fan. I'm a member of Costco. I shop at Costco. Costco and I are tight.

Here's what's great about Costco: in one singular errand, you can buy six hundred rolls of toilet paper, two hundred cans of La Croix, a hundred fifty individually wrapped pieces of snack nuts, and thirty-six boxes of mac and cheese and not have to buy that stuff again for years.

You know what I've noticed? Christians sometimes try to apply this model to their spiritual lives.

We say, "Eh, I don't have time to read the Bible today. Yesterday's reading will have to tide me over."

Or, "I had such a vibrant prayer life years ago. It's lasted me all this time!"

Or, "I don't feel very close to God these days, but I *used* to. That counts, right?"

When Jesus' disciples asked Jesus how they should pray, his answer included this line: "Give us today our daily bread."

He wanted them to come to God *daily* to ask God for *that day's* bread. None of this multi-loaf situation that you buy once a month and then coast. No, no: *daily*. The provision was day by day.

Listen, you will never meet a person who hates legalism and the religious spirit more than I do. I'm not asking you to follow a rule here. I'm inviting you to do yourself the *favor* of remembering where your help comes from.

It is God who provides for our daily needs.

One day at a time.

A BLESSING FROM PAM

May you establish the regular rhythm today of coming to God to say thanks.

Relationally Sound

You, my brothers and sisters, were called to be free. But do not use your freedom to indulge the flesh; rather, serve one another humbly in love.

GALATIANS 5:13

Once when I was visiting a church in another state, I recognized the young man sitting in front of me as a young superstar athlete who'd been featured in the news quite a bit. He was considered the most talented athlete his sport had seen in years, and everyone had high hopes for him. He was dating the pastor of the church's daughter, and those who knew them thought they'd be married by the following year. Everything was headed up and to the right for this kid, and as I sat there observing him interacting with people, essentially lighting up the entire room, I received what I believed was a word from the Lord.

After the service I approached the young man and asked if I might share the prompting with him. "Yes, yes, please do," he said. "I'd love to know what you heard."

I told him that he clearly had everything in the natural world required to be a great success and that I wished him a blessed future as he pursued his dreams in full. And then I said this: "Pay careful attention to guard the relationships God brings into your life. Your ultimate success will not be determined by how effective you are on the field. It will be determined by how effective your relationships are."

Before I left his presence, I asked if I could pray for him, and the theme of the prayer I spoke over him that day is the same thing I'd like to pray over you: *Heavenly Father, please help us to protect the relationships you bring into our lives.*

A BLESSING FROM PAM

May you steward your relationships with great care today.

Living Skillfully

*If any of you lacks wisdom, you should ask God, who gives generously
to all without finding fault, and it will be given to you.*

JAMES 1:5

Everyone I know says they're submitted to authority—that is, until they're told no. As believers, we understand the power of submitting to authority. As reasonable human beings, we understand the *benefit* of submitting to authority. It's just that most of us don't like submitting to anyone or anything unless they tell us what we want to hear. I think this dynamic is what's behind our resistance to asking God for help.

For years I've held to a definition of wisdom that I stand by still today. It's this: Wisdom is the art of living skillfully amid whatever conditions we find ourselves in.

Living skillfully. Who doesn't want to do that?

And yet time and again we let entire *seasons* pass without availing ourselves of the wisdom of God.

I'm not sure if you've ever considered this before, but wisdom is a spiritual gift. It is a gift of the Holy Spirit, a gift that we are allowed to receive once we invite him into our lives. To neglect to ask for wisdom, then, is to refuse to open that gift.

I say we open the gift.

What has you stymied today? What situation has you confused? Where do you lack wisdom? Will you finally ask for help?

A BLESSING FROM PAM

May you find the courage to seek wisdom today.

Training in Righteousness

But as for you, continue in what you have learned and have become convinced of, because you know those from whom you learned it, and how from infancy you have known the Holy Scriptures, which are able to make you wise for salvation through faith in Jesus Christ. All Scripture is God-breathed and is useful for teaching, rebuking, correcting and training in righteousness, so that the servant of God may be thoroughly equipped for every good wok.

2 TIMOTHY 3:14-17

I'm sometimes asked by new Christians why we look up the same Bible passages, revisit the same Bible stories, and talk about the same Bible figures all the time. "Can't we cover this stuff once and be done?"

The question always reminds me of parenting adolescents. I used to *fantasize* about telling Abram and Callie something only once: "Brush your teeth." "Make your bed." "Do your homework." "Clean your room."

Can you imagine issuing those directives once and then moving on with your life?

Yeah. Me neither.

No parent wants to be a nag. And yet every parent realizes that unless a little nagging happens, our kids don't do what they need to do. Their breath will reek. Their sheets will forever be grimy and tangled in a knot. Teachers will call about our delinquent children. Our offspring will live in squalor.

Unless we continue reminding them of the things that are important, they will not continue the process of growing up.

Same goes for revisiting the Word of God. We can't "continue on" in what we have learned unless we reinforce those messages regularly.

Again ... and again ... and again.

A BLESSING FROM PAM

May you rejoice in your spiritual training today.

Directable

*"For I did not speak on my own, but the Father who sent me commanded
me to say all that I have spoken. I know that his command leads to eternal life.
So whatever I say is just what the Father has told me to say."*

JOHN 12:49-50

In our early married life, after Pam and I had been living in Amarillo, Texas, for about three years, I got a job offer from a TV station that just about blew my mind. It was a six-figure offer. They would pay six months' rent for us. There were bonuses involved. And Pam and I would be able to move back to within thirty or forty minutes of both of our parents' homes. It was a no-brainer decision, but I told the station owner I needed twenty-four hours to think about it and would get back to him the following day.

I hung up the phone, and Pam and I laughed out loud. We *cheered* out loud. To be twenty-seven, twenty-eight years old and earn an income like this would set us up well for decades to come. We were over the moon.

I told Pam I was going to take a walk for a few minutes and pray about the offer. I expected it to be a very short walk because *of course we were going to say yes*. But three seconds after my feet left the front porch, I sensed God saying, "No, no, no."

"But *six figures*!" I said, to which God said, *No*.

"But we'll be closer to our parents," I clarified, to which I heard, *No*.

I turned around, went back inside, looked at Pam, and shook my head. "We can't take the job," I said, to which she said, "Yeah. I know."

God had said the same thing to her.

There was nothing wrong with the job. It's just that God had different plans for us. Three months later, Pam and I adopted our son, Abram. Two years later I became the senior pastor at a church in Hereford, which led to my working at Gateway, which led to my being qualified to come to New Life Church.

And it all stemmed from being directable by God back in Amarillo.

We see this quality of being "directable" modeled in the life of our Savior, Jesus Christ, who said and did only what his Father had him say and do. He is our Shepherd, but he also was a sheep. He is our Leader but a follower, too. He knew that despite his deep understanding of life, God had a plan he was wise not to thwart. For every desert place there would be green pasture. There would be restoration of his soul.

For every "no" obeyed there would be countless *yes* experiences.

And there would be victory in the end.

I know it's tempting to evaluate life on the basis of what we see and believe. *Who in a right mind would turn down a job offer like this?* I get it. I've *lived* it. Here's what I know for sure: We will never be more satisfied than we are when we're squarely in the will of God. We will never be more contented than when we're living directable by him.

A BLESSING FROM PAM

May God direct your every step today.

Good Grief

When Mary reached the place where Jesus was and saw him, she fell at his feet and said, "Lord, if you had been here, my brother would not have died."

When Jesus saw her weeping, and the Jews who had come along with her also weeping, he was deeply moved in spirit and troubled. "Where have you laid him?" he asked.

"Come and see, Lord," they replied.

Jesus wept.

JOHN 11:32-35

The last verse in this passage has the claim to fame of being the shortest verse in the Bible, but there's more to those two words—"Jesus wept"—than meets the eye. Three verses later, In John 11:38, we read this: "Jesus, once more deeply moved, came to the tomb. It was a cave with a stone laid across the entrance. 'Take away the stone,' he said."

If you know the story of Lazarus, then you know that Jesus was about to raise the man from the dead. The man's sisters were about to unwrap the grave clothes that had been placed on their brother, and a huge celebration would ensue.

But if Jesus knew that this was his plan all along, that he would not let Lazarus stay dead but would in fact raise him to renewed life, then why verse 35? Why did Jesus weep?

In those two words—Jesus wept—we are reminded not to skip over the sadness we inevitably face in life. It's true that in Christ we have hope—endless amounts of hope, in fact. But between the tragedy and the beautiful hope there is grief—good grief, according to our Lord.

If you're hurting today, pause and let yourself hurt. Embrace the sorrow. Let the darkness be dark.

Joy indeed will come in the morning. For the moment, allow the night.

A BLESSING FROM PAM

*May you take the time and space you need
to move through the pain of life today.*

Availability

*He will swallow up death forever. The Sovereign Lord will wipe away the
tears from all faces; he will remove his people's disgrace
from all the earth. The Lord has spoken.*

ISAIAH 25:8

On this topic of grief, one of the byproducts of taking time and space to genuinely grieve is that we become available to God once more.

A member of our church informed me that she'd lost her husband in Afghanistan during his tour there with the Air Force. She was devastated—of course she was. But as she recounted the sequence of events, I couldn't help but notice that she'd been intentional about grieving her loss. She asked friends and family members to come to her home and share memories of her husband with her. Over the ensuing months she asked people to tell her the stories about him that continued to come to mind. She wanted to understand the impact his life had had, and she wanted to experience the depth of the loss.

By engaging in the process of grief, she was able to make it to the other side of that pain. Instead of burying her head in the sands of denial or busying herself to the point of not having time or energy to grieve, she entered in. She sat with it. She allowed it to occupy her life.

For a while.

And then the day dawned when her pain was bearable for once. The sharp edges of that grief had softened some. She could hear her husband's name and not reflexively wince.

Part of what helps us sit with our pain is knowing that it won't last forever. So yes, let it in—all of in, in full force. But never forget that it's temporary. Brighter days will dawn.

A BLESSING FROM PAM

*May you find grace today to grieve the losses you've sustained
and encouragement to return to God eager to serve again.*

Real Potential

Be devoted to one another in love. Honor one another above yourselves.
Never be lacking in zeal, but keep your spiritual fervor, serving the Lord.
Be joyful in hope, patient in affliction, faithful in prayer. Share with the
Lord's people who are in need. Practice hospitality.

ROMANS 12:10-13

Years ago I was on a Southwest Airlines flight with Abram and Callie when the flight attendant came by with some pre-takeoff reminders. "Remember, Dad, to put on your own mask first in case of an emergency," she said, "and then put the next mask on whichever of these two kids of yours has more potential."

Pretty good, right?

We all got a chuckle out of that, but hours later the exchange came to mind in a more serious light. *Which of my kids does have the greater potential? I wondered. Closer to home, what's my own potential like?*

How do we tell what our potential is?

This passage from the apostle Paul is here to help.

In his letter to the Roman church, Paul wrote to remind them of the non-negotiables of our faith, and whenever I see these traits show up in someone's life, I know that good things are in store for him or her.

Before plowing ahead with all that waits for you today, consider spending a few minutes self-assessing: How well are you devoting yourself to others in love? How consistently do you elevate others' needs above your own? How fired-up is your spiritual fervor these days? Are you sharing or kind of hoarding things for yourself?

God loves growing us up in his Son's likeness, and Jesus was the master of this way of life. Ask your Father to shore up whatever is lacking, so that your potential can be realized today.

A BLESSING FROM PAM

May you know what's valuable as you walk through today.
And may you act on what you know.

You've Got What It Takes

For this reason I remind you to fan into flame the gift of God,
which is in you through the laying on of my hands.

2 TIMOTHY 1:6

I've always been drawn to this verse from 2 Timothy because I imagine Paul's words to that young man went deep. When Timothy came into Paul's life, Timothy was struggling. Thought to be only fifteen or sixteen years old, like most teens he needed guidance. He needed direction. He needed encouragement for the road ahead. And did Paul deliver on that!

He reminded Timothy that God had given the boy a gift, and that the gift could be fanned into flame. It could be seen. It could be developed. It could have *power* in the world. Timothy wouldn't always feel set adrift by life. He would be an outright world-changer someday.

When Abram was four years old, I looked right into his eyes and said, "You're going to invent something someday that will change the world."

I'd received that word from the Lord. I believed that word from the Lord. And years later, Abram still remembers that word. He remembers every syllable I'd said. We both believe it will someday come true.

If you're feeling set adrift by life today, please know this: There is a gift inside you, placed there intentionally by God. It can be developed. It can be fanned into flame. Your life can and *absolutely will* matter.

In Jesus, you have what it takes.

A BLESSING FROM PAM

May you set aside your insecurities today
and focus instead on the gifts God has given you.

Lunatic, Liar, or Lord

When Jesus came to the region of Caesarea Philippi, he asked his disciples,
"Who do people say the Son of Man is?" They replied, "Some say John the Baptist;
others say Elijah; and still others, Jeremiah or one of the prophets." "But what about
you?" he asked. "Who do you say I am?" Simon Peter answered, "You are
the Messiah, the Son of the living God."

MATTHEW 16:13-16

Famed scholar, theologian, and author C. S. Lewis was sitting around talking with a group of his students when the topic of Jesus came up. "Some of you know Jesus as a good moral teacher," he said, "even as you refute that he was God. But he himself told his followers that he was the Messiah they were waiting for, and that no man could access the Father apart from a personal relationship with him."

"You may like Jesus, admire Jesus, and think that he is good," Lewis continued, "but as I see it, the only options available to you are that he was a lunatic, he was a liar, or he is the Lord."

You and I stand at the very same crossroads. We can't think nice things about Jesus and then just carry on with our lives; we must reconcile in our minds and hearts what to make of the claims he made. He's either God, or he's not. He was either raised from the dead, or he wasn't. He's either the singular access to God's presence … or else he is not.

A BLESSING FROM PAM

May you gain whatever clarity is needed today,
to see that Jesus is Lord.

Convictional Christianity: Jesus' Existence

"Very truly I tell you," Jesus answered, *"before
Abraham was born, I am!"*

JOHN 8:58

I grew up in an era and in a part of the country where something called "cultural Christianity" was all the rage. It's not like people overtly signed up to become a cultural Christian; rather, by being lukewarm about their faith, they kind of slid into that status unwittingly. Cultural Christians are people who aren't mad at God but who also aren't going to sacrifice anything for his cause. They appreciate Christian values, as long as they can still eat what they want to eat, go where they want to go, see the movies they want to see, and spend their money however they please.

By contrast, many, many New Lifers and I long to be *convictional* Christians. If cultural Christians follow God when it's convenient, convictional Christians follow him even when it's not. They follow him because of their convictions, which begs the question, *What convictions are those?*

Here's the first of five I'll give you these next five days: To be a convictional Christian is to live by the conviction that *Jesus has always existed.*

He was not created. He has always been.

"Before Abraham was born, I am!" he said, which would have sounded scandalous to first-century believers. Abraham was their heritage, the origin of their people and faith. *You were around before Abraham?* they must have thought. *But that was eighteen centuries ago!*

We sing a song around New Life that has this lyric: "He was, he is, he is to come."

Why do we sing that? Why do we confess that? Because it's a conviction we hold to be true. It's theology we want active in our minds and hearts.

A BLESSING FROM PAM

*May you come to the place of bold confession that Jesus has always been,
that he is today, and that he always will be with us.*

Convictional Christianity: Jesus' Divinity

*In the beginning was the Word, and the Word
was with God, and the Word was God.*

JOHN 1:1

Yesterday we introduced the idea that earnest believers of God long to be not cultural, but *convictional*, Christians. The first conviction we hold is that Jesus has always existed. Ready for conviction number two? It's this: *Jesus is fully God.*

Jesus left heaven and came to earth in the form of a human, but not once in that entire process did he relinquish his divinity. He was simultaneously man and God. Both. Fully. At once.

This matters because when we pray "in Jesus' name," we're praying in the power of God. Not God, Jr. Not mini-God. Not a-little-less-than-God.

God.

Fully God.

This is why Jesus' sacrifice on that Roman cross was considered "perfect." He had to be fully human to absorb our sins and fully God to pay for them. And aren't we glad he did just that. He paid for the sins of yesterday. He paid for the sins of today. He paid for the sins you and I haven't even committed yet, if you can try to wrap your mind around *that*.

He has always been with God—that's conviction one.

He has always *been* God—that's conviction two.

Praise Jesus—*God*—for these truths.

A BLESSING FROM PAM

*May your confession today be that Jesus is not only Lord,
but also God himself. Jesus and God are one.*

Convictional Christianity: Jesus' Creation

For in him all things were created: things in heaven and on earth,
visible and invisible, whether thrones or powers or rulers or authorities;
all things have been created through him and for him.

COLOSSIANS 1:16

Here is conviction number three: *through Jesus all things were created.*

Let me come at this one with an analogy. Have you ever had a device that wouldn't hold its charge? Sometimes I think tech companies intentionally design our devices to peter out after a couple of years so that we will show up to buy a new one. But I digress.

You leave your phone plugged in all night, for example, but the next morning after an hour's use, the battery is back to 9 percent. Frustrating, right? For whatever reason, that device just won't hold its power, and good luck making it do anything worthwhile.

Similarly, when we are unwilling to receive power for living, our lives kind of sputter and stop. By acknowledging that through Jesus all things were created, we are recognizing that not only is he the source of life, but also that we intend to look to him to keep life in all its facets working right.

When Pam and I center our marriage on the person of Jesus, our marriage works as it is meant to work.

When I center my parenting on the person of Jesus, I'm able to be a wise and compassionate dad.

When I center my leadership on the person of Jesus, I become the leader God longs for me to be.

When I center my attitude and my speech and my actions on the person of Jesus, despite my own foibles and failures and brokenness I can be a loving neighbor, brother, citizen, and friend.

I wonder what your life is centered on here lately. Will you confess this conviction today?

A BLESSING FROM PAM

Today, may you invite Jesus the Creator into every created thing.

Convictional Christianity: Jesus' Headship

*And he is the head of the body, the church; he is the beginning and the firstborn
from among the dead, so that in everything he might have the supremacy.*

COLOSSIANS 1:18

Jesus has always been with God.

Jesus has always *been* God.

Through Jesus all things were created.

And now the fourth conviction: *Jesus is head of the Church.*

New Life church was started nearly four decades ago, and while many of those years
were wonderful, it's undeniably true that many were not so great. If you weren't there
for them in person, Google it. You'll see that I'm telling the truth. If you want to know
why we're not a used-car lot today, it's because Jesus is head of our church. Jesus
started the church in 1984 through a prayer movement in our city. Jesus has been
with us as our leader through good times and bad. And Jesus will sustain us into the
future because of the promise of Colossians 1:18: "He is the head of the body, the
church." *He* is our ultimate pastor. He is our ultimate guide.

If a human being believes that he or she is the "founder" of a church or the "leader"
of a church or the reason the church prevails, that church will eventually fail. It is only
because of Jesus that a church can survive and thrive.

Here's an interesting fact: guess where the fastest-growing churches in the world today
exist? They exist in countries where religious freedoms are nonexistent, in places such
as Iran and China and Northern India. Wait. So in these countries, Christian worship is
banned, and yet the Christian faith is growing by leaps and bounds?

Yep. Guess why. Because Jesus wants it that way, that's why.

There is no power of hell and no scheme of man that can keep the Church from
multiplying as long as Jesus remains its head.

A BLESSING FROM PAM

May you reconsider with fresh appreciation your enthusiasm for the body of Christ.

Convictional Christianity: Jesus' Reconciliation

For God was pleased to have all his fullness dwell in him, and through him to reconcile to himself all things, whether things on earth or things in heaven, by making peace through his blood, shed on the cross.

COLOSSIANS 1:19-20

The fifth and final conviction is that *Jesus reconciles us to God the Father.*

If you have ever interacted with a Hebrew person about Jesus, then you probably know that instead of calling him "Jesus," they call him *Yeshua.* This is Jesus' Hebrew name, and it means, "Jehovah saves."

Yeshua is as common to the Hebrew ear as the name Sam or Bob or Bill might be to ours. Still today, there are scores of little Yeshuas running around Hebrew primary schools. But *this* Yeshua? He is very different from all the rest.

For three thousand years the Jewish people had cried out for a Messiah. They longed for a Savior to come and redeem and restore them and establish God's rule in their world forever. Moses had led them out of Egypt, but he hadn't been Yeshua. King David had built the famed temple to God, but he hadn't been Yeshua. Would Yeshua ever come? As time went on, they must have had their doubts.

For five hundred years, God fell silent. Between what we know as the Old and New Testaments, not a word came down. But then, in the tiny, forgotten outpost called Bethlehem, in the middle of nowhere, a baby was born. Yeshua would be his name.

Jehovah has come down. Jehovah has come to save.

The part of the Nicene Creed I can barely recite without getting choked up is this one: "God from God, Light from Light, begotten, not made."

For us, and for our salvation, he came to set us free. This is our firm conviction. It is on this truth that all faith rests.

A BLESSING FROM PAM

May you delight in the utter gift of salvation today.

AUGUST

"As believers, we are the carriers of God's solution to every problem the world will ever face. Because we have the same power residing in us that raised Jesus from the dead, doing great works is simply our heritage. It's what we were made to do."

- Pastor Brady Boyd -

Perfect Peace

Then he got into the boat and his disciples followed him. Suddenly, a furious storm came up on the lake, so that the waves swept over the boat. But Jesus was sleeping.

MATTHEW 8:23-24

Even expert fishermen will tell you that storms on the Sea of Galilee are both sudden and fierce, which was exactly the disciples' experience here in Matthew 8. And yet Jesus remained fast asleep.

I absolutely love this scene.

If you were in a small, handmade, wooden boat on the open sea, and without warning the skies broke open and lightning was crashing and that vessel started pitching wildly this way and that, I'm guessing you'd feel just the tiniest bit vulnerable ... that you'd be a little *concerned*.

It's the idyllic afternoon that is interrupted by a medical crisis.

It's the record-setting quarter at work followed by an unexpected layoff.

It's the relaxing family vacation erased by divorce papers.

It's the million plans cancelled by a deadly global pandemic.

The waters are calm, and then they're not. We've now got a *typhoon* on our hands.

Jesus? Still asleep.

Here is what Jesus' actions that day model for us: we can claim peace even amid life's storms. We can conserve energy, choosing not to fret but to continue walking by faith. We can believe that God will accomplish what he said he would, which is to protect us and provide for us until we inhale our final breath.

> *"God will be worshiped. The only question is whether we'll be among those worshiping him ... among those who worship him, alone."*

> - Pastor Brady Boyd -

A BLESSING FROM PAM

May you rest in the perfect promises of your heavenly Father today, whose might is greater than the strongest storm.

God Does Not Hate Capitalism

"Do not store up for yourselves treasures on earth, where moths and vermin destroy, and where thieves break in and steal."

MATTHEW 6:19

Let's start here: God does not hate capitalism.

He doesn't. I've studied capitalism. I've read scores of books on economics. I've worked to understand from all angles how the free market works. And this is what I can say without any hesitation whatsoever: *God does not hate capitalism.*

Let me tell you what God does hate: a selfish, greedy child of his.

Whenever people seek my financial counsel, I start with this advice: Follow the words of Matthew 6:19, and then live however you please. It's good advice! As long as you and I are absolutely *refusing* to focus on consuming and acquiring and "storing up" things here on earth, by definition on attention will be on better, godlier aims. Like giving. And blessing. And serving. And meeting needs. We'll be focused on all the right things.

God does not bless believers materially so that they can exercise selfishness.

God does not intend for money to be a force for egotism and greed.

God blesses his children so that they can partner with him in accomplishing his good work in the world, and money is simply a quick and easy means for getting that good work done.

When you look at "your" money, see God's fingerprints all over it. It belongs to him. It came into your life from him. And he longs (through you!) for it to help out somebody in need.

A BLESSING FROM PAM

May you be freed from the tendency to view what's yours as yours,
instead seeing all things as generous gifts from God.

Seeing Rightly

*The person without the Spirit does not accept the things that come from the Spirit
of God but considers them foolishness, and cannot understand them because
they are discerned only through the Spirit.*

1 CORINTHIANS 2:14

Years ago Pam and I struck up a friendship with a woman who was new to Colorado Springs and who was involved with Eastern mysticism. For Eastern mystics, there is no reality, no material world. Nothing truly "exists," in the way that you and I might say that it does. This laptop I'm typing on isn't really *real*. The book you're holding your hands isn't really *real*. They aren't real, you and I aren't real, and nothing we think we see is real. It's all an illusion, they would say.

This belief system holds that since nothing is real, pain and suffering aren't real. And so adherents can ignore those things, living a completely passive existence—which is their goal. Eastern mystics believe in karma, the sort of cosmic tit-for-tat explanation for why good or bad things happen to us all. They believe likewise in reincarnation, which holds that we never die; instead, we return again and again in various forms.

You can imagine how Pam's and my minds whirred, each time we interacted with this woman. I had *rebuttals*. I had *opinions*. I had *thoughts*. And yet as often as possible, I poured that corrective energy into praying for her instead. I wasn't trying to win an argument here. I was trying to win a friend.

Whenever we encounter people who aren't enjoying a personal relationship with Jesus, guess what our number-one aim should be? *Praying that they come to know Jesus Christ.* Until we know Jesus, we can't rightly know spiritual things.

A BLESSING FROM PAM

*May you help lift the spiritual fog for someone today,
so that he or she can see clearly the things of God.*

All That We Need

His divine power has given us everything we need for a godly life through our knowledge of him who called us by his own glory and goodness. Through these he has given us his very great and precious promises, so that through them you may participate in the divine nature, having escaped the corruption in the world caused by evil desires.

2 PETER 1:3-4

What do you need today? I don't mean the question rhetorically. I mean it earnestly: What do you need today?

Relief from pain? Insight regarding a relational struggle you're in? A breakthrough parenting moment? Answers from medical personnel? Assurance that things will get better? Cash?

I know that when the practical needs of life seem to be outpacing adequate resources to meet them, the last thing we think we need is more of God. No, we think we need *money.* Or *answers.* More *time.*

I get that. I live that.

And yet the truth is still the truth: In Jesus Christ, you and I have everything we need to live a godly life.

Everything. What an all-encompassing word.

Throughout Scripture, in every single story told, God's Spirit is present with his people, helping them to navigate seemingly impossible times. He was with Moses. And Samson. And Rahab. And Elijah. He was with Matthew. And James. And John. Mary Magdalene. Mary, his mom.

He was there. Not as an accessory, but as the central force for good in their lives.

If you're in Jesus, God's Spirit is in you, too, guiding, comforting, steering, assuring, creating something from nothing in your midst.

A BLESSING FROM PAM

May you be aware with newfound perception today of God's Spirit at work in your life.

God, Working through You

Now about the gifts of the Spirit, brothers and sisters, I do not want you to be uninformed. There are different kinds of gifts, but the same Spirit distributes them. There are different kinds of service, but the same Lord. There are different kinds of working, but in all of them and in everyone it is the same God at work.

Now to each one the manifestation of the Spirit is given for the common good.

1 CORINTHIANS 12:1, 4-7

If you are a follower of Jesus, then you have been given the Holy Spirit to live in your total being. This is not an optional thing. You can't take Jesus and leave the Spirit. They are a package deal; you get Jesus, you get the full godhead, made operational in your life.

This ought to come as very good news because it is only by the Spirit that we can gain spiritual understanding. It is only by the Spirit that we can become who God longs for us to be. And then there's this: it is only by the Spirit that we can contribute to others' lives.

Yesterday we looked at the fact that God's Spirit is active in you. Today, we build on that idea with this one: God's Spirit is active *through* you as well.

Throughout Scripture we find that the two primary reasons for the Holy Spirit being active in a person's or group's life are to (a) glorify Jesus and to (b) make Jesus known. These goals remain true to this day; if you are a believer in Jesus, then these goals should be our goals too.

Are you allowing the Spirit to work through your words and actions these days, such that Jesus is being *glorified*, such that he's being *made known*? Your gifts are not intended to be hoarded. Your gifts are meant to bring others to Christ.

A BLESSING FROM PAM

May you live as a "common-good"
kind of person today.

The Gift of Wisdom

To one, there is given through the Spirit
a message of wisdom ...

1 CORINTHIANS 12:8A

One of the most powerful scenes in all of Scripture is found in Luke 2:46. The context here is that when Jesus was twelve years old, he and his family had headed up to Jerusalem for the annual Passover festival, a several-days' trek from home. After the festival had ended, the entourage, which would have included family, extended family, servants, and other traveling companions, began making its way back home. At some point someone must have wandered through the throng looking for Jesus and discovered that he was nowhere to be found. For nearly three days they searched, to no avail. And then they found him. In an unlikely place for an adolescent boy.

Now, to that verse: "After three days, they found him in the temple of courts sitting among the teachers, listening to them and asking them questions."

Put simply, wisdom is the Holy Spirit at work in a person such that he or she hears and then speaks godly counsel.

Jesus was impossibly wise.

I'll keep this brief: If you are wise, please find people less mature than you are to share your wisdom with. And if you are lacking in wisdom, please find people more mature than you are to gain instruction for godly life. Either way, begin with this simple prayer: "Heavenly Father, I long for the spiritual gift of wisdom. I long to acquire it, and then I long to share it with others. We need wisdom in our world today. Please help me to be one who is wise. Send wise people my way. Raise me up in wisdom. Send me people who need my wisdom. May your wisdom freely flow."

A BLESSING FROM PAM

May you prioritize both the receiving
and the releasing of wisdom today.

The Gift of Knowledge

*... to another, a message of knowledge
by means of the same Spirit.*

1 CORINTHIANS 12:8B

There is nothing better than knowing the truth. If you're like me, you can manage just about anything, as long as you know the truth. Granted, we might not like the situation we're in, but once we understand what it is we're dealing with, it's far easier to move ahead. Think about it: if your teen is inexplicably sullen, your mind will take you down some truly terrible paths. Once you learn that he's frustrated with a friend, well, now you can be of help. Same goes for chronic pain: we can tie ourselves in worried knots regarding all the possible things it could be. Once we discover that we just can't eat grains anymore, well, now we can chart a course.

When speaking to his Jews who had believed him, Jesus said it this way: "If you hold to my teaching, you are really my disciples. Then you will know the truth, and the truth will set you free," (John 8:31-32).

When we walk in the truth, we are free; the spiritual gift of knowledge is what paves that path.

Knowledge is the Holy Spirit at work through us to know what is true. To determine right from wrong. To have the ability to understand what God would have us do. So, how do we get more of this gift? We simply have to ask.

If you have been harboring a lie, ask God for the gift of knowledge to help you repent. If you sense that someone you know and love is being deceived, ask God for the gift of knowledge to prompt them to see what's true. If you feel stuck in a given aspect of life, ask God to reveal what's real to you through the gift of knowledge. Pray that he would give you spiritual insight you don't yet possess.

Pure freedom awaits you, and there's no better way to live than free. Claim the gift of knowledge for your life right now. Start your day off today perfectly free.

A BLESSING FROM PAM

May you walk in freedom, not bondage, today.

The Gift of Faith

... to another faith by the same Spirit ...

1 CORINTHIANS 12:9A

The gift of faith is the Holy Spirit at work through us to be people of simple trust in God.

The classic Bible verse on the topic of faith is Hebrews 11:1, which says, "Now faith is confidence in what we hope for and assurance about what we do not see."

Whenever I read that verse, two words jump out at me: *confidence* and *assurance*. Those are bold, strong words. It's wonderful to be confident about something, isn't it? To feel assured about a given belief. So, while we sometimes associate the concept of "faith" with things that feel nebulous or unknowable, this definition offers a different perspective, that of feeling confident, feeling sure, feeling strong.

Throughout Scripture, whenever Jesus and the apostles talked about a person's faith or the faith of a group of people, they used one of four descriptors: no, little, great, or "full of." They wound encounter a person and say that person had "no faith." They would encounter a specific group and say that group had "little faith." Regarding another person, they might say that he possessed "great faith," such as the centurion in Luke 7 who came to Jesus to see if Jesus would heal a servant of his who was sick.

No faith. Little faith. Great faith. And then there was this fourth level of faith that was reserved for the special few. Of those folks, Jesus would say they were "full of faith."

"You are just *full of faith*"—wouldn't that be a wonderful way to be known?

Depending on the situation, we can find ourselves jockeying between these four levels from one minute to the next. But who wants to stay at level 1 or 2 or 3, when we could be living life at level 4 all the time?

Let me tell you how to get to level 4, and how to stay there once you arrive.

Taking our cue from full-of-faith people in the Bible, here's what we need to do: *surrender*. That's it: surrender all to God. When we surrender our thoughts, our attitudes, our words, our actions, our decisions, our very *lives* to the lordship of Christ, we pretty much *have* to walk by faith. If we cede all control to him, we have no control left of our own! And it's at that time that we live full of faith.

When you walk through your days one baby step at a time, having no clue how things are going to unfold, how problems are going to be solved, how situations are going to work out, you signal to God and everyone watching that you are choosing to walk by faith. You signal to everyone—including yourself—that you may not know much about all the outcomes you're about to face, but of this you are certain and sure: God is good. God is with you. God is leading you. And in him you can put your full trust.

He's for you.

He has promised to guide you.

He is committed to providing for you.

He is worthy of your complete trust today.

He is worthy of your full faith.

A BLESSING FROM PAM

May you risk being level-four faithful to God today.

The Gift of Healing

... to another gifts of healing
by that one Spirit ...

1 CORINTHIANS 12:9B

Abram and I were at a gathering one afternoon, and while I was talking with a group of people, I noticed him approaching a man who had a cast on his arm. I couldn't hear the exchange but could tell that Abram was asking lots of questions. After a few minutes, Abram had his hand on the man's shoulder and was clearly praying for the man.

I thought, *my son has the gift of healing.*

The gift of healing is the Holy Spirit working through you to help bring about wholeness in a person's mind, body, and spirit. If you have the gift of healing, you'll know it: you'll be doing a lot of what Abram did that day.

When Jesus came out of his time of temptation in the wilderness, he was filled with the Spirit and went about laying his hands on people to heal them from their disease. Which is how I know that those with the gift of healing are a *lot* like Jesus Christ. They see people as Jesus sees them. They long for complete restoration for people, just as Jesus does. And just like Jesus, they are willing to invest time and energy in seeing people made well.

If you would like to cultivate the gift of healing in your life, a straightforward starting point whenever you come across someone in need of healing is to ask three questions:

"What's been going on?"

"How can I pray for you"

"When can I check in with you again?"

God longs to meet all people at their point of unwellness. You might just be part of that desire of his coming to pass.

A BLESSING FROM PAM

May you know healing in your entire being today. And may you
have eyes to see and care for another today who needs the same.

The Gift of Miracles

... to another miraculous powers ...

1 CORINTHIANS 12:10A

I'm often asked why Jesus performed miracles, and the answer is simpler than most people assume: he wanted to show that God is not distant, that God is willing to intervene in our human affairs.

The gift of miracles is the Holy Spirit working through us to anticipate divine intervention into human affairs.

Here's something that's interesting: Whenever I ask believers if they believe that they have been forgiven of their sin, they say yes. They can point to various Bible verses that prove this is true. Whenever I ask them if they know for sure that when they die they will go to heaven and live eternally with God, again they say yes. Again, more Bible verses. But when I ask believers if they believe that they can do miracles, all I get is hemming and hawing in reply.

I quote them the seminal Bible verse on this topic, and still they aren't so sure.

That verse, by the way, is John 14:12: "Very truly I tell you, whoever believes in me will do the works I have been doing, and they will do even greater things than these, because I am going to the Father."

As believers, we are the carriers of God's solution to every problem the world will ever face. We have the same power residing in us that raised Jesus from the dead. Doing great works is simply our heritage. It's what we were made to do.

A BLESSING FROM PAM

May you avail yourself of great works today, in accordance with God's activity in the world.

The Gift of Prophecy

... to another prophecy ...

1 CORINTHIANS 12:10B

I've been married to Pam for more than half my life, and despite being every bit as attracted to her, intrigued by her, and delighted by her today as I was the day we met, none of these things is the reason we've made it this long as husband and wife. The reason our marriage has lasted comes down to the use of our words.

Pam and I encourage each other. We call each other to deeper intimacy with Jesus. We know how to fight fair. In short, we behave *prophetically* in our relationship, and that is why it works.

To practice the gift of prophecy is simply to strengthen, encourage, and comfort another person with words that are true. Upon becoming a believer, the first thing that usually gets transformed in a person's life are the words they choose to speak. "A good man brings good things out of the good stored up in his heart," says Luke 6:45, "and an evil man brings evil things out of the evil stored up in his heart. For the mouth speaks what the heart is full of." When your heart changes, your mouth changes. You stop using your words to cut people down and instead work to build them up.

If you'd like to see the gift of prophecy cultivated in your life, check in with the Holy Spirit each time you're about to speak. Before you say anything to another person, pause momentarily and ask, "Will this strengthen, encourage, or comfort them?"

If the answer is no, don't speak.

Nearly every pain you and I have ever known was inflicted by someone's words—that's where it all began. Don't be the one to harm another person today. Use your words to build them up.

A BLESSING FROM PAM

May you carefully steward each word that you speak today,
trusting God to direct your speech.

The Gift of Discernment

... to another distinguishing
between spirits ...

1 CORINTHIANS 12:10C

If you fly much, then you know that even the smoothest flight can turn turbulent in a jiffy. On this particular flight, all I saw when I looked out the window was an endless span of blue. It was a gorgeous day, and all was well—until it wasn't. Over the next sixty seconds, the pilot turned on the seatbelt sign, the flight attendant came on the intercom and told everyone to buckle up, and the scene outside turned black as fat drops of rain pelted the plane. We were less than a hundred miles from the airport and needed to start our initial descent, but given the storm we'd happened upon, the pilot was going to have to land blind.

"Trust your instruments"—that's what it's called when a pilot has no visibility for flying and instead has to rely on what his or her instruments are saying is happening outside the plane. This approach works for pilots at thirty thousand feet, and it works here on the ground for you and me, too.

Whenever you find yourself in the midst of a terrifying storm and can't see what's in front of you or which way to go, you can look to the guidance of your internal "instrument," the Holy Spirit, living in you.

The spiritual gift of distinguishing spirits is God's Spirit working through you to make you aware of influences affecting you and to assure you of what to do. As much as we'd love to have clear, blue skies hanging over our lives at all times, that simply isn't how this world works. And yet with the Holy Spirit directing our every step, we will surely arrive at the right place every time.

A BLESSING FROM PAM

May you take heart in your storm that your Father is leading you.
What you cannot see, he can.

The Scam of Sin

They exchanged the truth about God for a lie.

ROMANS 1:25

In J. R. R. Tolkien's series *The Lord of the Rings*, the character Gollum starts out as a human being but over time devolves into something entirely different from that. Entranced by the ring, which he calls "my precious," Gollum is perpetually torn between his obsessive pursuit of it and his deep longing to be freed from that pursuit. I won't spoil things by telling you which of those things wins in the end, instead leaving it at this: when we start worshiping any creation with greater fervor than we are worshiping the Creator, things will go badly for us.

You and I were made in God's image and placed in a world entirely created by him. There are no cosmic mistakes in our midst; all came to us by God's divine hand. God formed it all. God enlivened it all. God sustains it all still today. He alone is worthy of honor and praise. He is the only one we are to adore.

Anything that takes our attention off God is sin, and the problem with sin is that it is a sham. It promises things it can't provide. It tells us it will fulfill. What believers understand is that only God can provide. Only God can fulfill. Only God can satisfy our souls.

We must be careful not to exchange the truth of God for a lie, no matter how alluring that lie seems to be. Keep the truth. Hold fast to the truth. Hang onto the truth. Fix your gaze on the truth. Never let the truth out of your sight.

A BLESSING FROM PAM

May you worship God as distinctive Creator today.

Unashamed

For I am not ashamed of the gospel, because it is the power of God that brings salvation to everyone who believes: first to the Jew, then to the Gentile.

ROMANS 1:16

There will come a day in this country when we will have to declare whether we are followers of Jesus or not, whether we've gone God's way with our lives, and based on the speed at which our culture is devolving, it might come sooner than we think. When the apostle Paul said he was not "ashamed of the gospel," he was referring to the story of Christ.

A man with brown skin, a man of Middle Eastern descent, who was on the bottom rung of society's ladder, came from heaven to earth by way of a virgin teenager and then lived a sinless life. When he was thirty-three years old, he was falsely accused by the governing authorities of no wrongdoing but was horrifically crucified on a Roman cross. He went there willingly, to pay the penalty of our sin, thereby bridging the gap between humans and God.

He was dead and buried and left in a tomb for three full days, but on that third day he rose from the dead.

Upon his resurrection, more than five hundred people witnessed his reappearance, and forty days later he returned to his Father's side. Before he departed he told his followers to go and make disciples in every country on earth, teaching them all that we'd learned from him. Still today he is alive and is seated at God's right hand, where he makes intercession for us.

This story is the central thrust of our faith. It is the story we're to carry to the world. Ashamed? No, no: we're not ashamed of this. We're *honored* to tell this tale.

A BLESSING FROM PAM

May you put voice today to the story of Christ, Savior of our souls.

An Answer for Bad News

*Do not repay anyone evil for evil. Be careful to
do what is right in the eyes of everyone.*

ROMANS 12:17

I grew up in the Deep South and was among the first generation of kids in our area who went to a desegregated school. I saw things and heard things and experienced things in that racial era that haunt me still today, and while I can cognitively and emotionally understand the temptation for Black America to respond to those injustices with vitriol and even violence, the truth of Scripture is that repaying evil for evil is never a good idea.

This line of thinking is true for us all.

I have known people who have suffered every form of mistreatment and even abuse imaginable, and you'd better believe that in many cases they were tempted to enact revenge and "get their due." I have felt in my own heart that pull toward retaliation upon being slandered or otherwise harmed. We want justice. We want the wrong made right. We want someone to pay.

This is not the way of Christ.

Let me give you a strategy that will serve you well for the rest of your life: when the choice is to fixate on the bad news or the good news, choose the good news every time.

There is plenty of bad news in our world today, injustices on every side. But for the believer there is plenty of good news too ... the gospel, God's grace, salvation available to all.

And because of the gospel message, when violence comes, we don't have to react. When we're slandered, we can bless. When we're wronged, we can forgive. When we're harmed, we can give grace. We can be light in the darkness today.

A BLESSING FROM PAM

*May you set your gaze on the good news of the gospel today,
regardless of the bad news you face.*

Why Jesus Came

But Christ has indeed been raised from the dead,
the firstfruits of those who have fallen asleep.

1 CORINTHIANS 15:20

A common misconception regarding why Jesus came to planet Earth centers on his wanting to turn bad people into people who are good. This is nothing more than religious moralism, and it couldn't be further from the truth. Jesus didn't die to give our behavior a boost; he died to *bring us to life*.

Let's think about why this is good news.

Have you ever heard the phrase, "I'm standing on the outside, but I'm sitting on the inside?"

If you're a parent, then you've probably seen that phrase played out in the life of your child. You can force behavior modification, but that doesn't always mean there's been a change of heart.

If the only thing Jesus' death accomplished was an uptick in the way we behave, you and I can fool the system by continuing to "sit on the inside" day by day.

In John 10:10, Jesus says, "I have come that they may have life, and have it to the full."

If he came that we may have life, then guess what we had *before* he came? Death. The apostle Paul confirms this line of thinking in Ephesians 2:4-5, which says, "But because of his great love for us, God, who is rich in mercy, made us alive with Christ even when we were dead in transgressions ..."

Jesus didn't come and die so that we'd act better. He came and died so that we'd *live*.

A BLESSING FROM PAM

May you know life to the full today.

Set Apart

*Know that the LORD has set apart his faithful servant for
himself; the LORD hears when I call to him.*

PSALM 4:3

Pam was making her way through the produce department at the grocery store in our neighborhood not long ago when she found a wad of bills on the floor. "Why didn't you use that money to pay for our groceries?" I asked her, to which she just grinned and shook her head.

Of course she had taken the money directly to the store manager, who stared at her like she'd grown a third eye. "Uh, thanks for turning this in," he said, as he glanced left and right to see if he was being pranked.

He wasn't being pranked.

Pam really was turning in hundreds of dollars, even though she could have quietly pocketed it without getting caught.

I tell you this story to demonstrate a simple fact, which is that this is just *how it goes* for a believer of Jesus Christ. We do things that the world may find peculiar. We take the path of righteousness as often as we can. We hear from God and actually do what he says. We prize excellence and honesty and being able to sleep at night.

We do these things because we are set apart.

We are set apart for God.

If you are ridiculed for being righteous, if you are called out for telling the truth, if you are mocked for loving Jesus, if you are derided for doing what's right, let me give you a useful reminder, one I hope you'll keep close all your life:

All is as it should be.

All is as it should be.

A BLESSING FROM PAM

May you make no apologies for doing what's right today.

Where Mercy is Found

*Whoever conceals their sins does not prosper, but the
one who confesses and renounces them finds mercy.*

PROVERBS 28:13

Whenever I have a friend I can trust with a secret, I know I have a really good friend. I think about all the times I've sat across from, say, Daniel Grothe and shot straight with him about something challenging I was walking through, and those confessions flowed so effortlessly. Why? Because Daniel is a really good friend.

What's true for us relationally is true spiritually, too. If we believe that God is a good friend to us, then confession will be natural—even sweet. But the inverse is also the case: If we believe that God is a tyrant, just waiting to unleash his wrath on us, then we'll never want to confess.

When was the last time you told a secret to God? When did you last confess something meaningful to him? To be sure, he already knows the deepest secrets of our hearts, but unless we own those secrets and confess them, we won't receive the mercy he longs to give. He has already made up his mind to forgive us. All we need to do is come.

If God is your intimate friend, confess to him. It's the most natural thing you could do.

If God is not your intimate friend, confess to him. That intimacy will show up fast.

A BLESSING FROM PAM

May you step out of the shadows and confess your sin to God today.

God's Intent

And God is able to bless you abundantly, so that in all things at all times, having all that you need, you will abound in every good work.

2 CORINTHIANS 9:8

Have you ever felt a little beat up by life, as though everything and everyone were somehow out to get you? Days can be long, and life can be hard. Plans sometimes don't work out. People sometimes let us down. Things cost more than we think they will. Projects take longer than we think they should. Children don't always make the right decisions. Highly anticipated events get cancelled. On and on it goes.

One of my favorite reasons to spend time with God is because what the world takes from me God replenishes. His intent toward me is *good*. His aim in my life is to *bless*. His hope for me is to *flourish*. And the same is true for you.

God wants to be present and active in our lives because he's looking to provide us with whatever we need—"all things at all times," this verse says. He loves it when we come to him with our needs. He loves it when we trust him with our truth. He loves it when we rely on his power working in and through us to accomplish his work in the world.

If you're feeling a little weighed down by the hassles and struggles of life, push pause on your stress and get alone with God. Ask him to remind you of his goodness. Ask him to refresh your understanding of his grace. Ask him to make his presence and power known to you somehow. Trust him to do what only he can do.

A BLESSING FROM PAM

May you be divinely refreshed by your heavenly Father.
May you sense that you're abundantly blessed today.

Leaving It All Behind

Then Jesus said to his disciples, "Whoever wants to be my disciple
must deny themselves and take up their cross and follow me."

MATTHEW 16:24

The disciples were talking with Jesus about salvation. "Who then can be saved?" they asked, to which Jesus said, "With man this is impossible, but not with God; all things are possible with God," (Mark 10:26-27).

"Peter then spoke up," verse 28 says. "We have left everything to follow you!"

This wasn't Peter complaining; this was Peter *declaring*. He was reaffirming the disciples' decision to leave everything behind to follow Jesus. He was reminding Jesus that when the Lord had told those men that if they came with him they'd be fishers of men, and that if they spoke to demons those demons would submit to him, and that if they prayed with even a seed of faith they could make mountains fall into the sea ... that when Jesus had told them these and a hundred other things, they'd actually *believed* him. They'd taken him at his word.

By way of reply, Jesus said, "Truly I tell you, no one who has left home or brothers or sisters or mother or father or children or fields for me and the gospel will fail to receive a hundred times as much in this present age: homes, brothers, sisters, mothers, children and fields—along with persecutions—and in the age to come eternal life," (vv. 29-30).

"We left it all to follow you!" we can one day say to Jesus, knowing it was worth it at every turn.

A BLESSING FROM PAM

May you take Jesus at his word today that no sacrifice you make
can ever outpace the sacrifice he's made.

God or Money?

*"No one can serve two masters. Either you will hate the one and love
the other, or you will be devoted to the one and despise the other.
You cannot serve both God and money."*

MATTHEW 6:24

After I graduated from college with honors, I thought I'd have all kinds of businesses vying for me to come work for them; in fact, I had only one job offer, and it paid $14,000 a year. Pam was trying to finish school by taking night classes and working at a dry cleaners during the day, and while I fully supported those plans, the hundred bucks she netted each week didn't ever go very far.

We were reading in the book of Matthew one day and came across a verse we knew well: "You cannot serve both God and money." We had a decision to make.

I was twenty-two, and she was twenty-one, and the line we drew in the sand during that season serves us well still today. "We will always give God our first and our best," we agreed. "We will never not give him our tithe."

When you're making what we were making—roughly five hundred bucks a week— you need to write out a fifty-dollar check every Sunday, which for us was painful to do. Fifty dollars feels like a small fortune, when you're subsisting on ramen and canned green beans.

I'm grateful we resolved in our hearts back then that we'd seek God's kingdom first. When you're clear on whom you're serving, other distractions fall away.

What line in the sand might you draw today that will serve you well for years to come?

A BLESSING FROM PAM

*May you get clear today on which master you'll serve in your life.
May you be courageous enough to choose God.*

Free from Fear

For the Spirit God gave us does not make us timid,
but gives us power, love and self-discipline.

2 TIMOTHY 1:7

When Callie was seven we had a mouse in our house. For many, many consecutive nights, the child refused to sleep in her room because her room was on the main level, and that's where she'd seen the mouse.

I sat beside her. "Callie," I said, "mice are not dangerous. That mouse is actually so afraid of you that if it catches even a glimpse of you, it will run for it's tiny little life."

She wasn't buying it.

"When you saw it the first time," I continued with Callie, "did it rush toward you with claws and fangs bared? No, it didn't, right? It will run *away* from you every time."

She looked up at me, still unmoved.

"Listen," I said, all but giving up, "please just sleep in your own bed. If the mouse gnaws your leg off, I promise I'll get you another one."

"Daaaaad!" she screeched. Well, yeah. I deserved that.

Here's what the enemy does to you and me, every chance he gets: he tries to convince us that the mouse is deadly, that the tiny little mouse will take us down.

Let me tell you how fear gets rightsized in our lives, regardless of what we're afraid of: we picture the God of the universe standing beside the object of our fear, utterly dwarfing that benign mouse.

I carry an image with me that I revisit from time to time, which is of me standing in God's presence in heaven someday considering all that terrified me in life, thinking, *Seriously? I was afraid of that? What a colossal waste of time.*

A BLESSING FROM PAM

May you step away from your fear and toward God today.
In his presence, there's no reason to be afraid.

All God Wants

You, God, are my God, earnestly I seek you; I thirst for you, my whole being longs for you, in a dry and parched land where there is no water. I have seen you in the sanctuary and beheld your power and your glory. Because your love is better than life, my lips will glorify you. I will praise you as long as I live, and in your name I will lift up my hands.

PSALM 63:1-4

If you ever want to delight the heart of God, just read this psalm to him aloud. These words must be such music to his ears, as he hears a child of his reciprocate his love. All God has ever wants from us is worship—earnest worship; whole-being worship; worship directed toward him, alone.

Around New Life we say that the way we're going to make disciples, according to our mandate known as the Great Commission, is through the practices of worshiping, connecting, and serving. Those three words—worship, connect, and serve—are a big deal for our congregation ... they're the sum of what we're all about. And the reason that "worship" comes first in that lineup is that you just can't connect properly with other believers or effectively serve the body of Christ unless you first learn to worship God. Once we worship well, connecting and serving come naturally as the obvious byproduct of all that praise.

If you're stuck in a bad place of trying to perform for God, set that self-imposed weight down and just worship. Worship the God you adore.

A BLESSING FROM PAM

*May you be unabashed in your worship
of the one true God today.*

Over the Top

But to each one of us grace has been
given as Christ apportioned it.

EPHESIANS 4:7

Have you ever been in a situation where someone was just over-the-top extravagant? I'm thinking of a white-elephant Christmas party that everyone is supposed to bring a gag gift to. The idea is that each guest spends maybe five, ten dollars on an item that nobody in a right mind would want to keep, and then during the gift exchange one person at a time chooses a gift from the pile, opens it, and either hangs onto the gift they've opened or else swaps it for a previously opened gift—the wall-mounted singing fish, or the whoopie cushion, or the wearable blanket that makes you look like you're three years old.

Everything is moving along hilariously, until someone unwraps the next gift to find a 24-karat-gold bracelet. "Wait, this looks real," the person says, flabbergasted.

It looks real, because it *is*, the giver of the gift confirms.

They can keep the valuable item, but it feels too extravagant even to keep. "Can I pay you for this?" the recipient asks, to which the giver just shakes his head.

"But it's too ... it's too much," the recipient says, which is her way of saying, "You totally broke the rules."

And this, my friend, is grace. Humankind was on the earth living and laughing and enjoying the party, largely unaware of the trinkets they were settling for, while God was wrapping his blow-our-minds present: the person of Jesus Christ. His gift was the gift of grace, undeserved merit, God's riches at Christ's expense.

Grace is real. It's extravagant. It's definitely over the top. And by it we are utterly saved.

A BLESSING FROM PAM

May you never get over God's gift of grace. Today or any day.

Big God, Little Devil

Finally, be strong in the Lord and in his mighty power.
Put on the full armor of God, so that you can take
your stand against the devil's schemes.

EPHESIANS 6:10-11

Years ago a man from our church approached me after a service and updated me on his wife, who had been dealing with severe abdominal pain for months, despite doctors telling her nothing was wrong. Her husband said, "I wondered if you and the elders would be willing to pray for her. It's the only thing we haven't done."

The next night the couple came to my office, where the elders had already gathered. We anointed the woman with oil and began praying, one at a time. As other elders prayed, I sensed the Holy Spirit saying, "This is a spirit of infirmity you're dealing with." Sickness isn't always caused by a spirit, but in this case, just as it happened with the woman in Luke 13, evidently a spirit was to blame. When it was my turn to pray, I said, "I believe an evil spirit has attacked your body. When did the pain begin?"

The woman explained that she'd been at a friend's house, praying for her to be healed from cancer, and that upon returning home the pain had hit her sharply. And it hadn't abated since.

I said, "In Jesus' name, spirit of infirmity, leave this woman alone."

The pain was instantly gone.

We will never know why some prayers for healing are immediately answered and others never are. Either way, it remains true that God is powerful enough to heal all disease, if and when he chooses to do so. He is a big God, and the devil is little. Satan's schemes cannot take us down as long as we faithfully take our stand.

A BLESSING FROM PAM

May you stand firm today against Satan's plans for your life,
resolved that those plans will fail.

The Immediacy of Heaven

*Jesus answered him, "Truly I tell you, today
you will be with me in paradise."*

LUKE 23:43

My uncle mocked God and mocked the church throughout his entire life, despite my parents praying fervently for him that he'd surrender his heart to the Lord. He didn't need God, he'd always say. He didn't want a "Christian crutch." He was fine on his own, thank you very much.

When I was in my twenties, my uncle became very ill. He'd been a chronic smoker for years and had been diagnosed with lung cancer. His prognosis was grim.

I went to see him, and as he lay there in bed, tubes coming out of his mouth and arms, I couldn't help but think about how small and frail he seemed. He opened his eyes and saw me standing there. "I want Jesus in my life," he said.

I led my uncle in a prayer of surrender, and not long after, he died. What a comfort it was to me to know that the moment he left this reality, he entered into the presence of God.

To the thief on the cross who had spent his life devising evil and denying his need for God, Jesus said, "Today you will be with me in paradise."

Not tomorrow.

Not next week.

Not after you enter a period of rest, which is what "soul sleep" adherents would have you believe.

Now. Immediately upon surrendering your life to me, you will enjoy my Father's presence in full.

A BLESSING FROM PAM

*May you rest in the knowledge today that for the believer in Jesus,
to be absent from the body is to be present with God.*

On Being the Clay

Yet you, LORD, are our Father. We are the clay,
you are the potter; we are all the work of your hand.

ISAIAH 64:8

It's a posture that never serves us well, the posture that says, "I'll trust you, God, as soon as you explain what's going on."

Life can be perplexing—that's true for us all. We don't understand why circumstances unfold the way that they do. Why things we thought were certain fall apart. Why people we thought we could count on betray us in the end. There are far more questions than answers, aren't there? We think God owes us something here.

It is spiritual arrogance to withhold worship of God until we get adequate explanations from God. It is the clay saying to the potter, "I'll tell you how to mold me."

It is actually the Potter who makes such decisions.

It is the Potter who calls the shots.

God doesn't mind our questions, so be bold in bringing yours to him. Just recognize that answers may not be forthcoming—here or in eternity as well. And isn't this how we want it to be, if we're honest about spiritual things? Who wants to follow a God whose knowledge can be matched, whose perspective can be so easily grasped?

A BLESSING FROM PAM

May your questions not frustrate you
but drive you deeper into God's presence today.

More Desirable Still

Choose my instruction instead of silver, knowledge rather than choice gold, for wisdom is more precious than rubies, and nothing you desire can compare with her.

PROVERBS 8:10-11

It is said that in a given day, you and I make upward of 35,000 choices, or one choice every two seconds during the hours that we're awake. Right now, you're choosing to read these words. You chose where to sit to read them. You chose the lighting or lack thereof. Is there a glass of water beside you? You chose that as well.

We put weight on certain choices, such as whether to go to the doctor to have that cough checked out, or what to say to a child who is racked by fear, or how to navigate stress at work. But I dare say the most important choice you and I make in a given moment is whether to go God's way or our own.

Here is something I've noticed about people who let divine wisdom guide their lives: they are calm in the midst of confusion, they are prayerful instead of stressed out, they are loving in the face of hatred, and they are hopeful when the outlook is bleak.

You can make a lot of important choices today, but none will be more important than the choice to follow God.

A BLESSING FROM PAM

May you choose wisely today, moment by moment,
action by action, breath by breath.

Believing God

God said to Moses, "I AM WHO I AM."

EXODUS 3:14

When I was growing up, my dad had a phrase he'd always say: "Brady, you've got to say what you mean and mean what you say." If I heard that counsel once, I heard it a thousand times: say what you mean, and mean what you say.

This input made sense to me, coming from my dad. For twenty years he was a used-car salesman in our small town, and an honest one, at that. If my dad learned that a car's transmission had started leaking, he wouldn't sell the prospective buyer that car. "You don't want this one," he'd say. "We need to find you something else."

Once Dad had been at that dealer awhile, people took note of his honesty. Car buyers would walk into the dealership, keep walking past all the other sales guys, and say, "Hey, point me to Leland Boyd."

Dad made a good living selling cars because he said what he meant, he meant what he said, and thus he was a trustworthy man.

Throughout Scripture God reveals himself to various people, always explaining that he, alone, is God. He always has been God. He always will be God. And no one is equal to him in the world. He said that he created his children and that he loves his children and that he has good plans for anyone who would follow him. He said that by simply trusting in his Son, Jesus, we can spend an eternity with him.

The question I have for you is, *Do you believe him?*

Do you believe that God has said what he means? Do you believe that he means what he says? Faith cannot exist without a yes to these questions. Faith starts with believing God.

A BLESSING FROM PAM

May you take God at his word today.

Clarity as We Go

Your word is a lamp for my feet,
a light on my path.

PSALM 119:105

If you're stumbling around in the darkness today, I have good news for you. You don't have to stay in the shadows; God has made a way for you to see.

If there is one verse I have leaned on throughout the course of my life, it is this verse in Psalm 119. Here, the psalmist assures us that our path can be illuminated, that we don't need to fumble through the dark. A light is available. A lamp can be turned on. We can actually see where we're going in life. We can be confident in each step that we take.

Here's how that gets done: *we fixate on God's Word.*

If you want to hear God's voice and sense God's presence and receive God's guidance today, let the holy Scriptures into your mind and your heart. Let their truth wash over you. Let them influence all that you do.

You may not sense the change immediately ... it might not seem that a switch gets flipped. But over time, with careful consistency, the path under your feet will be set ablaze in brightness. It will be clear which way to go.

A BLESSING FROM PAM

May you trust God to illuminate your journey today
as you look to his Word to be your guide.

You are Seen

*Then each of them was given a white robe, and they were told to wait
a little longer, until the full number of their fellow servants, their
brothers and sisters, were killed just as they had been.*

REVELATION 6:11

A friend was at the American Museum of Natural History in New York City with her family recently, waiting in line to gain entry as soon as the doors opened. There were hundreds of people snaked for at least a city block, everyone with the same goal in mind: getting into that museum.

A docent from the museum approached unexpectedly and said, "The three of you, come with me." He then led my friend and her husband and daughter to the very front of the line. A reason for their expedited entry was never given; he just picked them out and led them right in.

Whenever I read this part of the book of Revelation, I'm reminded that while we sometimes feel lost in a sea of humanity, to God we are individuals who matter deeply to him. When he looks at our swelling population, he sees distinctive people, each with a story, each with a soul. In heaven, each of us will receive a white robe, which means we'll be tended to, one at a time. And because we're seen as individuals in heaven, we can be assured that we're seen as individuals right now.

You're not lost in a crowd, my friend.

God sees you, just as you are.

God made you. God sees you. God values you. God loves you. God is committed to *you*—singularly wonderful you.

A BLESSING FROM PAM

May you know today that you are individually loved by God.

SEPTEMBER

"We make Christianity tougher than it needs to be when we make it about more than reflecting Jesus. He said the world would know us by our love—it's that simple. We will be known by our love."

- Pastor Brady Boyd -

A Peaceful and Quiet Life

*I urge, then, first of all, that petitions, prayers, intercession and thanksgiving
be made for all people—for kings and all those in authority, that we
may live peaceful and quiet lives in all godliness and holiness.*

1 TIMOTHY 2:1-2

Nineteenth-century English historian Lord Acton once wrote, "all power tends to corrupt and absolute power corrupts absolutely," and the reason that quote remains ubiquitous is because it's absolutely true.

I'm a student of church history, and one of my favorite things to study is when Christianity was at its best in the world—being the most effective, making the most progress in the name of Christ. It might seem that we've been at our best when we've been most powerful—when we've had control in a given culture. But that simply isn't the case. Each time Christianity has gained power, especially in this country, we have squandered that power. We've proven Lord Acton's words true.

Throughout history, Christianity has been the strongest when its adherents behaved as the loving, life-giving minority working the margins of the culture they served.

I'm certainly not suggesting that we discontinue fighting for what's right. We absolutely ought to stand up for what God says is good and pure and true. We should vote. We should care.

But also: if we want to see revival in our land, we will happily invest ourselves in the seemingly small work of helping those on the margins who can't otherwise get a hand.

We will live peaceful and quiet lives for the sake of Christ.

A BLESSING FROM PAM

*May you love well today—quietly, peaceably, gently—
bringing life and light wherever you go.*

Remembering Your Redemption

The Lord is not slow in keeping his promise, as some understand
slowness. Instead he is patient with you, not wanting anyone
to perish, but everyone to come to repentance.

2 PETER 3:9

Think for a moment about the kindest person you know—I mean the sweetest, most generous, most gracious, most loving person you know. Can you picture him or her? Maybe it's your grandmother. Maybe it's a neighbor who is just impossibly helpful all the time. Maybe it's your spouse. Sometimes it's a son or daughter who has a truly expansive heart.

Now, I'm sure this person you're picturing is wonderful—that's why they came to mind. But did you know that this person wasn't *always* wonderful, that they weren't born as wonderful as they are now? Your grandmother—even your sticky-sweet grandmother—got aggravated from time to time. She lashed out at someone. She said a word she shouldn't have said. (Gasp!) She wasn't born saved, is what I'm saying. She had to come to a point of decision in life and surrender herself to the Lord.

Here's why I bring this up: We all were born needing a Savior, and until we come under Jesus' authority, we are sinful as can be. God longs for each person to come to that place of decision, to cede control of their life to him. Aren't we glad he was patient enough to wait for us, so that we too could be redeemed?

When you catch your becoming frustrated with sinners because their lives are wracked by sin, consider pausing and praying for their redemption instead, that God would be patient with them.

A BLESSING FROM PAM

May you catch God's spirit of longsuffering today,
which hopes that everyone will come to know him.

Together, We Go Far

Greet Priscilla and Aquila, my co-workers in Christ Jesus.
They risked their lives for me. Not only I but all the churches
of the Gentiles are grateful to them.

ROMANS 16:3-4

In the final chapter of Romans, Paul took time to thank the people who'd helped him succeed. If my math was right, he expressed gratitude for a full thirty-six women and men from five different churches spread across Asia and the Middle East.

He thanked Phoebe, who had given financially to help support Paul's missionary journeys. He thanked Priscilla and Aquila, who had risked their lives on Paul's behalf. He thanked Mary, a hard worker. He thanked Andronicus and Junia, who had been in prison when Paul was there. He thanked his dear friend Ampliatus. He thanked Rufus's mom, who had been like a mother to him. On and on it went.

It's an easy chapter to skip over, but that would be a mistake. I think God is modeling something through Paul that we would do well to practice ourselves.

If you are a believer today, then you too have a "list." You have a list of women and men who had your back, who cared about your heart enough to tell you the truth, who saw potential in you and were willing to draw it out, who took time out of their own busy lives to teach you the ways of Christ. You have a Phoebe and a Mary and a Junia and "Rufus's mom."

So, who are they?

More importantly when was the last time you said thanks?

Consider those who have gone before you and walked alongside you, to help you get to where you are spiritually today. Maybe it's time to thank them for the significant role they've played in your life.

A BLESSING FROM PAM

May you take time today to say thanks
to those who made you who you are.

The Point of Church

Whoever claims to love God yet hates a brother or sister is a liar.
For whoever does not love their brother and sister, whom they
have seen, cannot love God, whom they have not seen.

1 JOHN 4:20

Most people are in love with what I call the *sensational* aspects of church. They love to come to church because the music is stimulating, and because the building looks orderly, and because the donut holes are delicious, and because the sounds of children playing on the playground remind them of being a kid themselves. They love the lights, and the comfy couches, and the coffee bar, and the jumbo LED screens. They love feeling inspired. They love being called to live beyond themselves. They love—to put it crassly—being entertained.

And while there is nothing inherently evil or even wrong about any of these things, these things aren't the primary point of church.

Would you like to know what *is* the point?

When Jesus established his church, he called a group of people together and told them to go minister to the world. People serving people: *that* was the point of church. Whenever someone these days tells me they want God to be more active in their lives, I tell them to go plant themselves in the soil of relationships. That is where God will be.

Focus on the relational more than the sensational. That is what church is for.

A BLESSING FROM PAM

May you prioritize people over pizzazz each time you engage with the church.

Gaining Christ

*But whatever were gains to me I now consider loss or the sake of Christ.
What is more, I consider everything a loss because of the surpassing
worth of knowing Christ Jesus my Lord, for whose sake I have
lost all things. I consider them garbage, that I may gain Christ.*

PHILIPPIANS 3:7-8

Building on what we talked about yesterday, let's look at how we steward our relationships in life.

If we're not careful, most of our relational world can become transactional in nature. We are nice to the gate agent at the airport because we're hoping that person will upgrade our seat. We take an interest in the colleague at work after learning he has season tickets to the Broncos games. We butter up our spouse in hopes of not having to clean the basement this weekend. We feign interest during a lecture so that our professor will find us deserving of the higher grade. Transactional relationships are all about giving something to get something: you scratch my back, and I'll scratch yours.

This doesn't work in our walk with Christ.

In the passage above, Paul wrote that the most important thing about his existence was the "surpassing worth of knowing Christ." All he wanted was *gaining Christ*.

To "gain Christ" isn't to get something, but rather to become someone—namely, him. When you and I elevate Jesus to the most important aspect of our lives, we erase all the transactions, instead simply receiving his gift of grace. We tell God we're done trying to get things from him. We long to become like Christ instead.

A BLESSING FROM PAM

May knowing Jesus more be your singular aim for today.

Humility for the Win

*Humble yourselves, therefore, under God's
mighty hand, that he may lift you up in due time.*

1 PETER 5:6

It's no stretch to say that self-promotion has become an epidemic in our culture, no doubt fueled by social media and life in general online. One study I saw reported that while 20 percent of Facebook and Instagram posts are posted by what they call "Informers," people sharing valid information, a full 80 percent are posted by "Me-formers," people just looking for an ego boost. I know there are all sorts of monetary reasons for people to be seemingly self-obsessed these days, but at its core it's not the fiscal repercussions I'm worried about. My worries are spiritually based.

I'm not anti-social media, I promise. What I am is anti-*pride.* In 1 Peter 5:6 we read this exhortation: "Humble yourselves, therefore, under God's mighty hand, that he may lift you up in due time."

Humble yourself. You don't have to think less of yourself, but how about thinking of yourself less?

Humility isn't pushing ourselves—our image, our opinion, our agenda, our knowledge, or our preferences—into the spotlight; it's forcing others to the front of the line.

This line of thinking always raises good questions for me, questions such as this one: *Have I been spending more time and energy promoting myself or promoting others lately?*

And this one: *Is my life more self-sustained or more God-sustained these days?*

And this one: *Would people who know me best in this season describe me as a humble person, or would the notion make them reflexively laugh?*

A BLESSING FROM PAM

*May you rest from your self-promotion today,
trusting that God will promote you in due time.*

The Test that Must be Passed

*Dear friends, do not believe every spirit, but test the spirits to see whether they are
from God, because many false prophets have gone out into the world. This is how you
can recognize the Spirit of God: Every spirit that acknowledges that Jesus Christ has
come in the flesh is from God, but every spirit that does not acknowledge
Jesus is not from God. This is the spirit of the antichrist, which you have
heard is coming and even now is already in the world.*

1 JOHN 4:1-3

We looked earlier at the spiritual gift of discernment, and the root word of that gift—
discern—means to test, approve, and allow. A real sign of spiritual maturity is the ability
to test accurately whether something is "of God" or whether it is "of the world," (or the
"spirit of antichrist," as it is called here in 1 John).

When you became a believer, God implanted the Holy Spirit to serve as a guard over
your heart and a guide for your life. In essence, from that day forward you were given
a built-up discernment meter, a real, living gauge for knowing what is of God. But
here John offers us another way for knowing whether a given perspective, opinion,
or worldview happens to align with God's. It's the only test that must be passed,
really, that of agreeing to who Jesus is.

As you go about your life, whenever you encounter the belief that Jesus is from God, that
he is God, that he came to the earth in the flesh after having been sent here by God, then
you know you're dealing with the Spirit of God. This is a spirit you can trust.

On the contrary, whenever you encounter the belief that Jesus isn't from God, that he isn't
God, or that he didn't come to earth in the flesh after having been sent by God, then you
know you're dealing with the spirit of antichrist, the spirit of the world. This spirit cannot be
trusted. This spirit stands opposed to all we believe.

What a useful, straightforward test. We don't have to fear being led astray in this world!
We can learn to test every spirit and then run that test as often as we please.

A BLESSING FROM PAM

*May you approach every input today with spiritual discernment on your side.
Learn the test. Run the test. Pay attention the results the test yields.*

Peace as Power

Do not be anxious about anything, but in every situation, by prayer and petition, with thanksgiving, present your requests to God. And the peace of God, which transcends all understanding, will guard your hearts and your minds in Christ Jesus.

PHILIPPIANS 4:6-7

When we read God's Word, a real danger is assuming that life for people in biblical times was easier than it is for us today. We come across Paul's directive here in Philippians 4 and think that it probably wasn't that hard for people to "not be anxious" because life wasn't stressful to begin with. We mistakenly believe that since our technology today is different from what those people had access to, our travails must be different too. But it simply isn't the case.

In ancient Philippi, believers there were regarded as slaves. They had virtually no money or other means for trade. They had no weapons to protect themselves from Roman officials. They couldn't vote and had few rights. They were spiritually overwhelmed by a culture that esteemed hundreds of gods and goddesses while disparaging the one true God. And yet they were supposed to fret about ... *nothing?*

The counsel Paul offered to those believers he offers to us today: whatever has you feeling marginalized, overwhelmed, ridiculed, outnumbered, or totally stressed out is precisely the thing Paul is telling us to lay down for the sake of picking up the practice of prayer instead. Upon doing so, a miraculous thing occurs, which is that our lives are flooded with peace. This peace cannot be grasped with natural understanding; it's a supernatural trade. Our burdens for God's blessing. Our panic for Jesus' peace. Our hopelessness for hope fully restored.

A BLESSING FROM PAM

As you choose to pray instead of panic today, may you have the very real sense that your heart and mind are being guarded by God, by his gift of perfect peace.

Better

*But grow in the grace and knowledge of our Lord and Savior
Jesus Christ. To him be glory both now and forever! Amen.*

2 PETER 3:18

Throughout history, God has looked for a group of people who will give themselves wholeheartedly to the idea of radically following Jesus. These people understand that the most powerful force on the planet is the Spirit's resurrection power, the power that raised Jesus from the dead and that raises us to new life still today. And so they seek that power in their lives day by day, always striving to get better, to do better, to look more and more like Jesus Christ.

What could use a little resurrection power in your life today?

Could your marriage stand to get better? I'm not suggesting that the thing is altogether falling apart; I'm just asking if there are some dings and dents that could be cleaned up and put back in shape.

Could your attitude toward work stand to get better? You may not be storming out of meetings these days, but you may not be known as a joyful blessing either to your peers.

Could your daily habits stand to get better? Covid did a number on all of us, and despite it (hopefully) being in our rearview mirror now, the lethargy so many of us succumbed to is still sticking around for some.

God is at work in the world today, wherever people and cultures will have him. The question I have for you and for me is whether we're asking him to work in our lives. Do you want to get better? Do you want to more accurately reflect the nature of his Son? Where do you crave his power in your life? Will you tell him so today?

A BLESSING FROM PAM

*May you chart a path for real growth today,
trusting God's power to take you there.*

Loving All

Jesus replied: "Love the Lord your God with all your heart and with all your soul and with all your mind. This is the first and greatest commandment. And the second is like it: Love your neighbor as yourself."

MATTHEW 22:37-39

This passage is well-known and oft-quoted, and yet in my experience believers are half-hearted about upholding what it says to do.

The injunction is crystal clear: love God with everything we have—heart, soul, mind ... also strength, according to some translations. And then love people as we do ourselves. Given that most people *deeply* love themselves, this means we're to *deeply* love others too.

Here's what I see happen too often: we do one or the other, but not both. We either really, really love God but don't do so well with people. (They're so messy. They're so annoying. They're so needy. They're so vain.) Or else we really, really love people but kind of cast God to the side most days. (He meddles. He pries. He thinks he knows what's best in our relationships. We just need a little *space*.)

And yet there the commands stand. Love God. Love people. Both, at the very same time.

As you consider the dynamic I describe here, which side of the issue needs the most attention in your life? As with all things, your heavenly Father stands ready to help you accomplish all that he has asked you to do in your life.

A BLESSING FROM PAM

May you be strengthened today in your ability to love both God and people well.

Found Favor

Moses said to the LORD, "You have been telling me, 'Lead these people,'
but you have not let me know whom you will send with me. You have said, 'I
know you by name and you have found favor with me.'

"If you are pleased with me, teach me your ways so I may know you and continue
to find favor with you. Remember that this nation is your people."

The LORD replied, "My presence will go with you, and I will give you rest."

EXODUS 33:12-14

Have you ever labored on behalf of a loved one in energy, in effort, and in prayer? I think of all the parents I've known who've had a prodigal child, and all the adults I've known struggling to care for aging parents and all the men and women I've known who desperately wanted a family member to surrender to Christ. These and so many other situations are gut-wrenching because they leave us feeling helpless.

All these centuries later, this exchange between Moses and God remains timely for us. Let me draw your attention to two truths here: first, Moses reminds us in that little phrase, "this nation is your people" that God cares more about our loved ones than we do. That seems impossible, but it's true. God designed those prodigal children and those aging parents and those beloved people who are living outside of his will. He created them. He gifted them. He sacrificed his Son for them. He loves them like only he can.

Here's the second thing: We can do anything for God when we have his presence and his rest. We must pray for these things every day. "Father, help me go where you already are working, so that I'll be ministering in your presence there. And help me do only what you ask me to do, so that I won't unwittingly overreact."

Let's entrust our loved ones to God's perfect care. And let's wait on God's presence before we act.

A BLESSING FROM PAM

May you be confident today that God's love envelopes those you also love,
and that his presence surely goes with you.

Mine, Mine, Mine

Do nothing out of selfish ambition or vain conceit.
Rather, in humility value others above yourselves.

PHILIPPIANS 2:3

If you've ever parented a toddler, then the Ten Commandments of Toddlerhood will resonate with you. Here goes:

Commandment 1: If I like it, it's mine.
Commandment 2: If it's in my hand, it's mine.
Commandment 3: If I can take it from you, it's mine.
Commandment 4: If I had it a little while ago, it's mine.
Commandment 5: If it's mine, it must never appear to be yours.
Commandment 6: If I'm doing or building something, all the pieces are mine.
Commandment 7: If it looks like it *could* be mine, it's mine.
Commandment 8: If I saw it first, it's mine.
Commandment 9: If you're playing with it and put it down, automatically it's mine.
Commandment 10: If it's broken, it's yours.

Toddlers get a bad rap for being selfish, but based on the apostle Paul's counsel in Philippians 2:3-4, it's a safe bet that selfishness doesn't end in childhood. After all, if we could simply grow out of this particular sin streak by letting chronology have its way, then why would Paul need to have issued the directive in the first place?

Here are some phrases that are worth putting into our rotation:

"I'm happy to wait. Please, go ahead."
"You seem stressed. How can I help?"
"Thank you for asking, but first, tell me how *you're* doing."

Whenever an opportunity to demonstrate selflessness surfaces, seize it in confidence, knowing that your Father is delighting in you.

A BLESSING FROM PAM

May you be at peace today as you humble yourself on behalf of others.

Them First

*"Therefore, if you are offering your gift at the altar and there remember
that your brother or sister has something against you, leave your
gift there in front of the altar. First go and be reconciled
to them; then come and offer your gift."*

MATTHEW 5:23-24

Many times when I'm called in to help settle a dispute, the people involved spend their time and energy blaming the other person and telling them why the problem is all their fault. It's uncanny. They both will have a perfectly thought-through argument regarding the ins and outs of the other person's culpability, but when I turn the conversation to what *their* role in the issue might be, it's crickets for minutes on end.

In Matthew 5, we're shown a different way.

The scenario is this: we are bringing a gift to the altar at church, and just before we place that money in the collection plate we remember that we're still sideways with someone we know. Now, you and I both would probably brush that recollection aside, thinking that this worshipful moment didn't need to be interrupted with something as trivial as that. Maybe we'd make a mental note to follow up with that person later, or maybe we wouldn't. Either way, we'd keep participating in the flow of the worship service, trusting that everything would be all right.

God says it won't be all right.

In plain language, Jesus says that in such a scenario, we are to leave our gift there at the altar and go make amends right away. Only then can we come and offer our gift. Only then can we enjoy the presence of God.

We don't wait for someone else to own their stuff and make the first move.

We make the first move every time.

A BLESSING FROM PAM

May you be diligent to keep short accounts with those you know.
May you be first to clear the air.

Forgiving, Loving, at Peace

*"By this everyone will know that you are my
disciples, if you love one another."*

JOHN 13:35

It's a bold statement, but it's the truth: the way that you treat other people is a
direct reflection of what you believe God thinks about you. If you believe that
God is angry with you and that he is withholding forgiveness from you and that
he is sitting in heaven just waiting for you to mess up so that he can condemn
and punish you, then those patterns are exactly what will come out of you as you
interact with those you know. You will be quick to get angry with your kids. You
will refuse to forgive your spouse. You will keep a skeptical eye on your colleagues,
your neighbors, your extended family members, even your friends, almost willing
them to make a misstep in life so that you can rub it in—or at least privately gloat.

But the inverse is also true. If you believe that God deeply loves you, and if you
believe that God has forgiven you for every last sin, and if you believe that God is
for you and is committed to setting you up for success, then guess what kinds of
things will come out of you, as you move about in the world?

You will love others well.

You will forgive others easily.

You will rejoice when others are successful.

You will delight in all the right things and grieve with God all the things that are wrong.

We make Christianity tougher than it needs to be when we make it about more than
reflecting Christ. He said the world would know us by our love—it's that simple. They
will know us when we speak and look and react and act like him.

A BLESSING FROM PAM

*May you concentrate your energy exclusively
on demonstrating Christ's love to the world today.*

Profitable Vows

Get rid of all bitterness, rage and anger, brawling and slander,
along with every form of malice. Be kind and compassionate to one
another, forgiving each other, just as in Christ God forgave you.

EPHESIANS 4:31-32

When I was in the fifth grade, I had a serious girlfriend named Wendy. Things were going really well until day four of our relationship, when I discovered that the only reason she wanted to be my girlfriend is to make the boy she *really* liked jealous. I was crushed. And as soon as that other boy started paying attention to Wendy, I also was dumped.

I know I was only ten or eleven at the time, but I really did care about Wendy. I was kind to her. I was respectful to her. I thought she was really great. Years later, by hindsight I could see that it was just after being dumped by Wendy that I made a vow to myself. *I'll never respect another girl,* I said to myself. *I'll just treat them the way they treat me.*

For the next decade, it is no exaggeration to say that I treated young women terribly. Throughout junior high, high school, and college, I took everything I could take from women and then dropped them like a hot rock. I never felt bad about my behavior. I never apologized for my behavior. And I never planned to change my behavior.

But then I met Jesus Christ.

And he interfered with that inner vow.

He helped me see that in him I could have new vows, vows that would profit my life instead of tearing it down.

If you're still being governed by vows that dishonor God and make life hard, it's time to adopt a new vow, a vow that agrees with what God says is true.

A BLESSING FROM PAM

May your agreements all bring you life today,
God-honoring, soul-expanding life.

A Worthwhile Reminder

*Now, brothers and sisters, I want to remind you of the gospel I preached
to you, which you received and on which you have taken your stand. By
this gospel you are saved, if you hold firmly to the word I preached
to you. Otherwise, you have believed in vain.*

1 CORINTHIANS 15:1-2

Often in my role as your pastor I find the best thing I can do when preaching is to remind you of what you already know.

In this passage from the apostle Paul, he too was reminding believers in the city of Corinth of what they already believed:

"For what I received I passed on to you as of first importance: that Christ died for our sins according to the Scriptures, that he was buried, that he was raised on the third day according to the Scriptures, and that he appeared to Cephas, and then to the Twelve. After that, he appeared to more than five hundred of the brothers and sisters at the same time, most of whom are still living, though some have fallen asleep. Then he appeared to James, then to all the apostles, and last of all he appeared to me also, as to one abnormally born," (1 Corinthians 15:3-8).

God sent his only Son to inhabit human flesh; to be misunderstood, mistreated, and brutally murdered. Jesus bore the full weight of every misdeed we'll ever commit. And he voluntarily suffered death on a cross to span the bridge between God and us. After three days, he was raised to life. He went on ministering for another forty days before taking his place at his Father's right hand, where he intercedes for us to this day.

This is the crux of the gospel message, on which we base our entire lives. May we never forget Jesus' sacrifice. May we never take for granted God's great gift of grace.

A BLESSING FROM PAM

*May you be reminded today that God finds you so valuable that he would send his Son to die
on a cross so that you could know him not only personally, but eternally as well.*

Not of Our Choosing

My brothers and sisters, believers in our glorious Lord Jesus Christ must not show favoritism. Suppose a man comes into your meeting wearing a gold ring and fine clothes, and a poor man in filthy old clothes also comes in. If you show special attention to the man wearing fine clothes and say, "Here's a good seat for you," but say to the poor man, "You stand there" or "Sit on the floor by my feet," have you not discriminated among yourselves and become judges with evil thoughts?

JAMES 2:1-4

I was talking with a young man who told me he wasn't "into the whole church thing." He said, "I mean, my friends and I hang out and hike on Sunday mornings ... *that's* my church."

I was kind but clear. "That's not church."

Even if he and his friends read the Bible, prayed, took up an offering each time they met, it still would not be church—or not how the New Testament defines church, anyway.

When we form a congregation, we pick people we know and like.

When God forms a congregation, he picks people we need. He brings into our lives people from different socioeconomic levels, different races, different backgrounds, to shape the group he longs to see.

We don't "do church" for what church does for us. We participate in church to be formed into the image and likeness of Jesus, our Head. We don't discriminate among ourselves by hand-picking the people we'll enter fellowship with. We don't show favoritism based on who we like and what we prefer. We trust God to place us in the right body of believers for our own development and for the growth of the whole.

A BLESSING FROM PAM

May you trust God to draw you to the exact body of believers he'd have you be a part of. And may you'd engage fully and joyously with them.

Frequent and Unhurried

Therefore confess your sins to each other and pray for each other
so that you may be healed. The prayer of a righteous
person is powerful and effective.

JAMES 5:16

A mom was telling me that the only way she communicated with her teenagers these days was by texting them. "Well, yeah," I said. "Nobody calls anymore." To which she said, "No, I don't mean texting instead of calling; I mean texting instead of *talking*."

She was chuckling as she said it, but she was serious: while they all were at home, she and her teens would text each other instead of talking face to face. "We're never in the same room," she said. "It's just easier this way."

In James 5:16, the apostle Paul explained that if we were going to be people who were shaped by the gospel, then certain things would be true of us. Such as this: we would practice confessing our sins to one another and praying for one another so that, as he puts it, we "may be healed."

These things are difficult to do via text. We need in-person conversation for that.

If we aren't connecting even with the people in our own homes, it's a good bet that we're passing by people out in the world with barely a cursory, "How are you today?"

God wants more for us.

He wants for us to know each other and to walk with each other and to spur each other on to loving him more. He wants our pace of life to be different from the world's. He wants our peace in life to be different from the world's. Divine power and effectiveness are ours to be had, when we yield to God's perfect will.

A BLESSING FROM PAM

May you enjoy intimate, unrushed conversation with your loved ones today.

Shortcuts and Secrets

But when you are tempted, he will also
provide a way out so that you can endure it.

1 CORINTHIANS 10:13B

Have you ever been watching a suspenseful movie, and just before the main character takes the deal or opens the door or dials the number, you find yourself saying, "Don't do it. Don't do it. Don't do it"?

Sometimes I wonder if God is sitting in heaven thinking the same thing about you and me, whenever we are tempted to sin. *Don't do it*, he whispers. *Don't do it.*

I want to give you two quick tests you can run that will tell you if you're being tempted to do something that God would not have you do. The first is to ask yourself, "Is what I'm about to do going to require me to take a shortcut?"

God is a god of process. There is a way that things are done. We are to be married before we have sex. We are to work diligently before we are compensated. We are to wait on him to exact retribution for evil instead of taking vengeance into our own hands. If you are presented with a shortcut to God's processes, be very suspicious. You're likely being tempted to sin.

Here's the second question to ask: "Is what I'm about to do going to require me to keep a secret?"

God does his best work not in the darkness but in the light. God does not ask us to hide in the shadows; he asks us to live in such a way that we shine brightly for the world to see. If you're being asked to keep something hidden, stop what you're doing and pray. God promises to provide a way of escape for every temptation we face.

A BLESSING FROM PAM

May you find confidence today to wait on the Lord
and to choose to live in the light.

Grateful for Grace

... give thanks in all circumstances; for
this is God's will for you in Christ Jesus.

1 THESSALONIANS 5:18

Whenever I meet people who are stuck in sin, my initial response is one not of judgment and condemnation, but of compassion. Why? Because I know how they feel! Before I knew Jesus, I was a world-class sinner who made poor decisions all the time. By God's grace, I'm no longer that man.

I have a theory, which is that you and I are only as thankful for what God is doing in the broken people around us as we are for what God did in our lives when we were broken ourselves. If we've kind of gotten over being saved, and if we look at our lives and say, "Yeah, I've got this Christianity thing *down*," then we'll be unmoved by what God is up to in the lives of people who need him most. We won't pray for that work. We won't join in on that work. We won't celebrate that work when it bears fruit.

If, on the other hand, you pause from time to time to consider just how wretched you were before you started going God's way in life, and if you regularly say thank you to God from the bottom of your heart, then your posture toward the broken people around you will dramatically start to shift. You'll hold out hope for them. You'll pray for them. You'll cheer for them as they take each step toward the redemption that all of us need. You'll be grateful for grace, not dismissive of it. You'll regard grace as the gift that it is.

A BLESSING FROM PAM

May you say thank you to God today.

Gentle Like God

*As a father has compassion on his children, so
the LORD has compassion on those who fear him; for he knows how
we are formed, he remembers that we are dust.*

PSALM 103:13-14

I was reading through the psalms one day, when I was arrested by fresh perspective. I was taken back to my early twenties, when I decided to go all-in with God. Back then, I told myself that I was going to follow God as hard as I'd followed the world. I was going to pour the same time, energy, and effort into being holy as I'd poured into being unholy. I'd done all the wrong things for all the wrong reasons, but now I'd reverse course. I'd do all the right things. I'd do them for all the right reasons. And I'd never, ever fail.

Well, that lasted about a day. And then I failed. I goofed up. I sinned. And I was crushed.

In fact, for years, every time I stumbled or fell, I would berate myself. I was so disappointing! Why couldn't I get this thing right?

I assumed God felt the same way about me.

Thankfully, he did not.

This passage reminded me that throughout my entire life, God has had compassion on me, because he knows that I'm a broken human living in a broken world, doing my best to follow him. He gets that. He sees that. And he has compassion for me, and for you.

I'm not suggesting that we use God's compassion as license to sin. I'm suggesting that maybe we take our stumbles and bumbles in stride, recognizing that we won't always get it right. Maybe we practice being gentle with our own hearts so that as others need our gentleness we'll be prepared to share it with them.

A BLESSING FROM PAM

*May you treat yourself with the same kindness
and compassion that God feels toward you today.*

No Effort Without Error

*Blessed is the one who perseveres under trial because, having
stood the test, that person will receive the crown of life
that the Lord has promised to those who love him.*

JAMES 1:12

In my line of work, being criticized is just part of the job. And while nobody enjoys being criticized, over the years I've learned that to dismiss the criticism wholesale is to miss development opportunities that God would have me seize. These days, whenever criticism comes my way, instead of reflexively ignoring it or countering it with justifications and excuses, I try to remember to pause and pray, asking God what I'm supposed to be learning from the critique that has come my way.

In his famous speech, "The Man in the Arena," former president Teddy Roosevelt wrote, "It is not the critic who counts; not the man who points out how the strong man stumbles, or where the doer of deeds could have done it better. The credit belongs to the man who is actually in the arena, whose face is marred by dust and sweat and blood; who strives valiantly; who errs, who comes short again and again, because there is no effort without error and shortcoming ..."

If we cave to criticism every time, eventually we'll quit showing up altogether. And then the mission of Christ dies—at least as far as our participation in it. Better to learn what we can learn from the criticism we receive so that we can stay in the arena and strive for this gospel message we so deeply prize.

A BLESSING FROM PAM

*May you release your grip on the fear of failure today,
boldly persevering for the cause of Christ.*

The Necessity of Open Doors

Now when I went to Troas to preach the gospel of Christ and found that the Lord had opened a door for me, I still had no peace of mind, because I did not find my brother Titus there. So I said goodbye to them and went on to Macedonia.

2 CORINTHIANS 2:12-13

This passage from Paul to the Corinthians is the kind of section of Scripture that most of us overlook. Genealogies and travel logs—who needs information like that?

We do.

I'll tell you why.

As we go through our lives, it is absolutely critical that we pay attention to where God is already at work. He is God. He has a plan. He is working to bring that plan to pass. Which means the surest way for us to succeed in life is to *join him in that work*.

Paul understood that he was not to minister in a setting that God had not appointed for him. Such settings, to him, were behind closed doors. Far better, Paul surmised, to wait for divinely *opened* doors, and then to be ready to serve.

Just as was the case for Paul, you and I have a calling on our lives. We have an assignment God wants us to complete. And God has committed to leading us each step of the way so that by his power and in his timing and according to his perfect will and ways, we will accomplish the mission he's appointed us for. We will succeed in his very good work.

A BLESSING FROM PAM

May you wait on the Lord today, never outpacing his perfect timing,
never overstepping the role he would have you play.

The Courage to be Average

Let us not become weary in doing good, for at the
proper time we will reap a harvest if we do not give up.

GALATIANS 6:9

You'd probably agree that today Pastor Jon Egan is one of the best songwriters on the planet. But he wasn't always as good as he is now. In fact, he would tell you that the first hundred songs he wrote were nothing short of *terrible*. He refuses to sing them to this day.

Still, Jon wrote songs every day.

He kept at it, diligently working, until a songwriting harvest showed up.

He trained in secret so that one day, on the heels of the worst day in New Life's history, he could lead thousands of heartbroken people in the anthem he'd penned, "Overcome."

Do you know why most people never do anything great for God? It's because they lack the courage to be average, to be *in process*, to be trained. They want to zoom past so-so and get right to spectacular. They want to skip diligence to get to *dope*.

God is a god of process—remember?

He says, "Don't grow weary putting in the paces, the reps. I'm forming something in you here."

And at just the right time God will reap a harvest in us—that is, if we don't give up.

A BLESSING FROM PAM

May you trust God's timing in your life today, never rushing him,
never questioning his process, never pushing to get your own way.

True Love

For God so loved the world that he gave his one and only Son,
that whoever believes in him shall not perish but have eternal life.

JOHN 3:16

It's the most famous verse in all of Scripture, the most memorized verse in Scripture, the verse that shows up on posters at every pro football game every played: "For God so loved the world that he gave his one and only Son, that whoever believes in him shall not perish but have eternal life." And while these words are deeply meaningful to most believers, they would have meant even more to the culture that received them first.

In the ancient world, Greeks saw love as a tool, as a weapon, as a means for pursuing selfish gain. Virtues were used to create personal heroes—in politics, in the military, in the world of entertainment, and more. This use of the concept of "love" for something other than garnering individual fame would have come as a real surprise to them. This idea would have blown their minds.

And yet there it stands, God exhibiting love not so that individuals can flourish, but so that a community can be gathered in his name.

The world is fed up with individuals who do things only to serve themselves. The world can sniff out selfishness; the world can smell a fraud. What the world is looking for right now is a new imagination, a new kind of community, a community that's formed around love.

The minute we elevate divine love to our highest priority, we'll see people coming to Jesus in droves.

A BLESSING FROM PAM

May you receive the love of your Father today,
and may you dispense it to those you meet.

In the End

Train up a child in the way he should go,
Even when he grows older he will not abandon it.

PROVERBS 22:6 NASB

I didn't know the couple, but God had given me a word for them. I walked over there to them and said, "If you're open to it, I feel impressed by the Holy Spirit to tell you something."

They said they were.

"A prodigal in your life is about to come home."

Tears sprang immediately to both sets of eyes. What I didn't know was that their daughter had just returned home after eight years of being away from them. She'd said she didn't want anything to do with them and then left with a rodeo star. But once on the road, he dumped her for someone else, and her life spiraled downward from there.

While I was listening to this story, a young woman sheepishly approached. "I'm the prodigal," she said.

I smiled and gave her a side hug. "I've got good news for you," I said. "I was the prodigal, too. From age sixteen to age twenty-two, I ran away from God. He'd called me into ministry, and I wanted nothing to do with that. I ran, I hid, and I broke all ten of the commandments except for murder."

I began to explain to her what the good news of the gospel involved, saying that God had his hand on her life and had a purpose for her to fulfill. Her parents beamed the entire time I spoke.

As parents we believe that our kids will grow up loving Jesus and will never stray from his way of life. But the reality is that even the kids who grow up in amazing homes with devoted parents will have to choose for themselves who they'll surrender to, day by day.

This counsel from Solomon in Proverbs 22:6 is filled with tension. We all love the first part: "Train up a child in the way he should go," it says, to which we say, "Yes! There is a way my kid should go, and I'm going to make sure he knows exactly what it is."

But then there's that comma. And we collectively hold our breath.

"Yeah? Yeah? We do our part with our kids and then ... what? *What can we expect?*"

So many parents have lost heart right there in that pause. *We did what we were supposed to do!* they think. And yet still their kids fell away.

If you need assurance today as a parent, please stick around for what follows that pause. Because here we are given a guarantee that our work is never in vain. The result of good, godly training? It's that "even when he grows older he will not abandon it."

I wish I could tell you that this guarantee always came immediately following the training, that there would never be a prodigal situation to pray and fret about. It simply isn't the case.

But this much I know: our kids will finish the way that we started them. They will honor their training in the end.

A BLESSING FROM PAM

May you take heart, mamas and daddies, that your children
will return to their training, that they will honor the Lord with their lives.

The Worth of You

*Do you not know that your bodies are temples of
the Holy Spirit, who is in you, whom you have received
from God? You are not your own.*

1 CORINTHIANS 6:19

For thousands of years the Jewish people associated God's presence with a building—a physical place, a tent, a tabernacle, a temple. But God was after their hearts, and proximity was key to that goal being met. He wanted intimacy. Face-to-face connection. An in-person deal. And so he would come closer—much, much closer to them.

After leaving the Dallas-Fort Worth area to come to Colorado Springs, friends I'd talked to multiple times daily I now spoke with twice per month. Makes intimacy a little tough. Which was exactly God's point. Granted, we cannot see God. But we surely can relate with him. We can come near to him. We can sit and talk with him. We can share intimacy with him because he is here. He is here inside of us. He has taken up residence in our hearts.

A BLESSING FROM PAM

*May you make time today to bask in God's presence. He is with you.
He is inside you. He is near.*

What Brings About Our Demise

*For everything in the world—the lust of the flesh, the lust
of the eyes, and the pride of life—comes not from
the Father but from the world.*

1 JOHN 2:16

If you're a sports fan, then you know that the greatest teams don't do everything well. Rather, they do a few things better than anyone else. They practice those things time and again until nobody can beat them when they run those particular plays. On game day, their competitor knows full well which plays they're going to run, yet *still* they can't take them down. Why? Because they've fine-tuned those three or four things to the point that they run perfectly every time.

Satan works like that.

In this verse, you and I are handed Satan's strategy: lust of the flesh, lust of the eyes, pride of life. Money. Power. Sex. We know the plays before he runs them, and we *still* get taken down.

Read the history of Napoleon, Alexander the Great, every American president we've had, the greatest female leaders the world has known, and to a person you'll see these strategies at work making their life a living hell.

If we want to stop playing into Satan's hand, a simple place to start is being on guard whenever any of these three things is at work: Money. Power. Sex. Tread lightly on these three roads.

A BLESSING FROM PAM

May you be wise to Satan's schemes today.
May you refuse to help him win.

Lone Cowgirl at a Princess Party

For we are God's handiwork, created in Christ Jesus to do
good works, which God prepared in advance for us to do.

EPHESIANS 2:10

When Callie was five years old, Pam bought her a beautiful princess gown to wear to a birthday tea party Callie had been invited to. Moments before Pam was due to drive Callie to the party, my daughter emerged in her princess gown with tears streaming down her face. "It's itchy," she said through sobs.

Pam fixed the problem by having Callie put on a tee-shirt underneath the dress, but still, the child was not happy. More tears. More whining. More angst.

"I don't want to be a princess," Callie finally said. Stupid me said, "But all the other little girls will have on princess gowns."

Insightful Pam said, "You want to be a cowgirl, don't you."

Callie returned five minutes later clad in cowgirl boots and hat, with a pink bandanna tied around her neck. "I'm ready to go, Dad!" she cheered.

A picture was snapped at that party that I have framed on my office bookshelves. It's of fifteen princesses and one cowgirl, and it always reminds me of Ephesians 2. We are God's workmanship, created by him to be exactly as we are. We need not apologize for ourselves. We need not change ourselves. We need only to live as God would have us to live.

A BLESSING FROM PAM

May you love the you that God has created you to be today,
nothing more and nothing less.

Look-Alikes

*See what great love the Father has lavished on us, that we should
be called children of God! And that is what we are!*

1 JOHN 3:1

My dad passed away in 2005, but when he was alive—and especially when I was a teenager—I distinctly remember thinking that I wouldn't be like him when I grew up. He was a great dad—that wasn't the issue. It's just that when you're a punk kid, you think you know it all. You're just sure you won't be like your parents someday.

I came across some old photos several years ago that took my breath away. I was forty-seven at the time. In the photos my dad was forty-seven, and you would have thought I was staring into a mirror, for the similarities we possessed. This is what happens in families all the time: we start talking like each other. We start acting like each other. We start eating like each other. We start looking like each other, too. We are designed to reflect our parenting, and here God is saying, "I'm your parent now."

To be in God's family is to start looking and acting like God. It's to start being like God in all his greatness and glory. It's to be instantly associated with him.

I can think of no better news to share with you, honestly.

Hang around God, and you'll start being just like him.

A BLESSING FROM PAM

May you be proud of your family ties today as a beloved child of God.

OCTOBER

"The reason we can quit striving
in this earthly existence is that
what we're looking for we've
already found. As believers,
we fit in with Jesus. We'll
always fit in with him."

- Pastor Brady Boyd -

Another's Battle

Therefore let us stop passing judgment on one another.
Instead, make up your mind not to put any stumbling block
or obstacle in the way of a brother or sister.

ROMANS 14:13

What are you struggling with today?

You may not be struggling with debt today, but someone you know probably is. You may not be struggling with an addiction to alcohol or pornography today, but someone you know probably is. You may not be struggling to overcome depression and finally get out of bed today, but someone you know probably is. We could keep going down the list, but the point would be the same: just because you aren't battling a particular demon doesn't mean that nobody is engaged in that fight.

Here, the apostle Paul reminds us to be gentle with those around us. "Be kind," author Ian Maclaren once said, "for everyone you meet is fighting a hard battle."[1] We're not to stand in judgment of other people, assuming we know the full story there. We're not to add fuel to anyone's raging fire. We should be careful not to multiply another's struggle, and the way we get that done is by being kind. By being loving. By being *generous* with our actions and words. So, in the choices we make regarding attire and beverage and attitude and recreational activity, we should think not just of ourselves but of all who are affected by us.

A BLESSING FROM PAM

May you be a blessing today instead of a burden.
May you deal tenderly with everyone you meet.

---

[1] "Ian Maclaren > Quotes > Quotable Quote," Goodreads, n.d.,
goodreads.com/quotes/436360-be-kind-for-everyone-you-meet-is-fighting-a-hard.

Activating Our Love

If anyone has material possessions and sees a brother or sister in
need but has no pity on them, how can the love of God be in that person?
Dear children, let us not love with words or speech but with actions and in truth.

1 JOHN 3:17-18

The biggest lie that we tell in church is, "I'll pray for you." Generally when we say, "I'll pray for you," what we mean is, "This conversation is over."

God expects more of us.

In this passage we learn that when we come across someone who is in real need, lip service won't suffice. God wants us to *get involved*.

Instead of telling someone you'll pray for them, pray with them now.

Instead of saying, "Let me know how I can help," act on that offer and *help*.

Instead of wishing someone well and walking away, *walk with them* through this challenging time.

A BLESSING FROM PAM

May you love today not with words, but with actions,
as you follow the promptings of God.

Count Us In

Religion that God our Father accepts as pure and faultless is this: to look after orphans and widows in their distress and to keep oneself from being polluted by the world.

JAMES 1:27

Years ago I sat across from a city official who said, "Brady, we have eight hundred moms right now in El Paso County who are the working poor. They go to work every day and are upstanding citizens, but they live in their cars with their children at night. We need the church to get involved."

I didn't need to pray about anything. I didn't need to go on a four-day fast to discern what to do. "Count us in," I said, having no idea how we would help.

Our congregation began praying for these moms and their daughters and sons, trusting that God would bring us exactly the opportunities he wanted for us to seize. We opened a medical clinic for under-insured women. We purchased and renovated an apartment complex so that those families would have actual beds to sleep in each night. We began a life-skills-training program to help those women improve their skills and hopefully get better jobs. And it all happened because we determined in our hearts to live out James 1:27 in Colorado Springs.

When we care for widows and orphans, our work will be acceptable by God. There are many unknowns in this life that you and I are living, but that statement will always be true.

A BLESSING FROM PAM

May you see women and children in their distress today.
May you refresh your commitment to lighten the burden they bear.

When Not to Give

... being confident of this, that he who began a good work in you will carry it on to completion until the day of Christ Jesus.

PHILIPPIANS 1:6

Pam and I love to give. Because you're part of New Life Church, you probably love to give too. Our church is wildly generous, which I know delights the heart of God. It's also why I always find it odd when God prompts me *not* to give, when he says, "Hang back, Brady. I'm up to something here."

The last time this happened was when I'd noticed a couple that needed money for rent. Reflexively I wanted to jump in and help relieve their burden a bit. I prayed about what to do, but truthfully it was kind of a throw-away prayer. I'd already decided to help.

God stopped me short. The prompting I felt was this: "Brady, I love your generous heart, but I'm doing something in that couple's life. If you give them money right now, it will shortcut my efforts to grow them up. Do not give. Their struggles are temporary, but if you bail them out, those struggles could become permanent over time. Stand down."

On occasions such as this one I am reminded of God's promise recorded by Paul in Philippians 1:6. For believers, God is always at work to shape us and sharpen us, to grow us up in his likeness, to finish what he started in our hearts. He is our good Shepherd. We can trust him to lead us where we're meant to go.

So, yes: always encourage other people. Always root for their success. But be careful not to interrupt God's divine activity to shape and sharpen others too.

A BLESSING FROM PAM

May you stay in step with the Spirit of God today, mindful that he is not called to bless our activity. We are called to be blessings in his.

To Know and be Known

So speak encouraging words to one another. Build up hope so you'll
all be together in this, no one left out, no one left behind.

1 THESSALONIANS 5:11 MSG

Every weekend at New Life, we spend a few minutes greeting each other during the worship service, and despite the deep respect for the practices of singing songs to God and reading the Scriptures together and taking Communion, week in and week out that time of greeting might just be the most important thing we do. Jesus has called us to be on mission together—as one unit, which he calls his Bride—and if we don't know each other, we won't care for each other, and our unity will collapse on itself.

At our North campus, we call our main auditorium the Living Room. It's a name I've always loved. When I think about the living room in my house, I think about family and close friends gathering to talk and play games and laugh. It's a welcoming place. It's a relaxing place. It's a place of intimacy, familiarity, and warmth. Which is exactly how church should be.

In the same way that you'd never allow someone to hang out in your living room at home without engaging that person in conversation to learn about their experience in life, don't let someone hang out in our Living Room at church without committing to doing the same. Treat your section like it's your house and those two hundred people like they're your neighbors and friends. Reach out. Dig deep. Ask a question. Extend a hand. Speak encouragement. Offer hope. Be good to them.

This is how we become a family.

This is how we stay on mission as one.

A BLESSING FROM PAM

May you risk getting to know someone new this weekend.
May you also risk being known.

Generous, Just Like God

In everything I did, I showed you that by this kind of hard work we must help the weak, remembering the words the Lord Jesus himself said: "It is more blessed to give than to receive."

ACTS 20:35

Every time God responds to human beings, it is through the practice of generosity.

When he created the natural world for us to enjoy, that was generosity at work.

When he sent his Son to die on a cross, that was generosity at work.

When Jesus accomplished his mission and achieved grace for humankind, that was generosity at work.

When God invited you and me through his Son's sacrifice to relate to him for all eternity, that was generosity at work.

The reason it is more blessed to give than to receive isn't merely because we experience an emotional high upon doing so, though that can often be the case.

It's because when we give, we are emulating our heavenly Father. We are quite literally becoming more like him.

A BLESSING FROM PAM

May you focus more today on what you're giving than what you're getting.

Weak Faith

*" ... Truly I tell you, if you have faith as small as a mustard
seed, you can say to this mountain, 'Move from here to
there,' and it will move. Nothing will be impossible for you."*

MATTHEW 17:20B

If your faith feels weak today, I come to you bearing good news: You don't need strong faith to follow Christ.

Do you know that your heavenly Father already knows what you need for this day and is prepared to supply those things?

Do you know that God is absolutely fine with your coming timidly into his presence and owning the fact that you're weak?

Do you know that God promises to show himself strong in the midst of our weakness, to be our boldness when we've been leveled by life?

You do not need great faith to follow Jesus. In fact, if you have faith the size of even a mustard seed—small, seemingly incidental—you can whisper to the giant mountain you're facing, "Move. In Jesus' name, *move.*"

A BLESSING FROM PAM

*May you hide yourself today in the unsurpassed strength of your Father,
who loves to battle on your behalf.*

Telling Our Story

*Let the redeemed of the LORD tell their story—those he redeemed from the hand
of the foe, those he gathered from the lands, from east to west, from north and south.*

PSALM 107:2-3

If I were to come sit across from you right now and ask you to tell me your story of salvation, what story would you tell?

Would you tell me of being selfish and prideful, and then being totally humbled by God?

Would you tell me of being wracked by addiction, and then being shockingly and unexpectedly set free?

Would you tell me of being greedy and materialistic, and then learning true wealth is found only in Christ?

Would you tell me of being aimless, and then finding deeper purpose via a personal relationship with Jesus?

What is your story of divine rescue? What story would you tell?

"Let the redeemed of the LORD tell their story!" the psalmist declares. Why? Because we've been *freed*. From our sickness, our Savior healed us. From our sin, our Savior delivered us. From our hopelessness, our Savior reminded us that in him all hope is restored.

Jesus.

Jesus.

Jesus.

He's the theme of the most important story we'll ever tell.

A BLESSING FROM PAM

May you gather the courage to tell someone your story today.

Supernaturally Raised

*Children are a heritage from the LORD, offspring a reward
from him. Like arrows in the hands of a warrior are children born
in one's youth. Blessed is the man whose quiver is full of them. They
will not be put to shame when they contend with their opponents in court.*

PSALM 127:3-5

Once a month at New Life we dedicate babies to the leadership of the Lord, and it's a scene I never get tired of, an experience that touches me every time. Even the strongest, most self-sufficient women and men are brought low by the realities of parenting, and every month they step forward and say, "We can't do this thing on our own."

It is a powerful sight to watch four or five thousand people stretch out arms toward these families, symbolically saying, "We're here for you. We've got your back. We'll walk with you as you raise up these precious children. We'll faithfully fight for you as you faithfully fight for their hearts."

In Psalm 127 the psalmist describes children as "arrows in the hands of a warrior," and often when I'm watching those families dedicate their babies to God's family, I imagine how each boy, each girl, will someday fight for God's will and ways to spread through the world at large.

Whenever you walk past children at New Life, I invite you to silently pray the prayer we often pray on those dedication weekends: "God, please guide and direct those boys and girls so that they'll spend their lifetime devoted to you. Please give them wisdom to detect your way of righteousness daily, and courage to follow that path."

A BLESSING FROM PAM

*May you gain strength and encouragement today from
the innocence and vast potential of the children in your midst.*

Of Good Courage

*Have I not commanded you? Be strong and courageous. Do not
be afraid; do not be discouraged, for the LORD your God
will be with you wherever you go.*

JOSHUA 1:9

My mom is seventy-five years old, drives a pickup, and is ridiculously skillful with a chainsaw. A full-size chainsaw, too, not the dinky ones that Coloradans use. Awhile back, she returned home from a Wednesday night prayer meeting and found a five-foot Burmese python at her back door. Now, I don't know what you would have done in that situation, but my mom did what any other East Texan woman would do: she headed into the garage, grabbed a garden hoe, headed right for that snake, and lopped its head off. She then threw the body into the lake behind her house, clapped the dust off her hands, and headed inside to go to bed.

She relayed that story to me the following day, explaining that (sorry, reptile lovers) the "only good snake is a dead snake," to which I said, "Mom, if only you knew how to use the camera feature on your phone, you would be an absolute Internet sensation today!"

"Pffft," she said. "That'll teach people to keep a better eye on their pets."

Say what you will about my mom's level of compassion for stray snakes. What you can't dispute is that the woman is *fearless*. My whole life, she's had courage to spare. Which is exactly how God wants us to approach challenges in this life, as though his power is a weapon in our hands.

The next time you're tempted to be afraid, I want you to remember this fact: When you fix your eyes on Jesus, it's impossible to fixate on fear as well. When you're afraid, remember God's power. Fix your gaze on his immutable strength.

A BLESSING FROM PAM

*May your efforts be divinely empowered today,
as you trust God to show himself strong.*

Choosing to Forgive

"For if you forgive other people when they sin against you, your heavenly Father will also forgive you. But if you do not forgive others their sins, your Father will not forgive your sins."

MATTHEW 6:14-15

In our culture today, it's a rare thing to see someone forgive a wrong done. Instead, we've caved to a cancel culture, where if you goof up, you're ostracized from society—digitally for sure, but sometimes literally, too. You're pushed out of the professional and social circles you once enjoyed and are for all intents and purposes dead.

This is not the way of Christ.

Jesus said during his Sermon on the Mount that if we would forgive people who sinned against us, then his Father would forgive us, too. The inverse was also true: if we withheld forgiveness from those who wronged us, our Father would withhold forgiveness from us.

This instruction is so straightforward that it is nearly impossible to mistake.

We either get serious about practicing forgiveness, or else we stand to be eternally ostracized from God.

We either commit ourselves to learning to *reflexively* forgive, or else we forfeit fullness of intimacy with Christ.

Who do you need to forgive today?

Who are you withholding forgiveness from?

Today is the day to make that right.

A BLESSING FROM PAM

May you release another from wrongdoing today.
May you totally and completely forgive.

How to Love Your Enemies

If you love those who love you, what reward will you get?

MATTHEW 5:46A

Whenever I preach on this idea of loving our enemies, I can all but hear the scoffing in the room. Here's what the scoffers are silently saying to me:

Yeah, right. Love them? If only you knew what they did ...

Listen, Pastor Brady, there's a reason they're my enemy. This is their doing, not mine.

I'll love them the minute they act lovingly toward me.

Who is your enemy today? Who has wronged you and refused to make things right? Who has offended you? Who has slandered you with no trace of regret? Who has wrecked your reputation without remorse?

Got someone in mind?

I want you to pray blessing for that person.

I'm not kidding here. I'll wait.

Here's what you can say:

"Heavenly Father, I pray that you will bless _____ and keep _____ and make your face to shine upon _____ and give _____ your perfect peace today. I pray that _____ will make wise decisions today. I pray that _____ will be shown love today. I pray that _____ will grow in Christlikeness today. I pray that _____ will sense your presence in a beautiful, powerful way."

You can't hate the people you're praying for.

So pray. And pray. And pray.

A BLESSING FROM PAM

May you loosen your grip on your annoyance
and anger and pick up divine love instead.

The Heart You're Responsible For

Above all else, guard your heart, for
everything you do flows from it.

PROVERBS 4:23

One of the lessons we all learn as we get older is that we simply can't change other people. This is as it should be. It's difficult enough to change ourselves; what business do we have venturing out?

What this means is that we cannot control anyone else's habits.

We cannot control anyone else's motivations.

We cannot control anyone else's decisions.

We cannot control anyone else's health.

We cannot control anyone else's attitudes.

We cannot control anyone else's assumptions.

We cannot control anyone else's actions.

We cannot control anyone else's reactions.

We cannot control what anyone chooses to say.

And we cannot control the purity of anyone else's heart.

Here is what we can control, based on Solomon's wisdom in the verse above: We can take responsibility for the state of our own heart, ensuring that it is clean and whole and centered on Christ.

We can guard it as though life itself depends on its health.

Because life itself does depend on its health.

A BLESSING FROM PAM

May you faithfully guard your heart today,
prioritizing that singular task above all else.

By God's Spirit

So he said to me, "This is the word of the LORD to Zerubbabel:
'Not by might nor by power, but by my Spirit,' says the LORD Almighty."

ZECHARIAH 4:6

Not long ago, I was asked to help resolve a dispute among a group of people, to be a referee of sorts. I traveled to the city where the situation was unfolding, I listened carefully to both sides, and I prayed through my thoughts and opinions, not wanting to botch the deal or speak out of turn.

This was to be a two-day session, and as I sat in my hotel room on the first night, having been with the two groups for many hours that day, I wracked my brain searching for wisdom, looking for clarity regarding what I believed.

And then God spoke.

It wasn't an audible voice, but it might as well have been. "Brady," I sensed him saying, "sometimes human effort isn't enough."

I couldn't help but grin. Of course, God was totally right.

When we face an untenable situation, our reflexive response is to conjure every possible solution, accounting for every eventuality, every angle, every aim. But roughly 100 percent of the time, I find that if I will simply take my hands off the steering wheel and slide into the passenger seat, God is perfectly capable of navigating the treacherous road I couldn't get my tires to grip.

Only God knows best how his work will be accomplished. We do well to entrust outcomes to him. Waiting on God's wisdom takes great faith on our part. God always responds kindly to faith.

A BLESSING FROM PAM

May you rest in God's wisdom today.
May you act only on what he prompts you to do.

The Jesus We Need

*When they brought the colt to Jesus and threw their cloaks over
it, he sat on it. Many people spread their cloaks on the road, while
others spread branches they had cut in the fields. Those who
went ahead and those who followed shouted, "Hosanna!
Blessed is he who comes in the name of the Lord!"*

MARK 11:7-9

When our kids were young, Pam and I took them to Disney World a few times, and on each visit, a favorite pastime was to sit outside at some restaurant on Main Street in the afternoon and watch all the little-girl meltdowns that invariably occurred. Because from about one p.m. until five p.m., every girl age three to eight who woke that morning with dreams of being a princess was absolutely coming unglued.

One afternoon after a full day of rides and food and sweltering Florida heat, our family took the shuttle bus that carts you from the theme park back to your hotel, and seated across from me was a little girl with a glazed-over look. Her hair was ratty. Her Cinderella tiara was askew. She had strawberry ice cream caked on her cheeks and chin. And she was holding a giant lollipop—not licking it, mind you, but rather staring at it blankly, as though contemplating whether she had the energy to bring it to her lips.

Why doesn't Disney show this picture in their marketing materials, I thought, *and save hard-working parents six hundred bucks a day?*

In first-century Jerusalem, the nation Israel firmly believed that their Messiah would be bringing Disney World to them. They thought that this Jesus would be the fulfillment of all their desires. But then they saw him arriving—on a young donkey, no less—and feared that things were about to head south.

Donkeys were only good for a leisurely stroll. *Horses* were made for war.

To the chagrin of every Israelite alive at the time, their long-awaited Messiah had no intentions of assuming political power. No, his mission was far broader than that. He'd come not to wage war, but to usher in peace. Not to flex his military might, but to demonstrate humility. Not to incite a radical revolution, but to whisper an invitation instead: "Would you like to be set free? I have come to set you free."

The Hebrew knew what they wanted in Jesus, but God had a much different plan.

God gave them the Jesus they needed.

He remains the Jesus we need.

We can be set free, if that's what we're after.

We can live free—free, indeed.

A BLESSING FROM PAM

Today, may you relinquish your illusions of what
Jesus should be and receive who he is instead.

Who's Shaping Whom?

And we all, who with unveiled faces contemplate the Lord's glory,
are being transformed into his image with ever-increasing
glory, which comes from the Lord, who is the Spirit.

2 CORINTHIANS 3:18

Several years ago while in the UK, I found myself inside an ornate chapel on whose walls were painted fifty or so nativity scenes. Mary and Joseph and Jesus as Guatemalans. Mary and Joseph and Jesus as Chinese. Mary and Joseph and Jesus as Ugandans. And my favorite: Mary and Joseph and Jesus as Aussies, complete with kangaroos at their side.

The point: In every culture, they had tried to make Jesus look like them. Which perhaps explains why in Western countries, Jesus has always shown up with blonde hair and blue eyes.

This might be the right time to confirm that Jesus was not from Norway. He was from the Middle East.

We all want Jesus to look like we look. To eat what we eat. To vote like we vote. To prize the same things that we prize. Unfortunately, this isn't the case. Jesus did not come so that he could be transformed into our likeness. He came so that we could be transformed into his.

A BLESSING FROM PAM

May you seek to be conformed
to Jesus today.

Make Jesus Easy to Find

*Jesus entered the temple courts and drove out all who were buying
and selling there. He overturned the tables of the money changers
and the benches of those selling doves. "It is written," he said
to them, "'My house will be called a house of prayer,'
but you are making it a 'den of robbers.'"*

MATTHEW 21:12-13

We know the verses. We're aware of the account. The question that remains is,
What made Jesus so mad?

As Matthew 21:12-13 tells it, Jesus entered the temple and erupted over what was
happening there. Money changers had set up shop in the outer court, something of
an ancient church lobby, there to help people who had come with their sacrifice of
a lamb or a bird to get the very best lamb or bird. "For a small fee," they'd heckle, "I
can get you the very best bird ... no issues, no blemishes, no spots."

Can you imagine coming to New Life for the first time and having to wade through
a veritable trade show of salespeople, each one looking to push goods on you?

At this point, it's easy to feel self-righteous, thinking, *I'd never do what they did.*

But we run the same risk as those money changers did, if we don't ever allow God
to tell us no.

Listen, Jesus did not come to make us comfortable. He came to disrupt us and free
us from sin. This often requires the turning-over of tables in our lives. This often
demands that we make it simpler for people to encounter the Son of God.

A BLESSING FROM PAM

*May you remove all barriers today for someone
who desperately needs to find Christ.*

Sanctified Through and Through

May God himself, the God of peace, sanctify you through and through.
May your whole spirit, soul and body be kept blameless at the
coming of our Lord Jesus Christ. The one who calls you is faithful, and he will do it.

1 THESSALONIANS 5:23-24

Christianity is a terrible hobby.

When you follow Jesus, you experience a radical conversion. You ask for the Holy Spirit to come into your life. You take up your cross and follow Jesus. You live an altogether different life. You are marked. You are shaped. You are sanctified through and through.

Hanging in my office is a quote attributed to sixteenth-century explorer, politician, and theologian Sir Francis Drake. Drake was a terrible human being for much of his life. He was a pirate, a slave trader, generally regarded as a thug. But then he met Jesus and went through a wholesale transformation. He came face to face with God and never returned to the man he once was.

During those later years, he wrote beautiful prayers, and my favorite of his says this:

Disturb us, Lord, when
We are too well pleased with ourselves,
When our dreams have come true
Because we have dreamed too little,
When we arrived safely
Because we sailed too close to the shore.

Disturb us, Lord, when
With the abundance of things we possess
We have lost our thirst
For the waters of life;
Having fallen in love with life,
We have ceased to dream of eternity
And in our efforts to build a new earth,
We have allowed our vision
Of the new Heaven to dim.

Disturb us, Lord, to dare more boldly,
To venture on wider seas
Where storms will show your mastery;
Where losing sight of land,
We shall find the stars.
We ask You to push back
The horizons of our hopes;
And to push into the future
In strength, courage, hope, and love.

This is exactly the kind of robust life that God is calling you and me to live—not to a boring, methodical existence but to an unpredictable adventure with him. Your relationship with Jesus isn't something you sprinkle over your current life, but rather the bedrock of holiness that affects everything you say and do.

A BLESSING FROM PAM

May you dream of eternity's reality today,
letting it affect your every pursuit.

Joined on the Journey

*Now that same day two of them were going to a village called
Emmaus, about seven miles from Jerusalem. They were talking
with each other about everything that had happened. As they talked
and discussed these things with each other, Jesus himself came up
and walked along with them; but they were kept from recognizing him.*

LUKE 24:13-16

Following Jesus' resurrection he appeared to two of his disciples as they were walking to a town just outside of Jerusalem. He'd been through a radical experience: death on a cross, three days in a tomb, divinely being raised from the dead. Had I been his PR manager, I'd have scheduled him for far more important things. But there he was, on the road to Emmaus, engaging two totally unsuspecting men in conversation.

The scene is a little bit creepy, if you ask me. Imagine that you're walking along a road with a friend of yours, when suddenly an unknown person appears by your side. He asks you what you're talking about, as though he's been invited to hang there with you. You'd probably side-eye your friend a look that said, "Uh, just curious, who's the dude?"

It wouldn't be until the men made it to their destination and broke bread with other believers that their eyes would be opened to who Jesus was. "It's true!" they'd cheer. "The Lord is risen!" (v. 34). They'd encountered the living Christ.

I envision this turn of events from time to time, remembering that wherever our journey takes us, Jesus has chosen to join us there. When we're wrestling, when we're disputing, when we're confused, and when we're at peace, Jesus has decided to be *right there*, to help us continue on the path that God's paved.

A BLESSING FROM PAM

*May you look up from your circumstances today
and see Jesus there by your side.*

Letting Our Words Be Few

And when you pray, do not keep on babbling like pagans,
for they think they will be heard because of their many words.

MATTHEW 6:7

If you're a parent, then you know that whenever your kids want something, they tend to overwhelm you with words. In our home, we call it the "sales pitch," and it's exhausting every time. *Stooooop*, I always want to yell. *I got it. I get that you want this thing.*

I think that sometimes God feels the same way.

I already know what you're going to ask me. I don't need more words. I just need your earnest heart.

When it comes to prayer, it's not the quantity of words that counts. It's the *sincerity* he's looking for.

That is all I have to say.

A BLESSING FROM PAM

May your words today be few.

From God's Generous Hand

Jesus said to them, "Very truly I tell you, it is not Moses who has given you the bread from heaven, but it is my Father who gives you the true bread from heaven. For the bread of God is the bread that comes down from heaven and gives life to the world."

JOHN 6:32

When that city official I mentioned earlier told me about the eight hundred families living in cars every night, it was obvious that despite our valiant efforts with the renovated apartment complex, we weren't going to be able to solve the whole problem in one fell swoop. Caring for that many families would necessitate hundreds of millions of dollars—money that New Life didn't have.

I was driving across the parking lot one afternoon and called out to the Lord. "Father, if you will give us the resources, we will help get those families off the streets."

We could be trusted. We would be faithful. We would be part of the solution, if only God would provide.

What if I have already given you the resources you need?

Huh? I drove to the back side of the property and stopped at the far southeast corner. There. That was the answer I sought.

Back in the day, our parking lot was laid out with the assumption that we'd have seven thousand people in our building at one time. On our highest-attendance Sunday, we run five, which means that a lot of parking spaces perpetually go unused. I thought about the ancient practice of farmers leaving the corners of their fields unharvested so that people who were hungry could come pick and eat the spare food. Were our parking-lot corners our "gleanings," areas we could develop for turning a profit so that we could care for those in need?

We look to human ingenuity for solutions, but God says, "look to me."

It is the Father who supplies bread from heaven. It is the Father whose hand provides.

A BLESSING FROM PAM

May you look not to your own clever solutions today, instead trusting God to direct your steps.

The Best Place to Be

However, I consider my life worth nothing to me; my only aim is to finish
the race and complete the task the Lord Jesus has given me—the
task of testifying to the good news of God's grace.

ACTS 20:24

My favorite thing to do during the Summer Olympics is to watch the marathoners complete their race. I don't love watching the entire three-and-a-half hours of coverage, you understand, but when it comes to those last few meters, I'm glued to the screen. In most cities, the marathon finishes inside a giant stadium that is packed with family members and sports fans cheering on the runners. And as the leader enters the stadium, the entire place erupts in praise. That runner senses all that enthusiasm as has fresh legs for finishing the final laps.

Similarly, you are I are running a race—not a physical one, but a spiritual one. And while economic downturns and housing crashes and global pandemics and wild inflation threaten to trip us up, in Christ Jesus we are destined to finish that race strong.

Whenever you're tempted to cave to the unfortunate circumstances life tends to present, I want you to think of that marathoner entering the stadium, legs pumping as the race concludes. You and I both want to be like that runner: gaze skyward, chest confident, stride long. Do you hear that applause? It's Jesus, reminding us that victory has already been secured in him. Keep running, believer, keep running. Now is not the time to give up.

A BLESSING FROM PAM

May you be given the strength you need today
to continue on righteousness's path.

A Great Cloud Indeed

Therefore, since we are surrounded by such a great cloud of witnesses,
let us throw off everything that hinders and the sin that so easily entangles.

HEBREWS 12:1A

It's been well over a decade since I lost my dad, but still today I sense his presence whenever I'm feeling a little less than strong. I don't get any visions of him. I don't hear his audible voice. It's nothing creepy like that—just an awareness, just a feeling, just a sense. Here is what that sense says: "Others have gone before you, Brady, who saw fit to stay the course. You don't have to bail just because things are hard right now. You can throw off hindrances as fast as they show up."

In this verse the writer of Hebrews assures us that as believers you and I have a whole gathering of fellow Christians who are watching us from above. They are encouraging us to persist in the faith. To keep going in life. To follow Jesus with all that we've got.

This is a timely reminder for you and me. We need not sink under the weight of sin and strain; we can toss those things aside. We need not fall prey to the entanglements of this temporal existence; we can keep running, keep moving ahead.

A BLESSING FROM PAM

May you be renewed today in your belief
that you are victorious over every last sin.

A Place for You and Me

*"Do not let your hearts be troubled. You believe in God; believe also in me.
My Father's house has many rooms; if that were not so, would I have
told you that I am going there to prepare a place for you? And if I
go and prepare a place for you, I will come back and take
you to be with me that you also may be where I am."*

JOHN 14:1-3

You and I exhaust endless energy in our day-to-day lives trying to fit into a world we were never meant to permanently inhabit. Even the speediest scroll through your social-media feed will assure you of this fact. We primp and pose and posture and post, all the while hoping that we'll be found worthy, that we'll be seen as important, that we'll finally fit in.

I'm here to tell you the effort is futile.

We're not *supposed* to fit in.

Much has been written on heaven and what we'll find there when we finally arrive. And while I'm sure the streets of gold will be fantastic and seeing all those angels will be cool, there is only one thing I'm anticipating in eternity: the never-ending presence of Jesus Christ.

I want to be where Jesus is. I want to see him face-to-face. I want to tuck myself into his sufficiency and exhale all worldly concerns.

John tells us in this passage that the reason we can quit striving in this earthly existence is because what we're looking for we've already found. As believers, we fit in with Jesus. We will always fit in with him.

Relax, Christian.

Quit seeking the approval you've already perfectly gained.

Jesus has graciously made room for you. You're good. You're beloved. You're in.

A BLESSING FROM PAM

*May you catch this idea today and never let it go: in Jesus,
all striving ceases. In him, we're eternally home.*

Belief versus Behavior

For the Son of Man is going to come in his Father's glory
with his angels, and then he will reward each person
according to what they have done.

MATTHEW 16:27

There has been longstanding confusion in Christian circles regarding what exactly will happen to us when we leave this earthly life and enter eternity with God. Here in Matthew 16, we see that we will be rewarded according to what we have done, and even though I've never seen the word "rewarded" used as a synonym for *punishment*, some believers have grown concerned that upon reaching God's glorious presence, bad news will be waiting for them.

This is not what will happen to us.

Let me back up a step and explain.

Your belief—and that alone—determines your eternal destination. "If you declare with your mouth, 'Jesus is Lord,'" Romans 10:9 says, "and believe in your heart that God raised him from the dead, you will be saved." Furthermore, in 2 Corinthians 5:8 Paul says, "We are confident, I say, and would prefer to be away from the body and at home with the Lord." So, for the believer, heaven is guaranteed.

That much, Christians are usually sure of.

It's the next part that trips them up: belief determines destination, but *behavior* determines reward. How you act does not affect your salvation, but it does alter how sweet that homecoming will be when you finally see your Lord.

So, yes: spend your time wisely, rightly assess the motivations of your heart, speak works that build up instead of tear down, seek to serve instead of being served. Do all that you can to live like Jesus, not so that you can earn salvation, (you can't), but so that you can relish the rewards he longs to bestow.

A BLESSING FROM PAM

May your salvation prompt life-giving responses in you today,
as you joyously give and serve.

Deeper Into God's Kingdom

"You're blessed when your commitment to God provokes persecution. The persecution drives you even deeper into God's kingdom. Not only that—count yourselves blessed every time people put you down or throw you out or speak lies about you to discredit me. What it means is that the truth is too close for comfort and they are uncomfortable. You can be glad when that happens—give a cheer, even!—for though they don't like it, I do! And all heaven applauds. And know that you are in good company. My prophets and witnesses have always gotten into this kind of trouble."

MATTHEW 5:10-12 MSG

I don't know how your commitment to God is showing up in your life these days, but if you're serious about following Jesus, I guarantee that it is.

You may be so committed to coming to church on Sunday that you've had to tell your boss or teacher that you're not available on that day.

You may be so serious about tithing that you've had to decline invitations to go out with friends.

You may be so fired up about how God has transformed your life that you're now being accused of "toxic optimism."

Jesus is clear throughout the New Testament that if we are going to follow him, we *will* be persecuted. We *will* be insulted. We *will* be ridiculed. He also is clear that the net effect of enduring these things is that we will be divinely *blessed*.

The next time you are mocked for your Christian beliefs, remember the long, arduous journey Jesus took to the cross, the Road of Suffering he was made to walk.

He knows how it feels to be scorned.

He's cheering you on even now.

A BLESSING FROM PAM

May you proudly step ever deeper into God's kingdom,
as you sacrifice all for him.

The Best Part of Your Life's Story

*"I am the Alpha and the Omega," says the Lord God, "who is,
and who was, and who is to come, the Almighty."*

REVELATION 1:8

We tend to think about life as a story—our story. We start new "chapters" of that story whenever we graduate from school, or get married or become parents, or begin a new business venture, or move to a new city. When we meet people and start getting to know them, we tend to define ourselves according to these various chapters, to the story we've crafted about our lives.

But for the believer, the best part of our life's story is that we're part of an even bigger story than that. We're part of God's story, which has been unfolding long before we arrived on the scene.

God always has been.

God always is.

God always will be.

And by his grace we are grafted into his story.

In his story, our stories make sense.

The next time you introduce yourself, start with the most important part: you met Jesus and gave your heart to him. His story is your story now.

A BLESSING FROM PAM

*As you consider your life may you consider Christ first,
your beginning and also your end.*

Jesus is Lord

Today in the town of David a Savior has been
born to you; he is the Messiah, the Lord.

LUKE 2:11

Like you, I've been through ages and stages with family and friends that make my heart leap into my throat. When my son was a new driver and was working, he'd often get home after dark. Just before he'd head out to his car each time, I said to him, "Abram, Jesus is Lord."

Years later, when Callie was trying to decide where to go to college and was up to her eyeballs in what-ifs, I said to her, "Jesus is Lord."

When a close friend had to walk through a terrible disease, I said to him, "Jesus is Lord."

When a colleague lost a parent unexpectedly, I said to her, "Jesus is Lord."

When my own heart would falter over the state of our nation, I said to myself, "Jesus is Lord."

And today, regardless of what is perplexing you, I say to you, "Jesus is Lord."

Sometimes we simply need to remind ourselves that Jesus, our Jesus, is Lord. He sees all. He knows all. He is above all.

We cannot control the world. But we can control whom we worship.

I choose to worship Jesus as Lord.

You can make that same choice today.

A BLESSING FROM PAM

May you take great comfort throughout your day
today that Jesus indeed is Lord.

Is Sin the Problem?

For the wages of sin is death, but the gift of
God is eternal life in Christ Jesus our Lord.

ROMANS 6:23

If you're like me, as you survey the landscape of our current culture you see problems on every side. You see families breaking apart. You see single moms unable to earn a living wage. You see kids struggling to find purpose in life. You see gender confusion creating anxiety in people of all ages. You see prominent leaders misusing their influence. On and on it goes.

To accept the culture's read on the situation is to be told that everything is just fine. As long as people are doing what they want to do, and as long as people are happy, and as long as people are being "true to themselves," well, then, what could be wrong with that?

Awhile back I had a revelation, which was that if we don't agree on what the problem is, we won't agree on the solution. If sin is not the problem, then the gospel is not the solution.

Which begs the question, *Is sin the problem here?*

The gospel is not here to make us feel good or to make us better people. The gospel is here to rescue us from the wages of sin, which is death.

Whenever you're tempted to let the problems we face leave you demoralized, disillusioned, and longing for a bit of hope, come back to the truth of the gospel, the solution we're dying for.

A BLESSING FROM PAM

May you take cover today under the protective wing of your Father.
In his presence, all problems get solved.

New Every Morning

*Because of the LORD's great love we are not consumed, for his compassions
never fail. They are new every morning; great is your faithfulness.*

LAMENTATIONS 3:22-23

If you do one thing today, let it be renewing your allegiance to God. We see
in Lamentations 3 that every single morning, God waits with compassion and
faithfulness in hand. He lingers, curious if we will show up, eager to know where
we stand. Christianity isn't like a retirement plan, where we can save up enough
to retire from God. No, no: each day that we are alive is a day when you and I
need grace. We need power. We need forgiveness. We need love.

And so we come to God tomorrow, and again the day after that. We say, "Father,
I need your presence today. I need your power. I need your grace."

We can't get by without these things. He knows this. And he loves to provide.

A BLESSING FROM PAM

*Today, may you receive the mercy
that God has in store for you.*

Secretly Faithful

*"Be careful not to practice your righteousness in front
of others to be seen by them. If you do, you will have no
reward from your Father in heaven."*

MATTHEW 6:1

I've long held the belief that when you and I get to heaven we will find a line of people being rewarded for things we never knew were being done. They will be the faithful followers of Jesus who served quietly, without praise.

They waited on a child with special needs morning, noon, and night, with no fanfare, no recognition, and no relief week after week.

They took in their elderly parents, monitoring their meds, helping with hygiene, loving them patiently, prioritizing their needs.

They cooked meals for families that were hungry. So many hours, so much money, so much care.

They will be there before the throne of their Father, eyes wet with gratitude and relief. They served well. They lived well. God knew it the entire time.

If you are serving in secret today, can I tell you something? God sees what you're doing, and he's proud. What a perfect reflection of Christ's love you are. What light in the darkness you've been.

Keep going, faithful servant. Keep caring as Jesus cared. The reward you'll receive in heaven is far better than any you could get down here.

A BLESSING FROM PAM

May you stay the course today, serving wherever God has asked you to serve.

NOVEMBER

"The greatest decision you'll
ever make is to devote yourself
to the Church, to plant your feet
among a group of people who are
wildly diverse and fantastically
messy. Stand with them. Eat
meals with them. Pray with
them. Love them well."

- Pastor Brady Boyd -

What God Intends

You intended to harm me, but God intended it for good to accomplish
what is now being done, the saving of many lives.

GENESIS 50:20

I still remember exactly how I was feeling on March 13, 2020, when government orders came down that we couldn't meet in person for worship services that weekend. None of us on staff knew how we were going to pull off online services, so a handful of us gathered on Saturday morning to sort things out. Standing in front of those cameras in a totally empty auditorium felt more than a little strange, and I couldn't help but wonder if we'd ever come together as a congregation again.

Now that things have largely resumed as they were pre-Covid, it seems a little melodramatic to write that, but in the moment we really didn't know what we were facing, or if things would ever feel normal again.

Those months when we were a virtual church were tough—there's no doubt about that. But God was on the move. Each week, upward of forty thousand people from thirty-five states and multiple countries watched our services online. Our team received countless calls and texts and letters from people who were making decisions for Christ. Weeks into this process I received an email from a man in St. Louis, Missouri, who had stumbled onto our service via a Facebook link. "Pastor Brady," he wrote, "I haven't attended a church service in twenty years, but for whatever reason last month I watched one of yours. And something happened in my heart. I've been watching you every Sunday, and I can feel myself changing. For the first time in my life, I'm open to God."

I shook my head in wonder, resolving in my heart to judge things more slowly in the future. Who knows what God's up to? Who knows what good he's bringing about?

A BLESSING FROM PAM

May you pause in the face of "unfortunate" situations
to ask God where he's at work.

Two Things God Seeks

Even in darkness light dawns for the upright, for those who are
gracious and compassionate and righteous. Good will come to those
who are generous and lend freely, who conduct their affairs with justice.

PSALM 112:4-5

Nobody sits around wishing for bad things to come to them, for evil to unfold. You and I both want good things for our lives, and here in Psalm 112, God (inspiring the words of the psalmist) tells us exactly what to do, to attract the goodness we seek.

First, we are to be generous people, people who lend freely. What this means is that when God allows resources to flow into our lives, he knows that he can trust us to steward them in a righteous way.

When God blesses your business financially, are you faithful to spend those additional monies in a way that honors him? Are you consistent about tithing to a local church? Do you stay out of debt, as Scripture exhorts us to do, so that you have margin in case of an emergency? Are you constantly looking for ways to help others out?

These are great questions to ask, when assessing how generous we are.

Here's the second thing we must do, if we want to attract goodness to our lives: we must be people of integrity.

Living with integrity simply means living an *integrated life*. It means we're the same people when we are in private as we are when others are around.

If you're in need of a little goodness today, you now know where to begin: practice generosity by extending a helping hand; and live with integrity today, upholding the same values whether people are watching or not.

A BLESSING FROM PAM

May you be supernaturally equipped today to live an integrated life,
and may you be as generous to others as God has been to you.

Choosing Freedom Instead

So if the Son sets you free, you will be free indeed.

JOHN 8:36

As the story goes, the wild monkeys were totally taking over the town. They were inundating local shops. They were ransacking village streets. They were dragging garbage from the cans they'd destroyed. They were generally just wreaking havoc on a frustrated South Asian town.

Interestingly, wild monkeys are tough to catch. They're relatively smart. They're super fast. And they tend to work in packs.

One villager had a brilliant solution. He drilled a hole in the base of a coconut, drained the coconut of its milk, and inserted a small piece of unwrapped candy. The hole was just big enough for a monkey to cram its hand into but no bigger. So when the monkey put his hand inside the coconut and made a fist around the candy, he couldn't get his hand back out.

What the monkey didn't know was that the villager had laced a rope through the other end of the coconut. As soon as the monkey took the bait, the villager pulled the cord, captured the monkey, and headed off to set another trap.

You and I look at that situation and think, *What a dumb monkey. I'd never hang onto something that was costing me my freedom.*

But not so fast: if we're not careful, we'll hold fast to that fear or worry or greed or addiction or propensity or fixation or doubt, and before we know it we too will be captured. Like those monkeys, we'll be enslaved.

The truth is that for the believer, freedom is ours. We don't have to beg for it or try to earn it. We have it, through Jesus Christ. The question that remains is, *Will you live as those who are free?*

Free people ought to always live free. Freedom is for those who are free.

A BLESSING FROM PAM

May you enjoy perfect freedom today.

Completely Restored

*Then I saw "a new heaven and a new earth," for the first
heaven and the first earth had passed away, and there was no
longer any sea. I saw the Holy City, the new Jerusalem, coming
down out of heaven from God, prepared as a bride beautifully
dressed for her husband. And I heard a loud voice from the
throne saying, "Look! God's dwelling place is now among the
people, and he will dwell with them. They will be his people, and
God himself will be with them and be their God."*

REVELATION 21:1-3

Growing up, my grandparents lived right across the street from us, and on
many occasions my grandfather would pick up my sister and brother and me
in his bright-red 1949 Ford pickup truck and drive us the three miles to the
little general store in town, where he'd buy us frosty root beers in those
thick glass bottles.

Recently I was scrolling through a car-restoration website that I like to look at
and stumbled upon a blog written by a man who was restoring a 1949 Ford
pickup. He said he'd found it in the middle of a pasture and that the whole thing
had been rusted out. A family of raccoons was probably living under the hood,
as wild animals are want to do. But when the man saw that truck, he didn't see
all that was wrong with it; he saw it in its perfect state.

He loaded it onto a trailer, hauled it to his shop, spent months fixing every last
problem, and was beaming in the picture on his website that showed the truck,
completely restored.

When John, who wrote the book of Revelation, looks at the world around him,
nothing is as it should be. He has been exiled to an island, where he lives as
a prisoner. The Roman government wants him dead. And he's separated—
perhaps permanently—from the churches he longs to serve.

But suddenly, in a divine vision, John sees things as they once will be. He sees
a beautifully restored creation. He sees everything working just as it should
work. He sees the Bride of Christ in all her radiance. He sees God and people,
living as one.

If things in your life aren't as they should be, I have good news for you today: better days are coming, and they are coming very soon. We will one day be freed from our pain and our groaning, and we will be cured of our every disease. We will enjoy unhindered intimacy with our Father, as he dwells with us and us with him.

A BLESSING FROM PAM

May you resolve to stay the course today, knowing
that any frustration you feel today is temporary at best.

Battles Yet to Fight

*When you were dead in your sins and in the uncircumcision of your flesh,
God made you alive with Christ. He forgave us all our sins, having
canceled the charge of our legal indebtedness, which stood against us
and condemned us; he has taken it away, nailing it to the cross. And
having disarmed the power and authorities, he made a public spectacle
of them, triumphing over them by the cross.*

COLOSSIANS 2:13-15

When I was a kid, a neighbor who had fought in World War II used to tell me stories about D-Day, June 6, 1944, and about the torpedo boat he was in when he landed on Omaha Beach in France. It was the first time that old boy from Louisiana had ever seen a real beach, he'd tell me.

World War II experts say that D-Day was the day when the war was technically over. Allied troops celebrated that day as German fighters began their epic retreat back to Berlin. But it wasn't until nearly one year later, on May 8, 1945, that Europe was declared truly free. The war had ended long before, but there were battles yet to fight.

Spiritually speaking, this is exactly the state we're in.

Because of what Jesus Christ did on the cross, the war over sin and death has been won. But while we have been declared ultimately victorious, there are battles yet to fight.

In this passage from the apostle Paul, we see that every force that seeks to take us down has *already been disarmed*. Which is why we can enter into the battles we're called to fight with courage and confidence and grace.

As you stand up for what is right today, engage not from a place of vulnerability, but from eternal victory's seat. The outcome has already been decided, and you're on the winning side.

A BLESSING FROM PAM

May you exude confidence today as you fight for divine righteousness, justice, and love.

Joy and Pain

"A woman giving birth to a child has pain because her time has come; but when her baby is born she forgets the anguish because of her joy that a child is born into the world."

JOHN 16:21

If you've ever seen a photo of a woman just after she has given birth, then you have caught the intent of this verse. Pam and I always rejoice when we see on social media that a New Lifer has had a baby, and every time I look at the pictures of the mother, I see two distinct emotional states reflected in her eyes: there is the residue of great turmoil and anguish, while simultaneously there is great joy.

Similarly, John is telling us that since we know a new creation is being birthed all around us, we can let joy eek into the sorrows we carry in this world. We can balance our grieving with hope.

Here's what Jesus wants us to know today: this reality we're experiencing isn't the only reality there is. He is coming back. Do you believe that? He is coming to get his Bride. And until then we can rest in the perfect assurance that things are about to get *good*.

A BLESSING FROM PAM

May you find courage today to let your heart hope again. Hope is the birthright of every believer because of the sacrifice that Jesus made.

Grafted In

*But when the set time had fully come, God sent his Son, born of
a woman, born under the law, to redeem those under the law,
that we might receive adoption to sonship.*

GALATIANS 4:4-5

Abram was eight or nine years old, and like every other night, I came in as he was settling into his bed, to pray over him and tell him good night. As I headed back to the living room, I heard his sleepy voice say, "Dad?"

I stopped at his door and turned toward him. "Yeah, Abram?"

"Dad, I just wanted to say thank you for adopting me."

"Well, you're welcome. Why do you say that?"

"Because if you hadn't adopted me, then we couldn't be buds."

And then he rolled over and went to sleep.

I stepped into the hallway, shut his bedroom door behind me, and felt tears spring to my eyes. What a thing to say, right? I'll never forget that night.

You know what else I'll never forget? That the God of the universe saw fit to adopt me so that he and I could be buds.

If you are a follower of Jesus, then you are his daughter or son. You have been grafted into his family. And now, you can be his friend.

A BLESSING FROM PAM

*May you never, ever get over the joyous feeling of being welcomed
into a forever family, the beautiful family of God.*

Still Parting Waters Today

Then Moses stretched out his hand over the sea,
and all that night the LORD drove the sea back with
a strong east wind and turned it into dry land ...

EXODUS 14:21

Whenever I stand in front of our congregation and look out at the faces looking back at me, it's not uncommon for this verse from Exodus to come to mind. God had freed his people from Egyptian slavery, and now they were on the run from Pharaoh and his massive armies, who were closing in on the nation Israel.

God's people came to the edge of the Red Sea and stopped abruptly. There was no way to get across. But then God intervened. Moses stretched out his hand, a strong wind blew, and the waters separated, revealing dry land.

When I look at you, I see a similar story. I see the man who just celebrated twenty-one years sober, after nearly losing his life to drugs. I see the eighty-year-old woman who finally got a cancer-free diagnosis three days before coming to church. I see the couple that recently celebrated twenty-five years of marriage, despite nearly losing everything after dealing with an affair. I see the teenage daughter who was on the run from her parents and from God but who made her way home days before. I see God parting the seas in a hundred ways, as though just to prove that he still can—and still will.

A BLESSING FROM PAM

May you put complete trust in your Father today,
who loves to intervene on your behalf.

What Follows the Darkest Dark

*And you, my child, will be called a prophet of the Most High; for you
will go on before the Lord to prepare the way for him, to give his people
the knowledge of salvation through the forgiveness of their sins, because
of the tender mercy of our God, by which the rising sun will come to us
from heaven to shine on those living in darkness and in the shadow
of death, to guide our feet into the path of peace.*

LUKE 1:76-79

I'd been speaking all week in Kenya when a pastor invited my traveling companions and me to go on a safari near Tanzania. That night, he drove us into a fenced-in area on the park's grounds, not far from where the giraffes and elephants and lions all roamed freely. We'd be sleeping in tents, he explained, and once the sun had set, we were to stay inside our tent for the rest of the night. The generators that were on timers would shut down, the lights would go out, and our safety would evidently be compromised should we choose to break this rule.

"I cannot emphasize this enough," he said, eyeing me soberly. "Once you're in your tent for the evening, do *not* come out. Baboons climb these fences and roam through the campgrounds at night. You do not want to take them on."

I have to tell you: that night, every time I heard a single branch rustle, I jolted upright in bed. It was dark—too dark for my comfort. I'd place my hand directly in front of my face, yet I couldn't make out its shape. But then came six a.m.

I'd never been so happy to see six a.m.

The generators kicked in. The lights flickered on. And I could make out my hand once more.

This is a useful image for you and me. I know that on some days it can feel like the baboons in our culture are running rampant, and that we're going to be mauled for sure. On those days it's helpful to remember that the light will shine once again.

A BLESSING FROM PAM

*May you know the perfect peace of God today as you face life's challenges.
May you rest assured that the sun will shine.*

Beware the Lie

He [the devil] was a murderer from the beginning, not holding
to the truth, for there is no truth in him. When he lies, he speaks his
native language, for he is a liar and the father of lies.

JOHN 8:44B

Have you ever played that game, "Two Truths and a Lie"? It's often used as an icebreaker for groups that don't know each other well, and the idea is that as you introduce yourself, you say two truths about yourself and one lie. The rest of the group is supposed to guess which statement was the lie.

For example, someone might say, "I'm originally from California, I almost majored in surfing in college, and I've biked the entire Pacific Coast Trail."

Now, if the person said something outlandish in there, like, "I've won the lottery six times," then you'd pretty much know the lie. The key to stumping the group is to say things that could *conceivably* be true.

Which is how it goes for all lies, by the way.

When he's trying to trip us up, Satan doesn't trot out unbelievable enticements. Instead, he puts a lie in front of us that seems like it could be true.

He puts out a plate of oatmeal-raisin cookies and says, "Look! Your favorite: chocolate chip."

But then you bite into that thing and reflexively spit it out. Because (repeat after me), "raisins have no business being in cookies. Raisins have no business *anywhere*."

Sin promises us something that it never can fulfill. It is always a false assumption. It always an outright sham.

Do not be fooled, believer. Make sure those cookies are chocolate-chip.

A BLESSING FROM PAM

May you be granted an extra measure of wisdom today
for spotting the difference between truth and lie.

The One Thing that Works

"Come to me, all you who are weary and burdened, and I will give
you rest. Take my yoke upon you and learn from me, for I am gentle
and humble in heart, and you will find rest for your souls.
For my yoke is easy and my burden is light."

MATTHEW 11:28-30

I know that sleep is a huge issue for many, many people, but personally I have slept well for years now. And I "blame" my condition on God. Here's what I've been doing that has helped me sleep so well: I've been practicing what Matthew 11 says to do regarding giving God my concerns.

If this sounds too simple to be effective, it's because it kind of is. Before my head hits the pillow each night, I think back on my day. I ask God to help me assess how things went. I praise God for the protection and provision he afforded me. I claim forgiveness for any mistake the Spirit brings to mind. I renew my commitment to following hard after God. I pray for people whose needs I'm aware of. I pray blessings on the lives of my enemies. I think through the following day's obligations. And then in thirty seconds, I'm fast asleep.

If you're skeptical of this approach, I dare you to try it—even for a night. Lay down the burdens that threaten to distract you from rest. Pick up God's weightless burden instead.

A BLESSING FROM PAM

May you know peaceful, perfect rest tonight,
as you entrust every last care to God.

God's to Repay

Do not take revenge, my dear friends, but leave room for God's wrath,
for it is written, "It is mine to avenge; I will repay," says the Lord.

ROMANS 12:19

When Dr. Martin Luther King, Jr., launched the Civil Rights movement in the mid-1950s, some of the leaders he'd recruited to his team tried to convince him that the right course of action in response to the oppression their people faced was violence. "Violence beats violence!" they told him. But Dr. King knew this wasn't the case.

One Sunday morning when he was preaching, he said, "The ultimate weakness of violence is that it is a descending spiral, begetting the very thing it seeks to destroy. Instead of diminishing evil, it multiplies it. Through violence you may murder the liar, but you can't murder the lie. You may murder the hater, but you do not murder hate. Returning violence for violence multiplies violence, adding deeper darkness to a night already devoid of stars. Darkness cannot drive out darkness. Only the light can do that. Hate cannot drive out hate. Only love can do that."

It is a radical truth of our faith that we are not to exact revenge on those who do harm to us. We do not return hate for hate. Instead, we entrust our situation to the God of all justice, the God who promises that in his time, and in his way, he always will repay.

A BLESSING FROM PAM

May you exhale your rage against those who have harmed you
and inhale God's commitment to making things right.

Greater Still

You, dear children, are from God and have overcome them, because
the one who is in you is greater than the one who is in the world.

1 JOHN 4:4

My first three months at New Life were life-giving and sweet, but by my hundredth day our entire world felt like it was tumbling into a freefall, and truthfully, I wanted out. Sure, it had been fun getting to know you, telling stories, preaching to a packed house. But as the full impact of the shooting that happened on our campus hit me, I told Pam that I believed the reason God had brought me to this church was to be a hospice pastor tasked with giving a once-great congregation a dignified death.

My faith felt flat. I was crushed. I didn't see how God could redeem what had occurred.

A few months ago we baptized 268 people on a single Sunday morning, and as I stood in the midst of our people, cheering on each person who was entering those waters, I thought, *I'm so glad I didn't bail fourteen and a half years ago.*

If your faith is feeling flat today, I hope you'll lean in and look carefully at these words:

Because of your spiritual heritage, you are destined to overcome.

Do you believe that today? Because of who you are in Christ Jesus, you are destined not to fail. You don't have to bail on your assignment. You can persevere in Jesus' name.

I wouldn't trade the miracles I see around New Life these days for anything in the world. I'm so grateful I get to see them. I'm so grateful I stayed to see.

A BLESSING FROM PAM

May your faith be divinely boosted today
so that you can persist and not fall away.

Poetry Not Required

In the same way, the Spirit helps us in our weakness. We do not know what we ought to pray for, but the Spirit himself intercedes for us through wordless groans.

ROMANS 8:26

Pam's and my first pastor was Rodney Duron, a gentle, former-athlete father-figure who always gave rib-crushing hugs. Pastor Rodney was a prayer warrior unlike anyone I'd ever met. Whenever he prayed aloud, Scripture passages would flow like a stream from his heart and by the time he was done talking, you'd have thought you'd attended a poetry reading. His prayers were beautiful. His prayers were passionate. His prayers were *smooth*.

I loved his prayers. But I have to admit that sitting in his congregation as a twenty-something who was relatively new to the faith, I started telling myself that since I'd never be able to pray like Pastor Rodney, I should just give up on prayer for good.

Then I found Romans 8.

Listen, there is absolutely nothing wrong with praying lovely prayers. But equally true is that if you're a lovely pray-er, you should know that God's got your back. His Spirit is praying on your behalf whenever you have no clue what to say. He's always pleading with the Father to take good care of you.

So: come. Come before the Father and pray your imperfect prayers. They need not be poetic. They need only to be sincere.

A BLESSING FROM PAM

May you confidently make your requests of God today,
ineloquent though they may be.

Hungry

After fasting forty days and forty nights, he [Jesus] was hungry.
The tempter came to him and said, "If you are the Son of
God, tell these stones to become bread."

MATTHEW 4:2-3

After Jesus was baptized, he was led into the desert to be tempted by Satan. He fasted during that entire span, which is why Matthew 4 tells us that Jesus was hungry. I would have been hungry too.

There are scores of implications regarding what happened to Jesus in the desert—how Satan tempted him, how Jesus responded, what those responses mean for you and me. But there's something about that simple phrase that gets me every time: "he was hungry."

During the early days of the Covid shutdowns as a church we were distributing thousands of pounds of food to people in need. One day I received an email from a college student, and she explained that while she was still on campus, student services were all shut down. Her parents were struggling to get groceries themselves, and given her dwindling checking account, she also couldn't eat. She'd found out through the media that our church was sending packages of food and asked if she could be put on the list.

I instantly thought of this passage from Matthew. Jesus knew how it felt to be hungry. He'd want us to get her some food.

A week later I received another email. "Pastor Brady," it read, "I have enough food here to last me two months and feel at peace for the first time since all these shutdowns took hold. Thank you. Please, thank your church for me."

I know it seems incidental to people who are used to three meals a day, but whenever you encounter someone who is hungry, carve out time to get them a meal.

A BLESSING FROM PAM

May you tangibly show the love of Jesus today
by feeding someone you meet.

If Jesus Did It, Do It.
If Jesus Didn't, Don't.

Whoever claims to live in him must live as Jesus did.

1 JOHN 2:6

Not to throw stones, but one of the most life-giving decisions I made this past year was divorcing my Facebook account. I thought I'd wake up the next day feeling regretful, but the opposite was true. I'd seen so many professing Christians with bios calling themselves "Daughter of the King" or "Highly Anointed" or whatever spreading vitriol for so long that now that the input was out of my life, I felt like I could finally breathe.

At issue was blatant hypocrisy: *Don't claim to be associated with Jesus*, I'd think, *and then talk to people like that.*

I'd think of rebuttals to those people's posts but then realize that in posting my remarks, I'd be caving to the very same sin. And so I ditched the thing altogether. I left Facebook and never looked back.

If you were to ask me what I'd put on a billboard that the entire world would see, I'd say this: "If Jesus did it, do it. If Jesus didn't, don't."

My point: Whatever is keeping you from following Jesus intimately, get rid of that thing right now.

And also: Whatever is causing you to lean hard into him, well, that thing gets top spot.

A BLESSING FROM PAM

Today, may you live a life worthy of your calling.
May you lovingly reflect the Savior of your soul.

Unwavering

Against all hope, Abraham in hope believed and so became the
father of many nations, just as it had been said to him, "So shall your offspring be."
Without weakening in his faith, he faced the fact that his body was as good as dead—
since he was about a hundred years old—and that Sarah's womb was also dead. Yet
he did not waver through unbelief regarding the promise of God, but was strengthened
in his faith and gave glory to God, being fully persuaded that God had power to do
what he had promised. This is why "it was credited to him as righteousness."

ROMANS 4:18-22

Somewhere between the time when Pam and I found out we were both infertile and the time when we adopted our son and daughter, the Lord spoke to me one morning at six a.m. *Pray for a little girl with red curly hair and blue eyes*—that's how the prompting went. And so I prayed. And nothing happened.

Five years later, a nineteen-year-old woman approached Pam and me and said, "I'm three weeks from giving birth. Would you take my baby? Would you raise my baby for me?"

We prayed about it and said yes. That baby has curly red hair and blue eyes to this day, and Callie is her name.

You may recall that in the book of Genesis, God had promised Abraham that he would be the "father of many nations," and yet there he stood at one hundred years old, having not birthed a single child.

I don't mean to project onto Abraham what Pam and I went through, but to be candid there were many sleepless nights, wondering if God would come through for us. We wrestled with doubt. We wrestled with unbelief. We wrestled with taking God at his word. Would he actually provide for us? Would he give us the desire of our hearts?

It's all that Pam and I would talk about—our fears, disappointments, hurts. Looking back, we wouldn't change a single thing, for the intimacy we gained with Christ.

What are you waiting on God for today? Someday when you look back on this season, will you see that you were unwavering in your faith, or that you lost confidence in him?

A BLESSING FROM PAM

May you be strengthened in your faith today, as you give all glory to God.

Re-Imagined

*She [a wife of noble character] is clothed with strength
and dignity; she can laugh at the days to come.*

PROVERBS 31:25

In Proverbs 31, we find a whole litany of ways that a wife of noble character should behave. What's not as commonly understood is that the instruction was given from King Lemuel's mother to King Lemuel, and only after she'd told *him* how to behave. "Speak up for those who cannot speak for themselves," she said, "for the rights of all who are destitute. Speak up and judge fairly; defend the rights of the poor and needy," (Proverbs 31:8-9).

If you do these things, she implied, then maybe the kind of woman I'm about to describe to you will be attracted to you.

Of all the instruction King Lemuel's mother then lays out, I've always loved this particular piece of advice: be clothed with strength and dignity; and laugh at the days to come.

Over the past almost-fifteen years, we've seen our fair share of families walking through difficult times. Families lost loved ones in tragic shootings. They lost businesses in economic droughts. They lost aging parents due to Covid. They lost hope because all seemed lost.

If you represent one of those families that has lost something meaningful recently, please know that I'm praying for you. I'm praying that you have patience to walk through this struggle. And resolve to stick to what you believe. And imagination to help you envision a future apart from the stability you so dearly miss.

I'm praying strength and dignity over your household. And that laughter will fill your heart. And that the God who has promised to sustain you will show himself strong in your weakness today.

A BLESSING FROM PAM

*May you be steadied today as you traverse uneven terrain.
May you sense God's presence leading you on.*

Choosing to be Content

LORD, you alone are my portion and my cup; you make my lot secure. The boundary lines have fallen for me in pleasant places; surely I have a delightful inheritance. I will praise the LORD, who counsels me; even at night my heart instructs me. I keep my eyes always on the LORD. With him at my right hand, I will not be shaken.

PSALM 16:5-8

During that season when I wanted to walk away from ministry I described a few days ago, God laid a passage of Scripture on my heart. I was weary from the aftermath of the shooting and the founding pastor's scandal. I was stressed over the state of our national economy. And to add insult to injury I had to lay off many staff members because, simply put, we couldn't afford to pay them anymore.

It started to feel like God had placed me in a role in which I'd never be able to succeed.

One morning I was sitting beside the windows in my second-floor office and caught sight of Pikes Peak. It was a classic Colorado morning: bluebird skies, bright sunshine, snow on the tip of the peak.

I was feeling demoralized. I remember sitting there, complaining to God.

"Look up," he seemed to be saying. "Look up, and see where you are."

As I took in the scene afresh, just then a parachuter leaped from a plane.

"Do you see the beauty around you? Do you see that I brought you here?"

I thought of this section of Psalm 16.

My boundary lines indeed were in pleasant places. I was in Colorado Springs, for crying out loud.

I came to a realization that morning, which serves me still today. If we choose contentment, there is always enough. If we choose discontentment, there never is.

A BLESSING FROM PAM

May you have eyes to see the blessings God has ushered into your life instead of fixating on all that is wrong.

The Battle for Your Worship

I rejoiced with those who said to me,
"Let us go to the house of the LORD."

PSALM 122:1

I can't tell you how many people have confided in me that their family always seems to get into an epic knockdown-drag-out meltdown on the way to or from church each weekend.

Isn't that the way things go? We're believers in Jesus Christ. We're heading to or from our house of worship, where we gather with other believers to pray and sing and learn the Scriptures and celebrate amazing grace. This is the highlight of our week, the fuel we need for our souls. And then we botch the whole experience by being testy with the ones we love.

I've long believed that as believers there is a significant battle attached to our worship. Think of it: the last thing the enemy wants us to do is gather and worship God. He absolutely hates it when we drop our differences—our politics, our parenting styles, our taste in music, our beliefs about how the nation should run— and link arms in holy unity, declaring Jesus sufficient for us all. And so he does all he can to derail it. He does all he can to pull us apart.

My counsel to you and me both is this: be on guard as you're making your way to and from worship each time. *Rejoice*, and don't pick a fight.

A BLESSING FROM PAM

May you be the model of encouragement and peace
as you engage in worship this week.

Enough? Then Share.

John answered, "Anyone who has two shirts
should share with the one who has none, and
anyone who has food should do the same."

LUKE 3:11

As Daniel Grothe told the story, a single mom in the Friday-night congregation he serves had been struggling for quite some time, and things were only getting worse. As he walked out to his car after services one weekend, a lady he didn't know approached him and slid an envelope into his hands. "It's for the single mom we were praying for tonight," she said. "I hope that it will help."

Inside the envelope was a check for three thousand dollars.

Uh, yeah. I'd think that would help.

If there's one thing I love about New Life, it's our nearly obsessive commitment to prayer. If there's a second thing I love about New Life, it's our spirit of generosity, our propensity to give.

As I think on Luke 3:11, I'm aware that 99.9 percent of people who will ever read this devotional have far more than two shirts hanging in their closet right now. It's easy to think that Luke is being metaphorical, but what if he's being sincere? In his day and age, people didn't have multiple outfits to choose from; to have two shirts would have been luxurious. It would have meant you were the richest of the rich.

You and I? We are the richest of the rich today.

It begs the question: What are we willing to sacrifice so that those in pain in our community can finally get their needs met?

A BLESSING FROM PAM

May you see and really see the needs around you today.
And may you jump at the chance to meet them.

With Us Always

He says, "Be still, and know that I am God; I will be exalted
among the nations, I will be exalted in the earth." The LORD
Almighty is with us; the God of Jacob is our fortress."

PSALM 46:10-11

In Texas, springtime is marked by thunderstorms. Wild, wooly thunderstorms that make you wonder if the end is near. You've seen *Twister*? That movie is based on fact.

When Abram and Callie were four and two years old respectively, Pam and I were living the Dallas-Fort Worth area, and on many occasions one of those thunderstorms would rumble through town during the darkest black of night. Flashes of lightening would rip the sky in two, and then thunder would barrel across the cosmos like a freight train out of control.

Invariably, about three seconds following the first thunder-boomer, Pam and I would hear the pitter-patter of tiny feet racing down the hallway toward our bedroom. Our kids' faces would have that look that said, "We're under attack, right? Tell us the truth. We know we are."

They'd climb into our bed, attach themselves to our sides, and exhale their grave concern. In a matter of moments, they'd both be fast asleep.

It's natural to look at the world around us and start shaking in our boots, when all we can see is the storm. But I'm here to echo what the psalmist said here, which is that the Lord Almighty is still nearby.

God is with us.

God is *for* us.

God has promised not to leave our side.

The storm has zero sway over him. He's still steady, confident, and calm.

A BLESSING FROM PAM

When you look around your life today, may God be all you see.

Loved

Give thanks to the LORD, for he is
good; his love endures forever.

PSALM 118:29

Have you ever seen a baby wombat? Born with no fur, fire-red paws, and ears that are way too big for its head, it might just be the ugliest creature alive. I'm telling you, only a mama wombat could love a baby wombat. Looking at that thing is *tough*.

And yet you and I aren't much better than that.

When we start out on our spiritual journey, we too are ugly, messy, ill-formed, and tough to take. Sure, we get better as we go—God's Word promises that much is true. But in those early days, someone has to choose to love us and help us when we're still stuck in our worst-case state.

That somebody? It is God.

One of my all-time favorite psalms is this one, Psalm 118:29. To think that regardless of how bad I look, how bad I *am*, God's love for me endures even so ... well, it's enough to blow my mind. For God to love me on my best day, when I'm put together, when I'm hard at work, when I'm slaying it hour after hour, is one thing. But for him to come close to me and commit himself to my transformation when I'm flubbing left and right? What a gracious choice to make.

Whenever I talk with someone who is new to the faith, I reflexively think back to how I was, when I first surrendered to Christ. I tap into the compassion others showed me back then and extend the same good will toward them.

A BLESSING FROM PAM

May you be a person of boundless patience and grace today
with those who are younger than you in the faith.

Face to Face

Practice hospitality.

ROMANS 12:13B

A few years ago when Pam and Callie were on a college visit, Abram and I were home alone. At some point during the evening, my son looked at me and said, "What's for dinner?"

I was tempted to say what I was thinking: "You're nineteen years old. What's for dinner is whatever you decide to cook." But I thought better of it, seeing as he and I rarely got time alone. Taking in my blank expression, Abram then said four words that would revolutionize my life: "We could DoorDash something."

The service was new at the time, and despite my skepticism that we could stay home in sweatpants and make someone else go through the drive-thru for us, sure enough, twenty-four minutes later, we were eating Popeye's chicken in front of the TV. It was truly fantastic. Also true: it would make for a dangerous habit for me.

I'm getting to the point where if I'm not careful I will have 100 percent of my life automated and will need to interact with exactly zero human beings. Between Amazon, grocery-deliver services, online banking, and now DoorDash, I guess, why would I ever need to leave my home, let alone interact with another person?

Ah, but then there's Romans 12, and those two inescapable words from Paul: "Practice hospitality," he plainly says.

Two hundred years after Jesus walked the earth a church father was asked for the most important advice he'd offer to Christ followers who wanted to make a real different in the world. He said, "Come together as often as possible."

That's it. Keep meeting, *face to face*. I'll never get over the fact that Jesus saw fit to come live and in person to rescue us from our sin. I think there's something to model there, something we're wise to prioritize.

A BLESSING FROM PAM

*May you forego the efficient and easy solution today
in favor of connecting with a real human being.*

Confronted by Holy God

In the year that King Uzziah died, I saw the Lord, high and exalted, seated on a throne; and the train of his robe filled the temple. Above him were seraphim, each with six wings: With two wings they covered their faces, with two they covered their feet, and with two they were flying. And they were calling to one another: "Holy, holy, holy is the LORD Almighty; the whole earth is full of his glory." At the sound of their voices the door posts and thresholds shook and the temple was filled with smoke.

"Woe to me!" I cried. "I am ruined! For I am a man of unclean lips, and I live among a people of unclean lips, and my eyes have seen the King, the LORD Almighty."

ISAIAH 6:1-5

In the life of a believer, an interesting progression occurs. Baked right into our DNA as followers of Jesus is the desire to worship holy God. It's what we were made for. It's what our hearts long for. Spending time in his presence praising him is the most meaningful thing we do.

The only problem, then, is this: Whenever we move toward God in a posture of worship, the Holy Spirit moves toward us. (James 4:8 confirms this truth.)

Which would be well and good and even absolutely amazing, except that the closer the Spirit gets to us, the more in touch with our shortcomings we are. We start seeing our brokenness in greater relief, when compared with the stunning presence of holy God. "Woe to me!" the prophet Isaiah put it. "I am a man of unclean lips!"

Even the sharpest, savviest, most righteous among us understand exactly what he means. Who can stand next to the perfection of God without feeling pretty puny about themselves?

This sounds like a downer of a story, I realize, but in fact it's a good-news tale. Because this progression is exactly the thing that makes worship such a transformational experience every time. Worship brings us out into the open—warts, mess-ups, and all. Worship keeps us from hiding behind our good behavior, good intentions, and good looks. Worship says, "It's all or nothing here. Either get real with God or get yourself something else to do."

A BLESSING FROM PAM

May you enjoy a radical encounter with the Lord today, as you let him grow you up in him.

The Power of Place

*Even the sparrow has found a home, and the swallow a nest
for herself, where she may have her young—a place near
your altar, LORD Almighty, my King and my God.*

PSALM 84:3

When we first opened Mary's Home years ago, our long-term residential program offering trauma-informed services to single-mom-led families exiting homelessness, one woman was taken to her new apartment, and upon entering the space she fell apart in waves of tears. The place had been completely remodeled and beautifully outfitted with furniture, dishes, the whole works, and she was so overcome by the thought that she finally had a home after spending so many years on the streets, living in her car, that she could barely breathe. "Tonight will be the first night that my children and I go to sleep feeling protected," she said—"feeling safe."

Places of residence, places of worship, places of fellowship, places of prayer—they all provide that sense of protection for us insofar as they point to the protection of God. When we invite people into our homes and our churches, into our gatherings and into our groups, we may have no clue how significant those places become for those people. But God knows. He sees. And just as he finds places for every last sparrow, he's constantly at work to secure his children in safe places too.

A BLESSING FROM PAM

*May you welcome someone into your world today,
into your environment, into your place.*

You Need You Here

So the churches were strengthened in
the faith and grew daily in numbers.

ACTS 16:5

Every spiritual story started in the church.

The church would gather and tell the stories. And out of those stories, people would scatter to their daily walk and then they would come back at night and they would tell more stories. And they would come around the Lord's Table and they would worship together and they would pray for the sick and they would be together. And out of that sense of community, everything began to spread.

But despite its wild popularity through the ages, today we're living in a time when people are giving up on church. The average self-identified Christian attends a church service only twice a month, on average. Which I find flabbergasting, truth be told. In the nearly four decades that I've known Pam, we've missed *maybe* three services a year each year in all that time. I don't say that to make you feel guilty; I say it to simply call you back to church.

I don't need you here at church as much as *you* need you here.

I will make you this guarantee: if you devote yourself to church participation, you will come back and find me in fifteen years and will say, "Pastor Brady, the greatest thing that I ever did for my personal faith was to plant my feet among a group of people who were diverse, imperfect, and messy. Still, I stood with them and began to love them. I ate meals with them. I prayed with them. I served alongside them. And I'm better for each of those things."

Test me in this and see if you don't agree that as you invest yourself wholeheartedly in the life of our church, your story is deeply enriched.

A BLESSING FROM PAM

May you be drawn back to the church today.
May your roots run deep in that place.

Count Your Blessings

I will give thanks to you, LORD, with all my heart;
I will tell of all your wonderful deeds.

PSALM 9:1

It's just a silly little Sunday school song from years and years past, but for me it packs a punch. (Be grateful you can't hear my singing here. You're welcome.) It goes like this: "Count your many blessings, name them one by one. Count your many blessings, see what God has done. Count your blessings, name them one by one. And it will surprise you what the Lord has done."

I wonder, how often do you literally count your blessings and attribute all praise to God?

Grateful people are happier.

Grateful people forgive more quickly.

Grateful people are quicker to repent and go God's way.

Don't be stingy with your gratitude today.

Say thank you from the bottom of your heart.

A BLESSING FROM PAM

May you be led today by generosity of spirit,
and may thanks flow freely from your life.

The Great Adventure

*And he said: "Truly I tell you, unless you change and become
like little children, you will never enter the kingdom of heaven."*

MATTHEW 18:3

When my kids were small, I could spontaneously say to them, "Hey, guys! Do you
want to go to the mountains and hike around?"

Or, "Do you want to go fishing with me?"

Or, "Should we go on a bear hunt?"

Or, "Who wants to go have an adventure today?"

And guess what their answer would be?

"Yeah! Of course! We're ready, Dad! Let's go!"

As we become adults, we learn to start playing it safe. But I'm convinced that one of
the main reasons you and I are told to "change and become like little children" if we
hope to enter the kingdom of God is that children are ready for adventure. They're
ready to go places, see things, dig in. They're ready to throw caution to the wind for
the sake of experiencing something that matters. They're eager to take the plunge
and soak up life.

Oh, that we would view our walk with Jesus that way, that we would quit hedging
and just dive in. That we'd become like children, one and all.

A BLESSING FROM PAM

May your answer to Jesus today be yes.

The Covering You and I Need

Do not forsake wisdom, and she will protect you;
love her, and she will watch over you.

PROVERBS 4:6

A man I know who was raised in a Christian home over time became hardened to the things of God. One year when a large men's conference was convening in D. C. this man decided to attend with his father, since the two of them rarely got time alone. Unbeknownst to this man, his dad was praying for him each day of the conference, that he would surrender his life to Jesus. But the only thing the man was interested in was escaping to a restroom every hour or so and smoking pot.

For three days this went on, with his father attending sessions and workshops and the son holed away smoking weed. But on day four the younger man headed outside to walk around during a break and had a full-on panic attack. For nearly a full minute, the man was wracked by fear, something he'd never experienced before.

Having no idea what else to do, and being pretty freaked out by the ordeal, the man sat on a park bench and asked God for help. "What on earth was that?" the man said, to which God said, "Son, I wanted you to know what it feels like to be outside the covering of my hand. I have kept my hand on you all this time because of your parents' faithful prayers. Without my protection you will surely fall. You will be turned over to your own ways."

He surrendered to Christ right then.

We may never know just how protected we are from calamity that waits for us on both sides. Thank God for his guidance and guardianship. He is watching over you now.

A BLESSING FROM PAM

May God never remove his divine protection from our lives.
And may we be grateful for his shield of strength.

DECEMBER

"What knots are you struggling
to untie these days? Have you
sought help from your heavenly
Father? He longs for you to
walk in wisdom! He'll share
his wisdom with you."

- Pastor Brady Boyd -

Relishing the Plenty

*When the woman saw that the fruit of the tree was good
for food and pleasing to the eye, and also desirable for gaining
wisdom, she took some and ate it. She also gave some to her
husband, who was with her, and he ate it.*

GENESIS 3:6

Just after God created Adam and Eve, he placed them in a gorgeous garden, where they could enjoy his intimate fellowship day after day. Here, they had access to enormous wealth because everything on the earth was theirs. God had made it all for them, and for the generations that they would birth.

But this offer was conditional. It was based on their distinctive devotion to God. God had set the parameters: they could enjoy the fruit of any tree in the garden, as long as they left one singular tree alone. That tree was called the Tree of the Knowledge of Good and Evil—the tree that represented what was God's to know, alone.

Instead of relishing the plenty they'd been handed, they fixated on that forbidden tree. Like fingers that just can't resist touching the bench that the "wet paint" sign is on, Eve approached the tree. She took of its fruit. And she ate.

Soon thereafter, Adam followed suit.

In the beginning, God was their sole desire. But along the way, that changed. Tempted with the one thing that God said should not be theirs, they chose to pursue their selfish aims.

Their decision is instructive to us today: Will we relish the plenty God has afforded us or let greed run roughshod in our hearts?

A BLESSING FROM PAM

*May you fiercely protect your intimacy with Jesus today,
refusing to let anything get in your way.*

He Builds Joy

For the kingdom of God is not a matter of eating and drinking,
but of righteousness, peace and joy in the Holy Spirit.

ROMANS 14:17

For a while, every time a certain commercial for a luxury-car company came on TV, I would viscerally recoil. I can't remember the entire ad script, but the tagline was this: "We don't just build cars. We build joy."

I hated that phrase with a passion. It was presumptuous—not to mention untrue.

I'm well aware that this is how advertising works: some agency makes claims on behalf of a company that while false are not legally errant, and we, the unsuspecting consumer, are emotionally driven to buy their thing.

I get it.

I just don't like it.

Especially when the ad usurps God's role in the world.

In case you haven't stumbled upon this truth already, let me state it plainly: Only by relating with the One who invented joy can you ever experience joy. We find joy not in an automobile, but in Jesus Christ, alone.

A BLESSING FROM PAM

May you look to God today to provide what only he can provide.

The Gift of Tears

As he approached Jerusalem and saw the city, he wept over it and said, "If
you, even you, had only known on this day what would bring you peace—but
now it is hidden from your eyes. The days will come upon you when your
enemies will build an embankment against you and encircle you and hem you
in on every side. They will dash you to the ground, you and the children within
your walls. They will not leave one stone on another, because you did not
recognize the time of God's coming to you."

LUKE 19:41-44

As Jesus approached Jerusalem and took in the city, what he saw was the depravity of the Church and of people. He saw the practice of slavery running rampant. He saw the Roman bondage inhibiting freedom throughout the land. He sorrow in the hearts of his people. And the text says that "he wept."

Truth be told, I'm not much of a crier. But years ago I was struck by an old Puritan prayer I came across. "God, help our hearts to be broken for the things that break your heart," it read. "Give us the gift of tears."

If you and I had spiritual eyes to see the denigration, deprivation, and degradation in our city today, would the realities stir in us any emotion at all? Maybe we wouldn't necessarily weep, but would we even stop to care?

As I pray for our church, I often ask God to help us to be Christians who are sobered by what sobers him. I pray that as a people we wouldn't be hardened, but that instead our hearts would be soft.

A BLESSING FROM PAM

May you be moved to compassion today
as you take in the needs you see.

Eyes on Me

*But my eyes are fixed on you, Sovereign LORD; in you
I take refuge—do not give me over to death.*

PSALM 141:8

When I was a kid my family went to the Louisiana State Fair almost every year. My dad would load us kids into the car, drive out to the fairgrounds, and give us the same spiel he always gave us, as we made our way across the massive parking lot. "Eyes on me the whole time, kids. There are lots of people here. Stay close, and don't go wandering off, okay?"

Yep. Got it, Dad.

One year, I got sucked into the grandeur and excitement of the midway. There were games chiming, bells ringing, people hollering and laughing, food vendors calling out their specials, and lights blinking everywhere I turned. It was *amazing*—especially for a seven-year-old. I'd followed the sights and smells for quite some time before realizing that I'd wandered off from my dad. And still today I can remember how terrifying that felt, to look up and not see him there.

As the color drained from my face and neck, I turned in slow circles, wondering if I was going to be kidnapped and held for ransom and never see my parents again. As I laid out my fatal hypothesis, a distinctive whistle caught my attention.

My dad had trained bird dogs on that whistle. He'd trained my siblings and me on that whistle. I'd know that whistle anywhere. That whistle belonged to Dad.

I ran as fast as my little legs could take me, closing the thirty-foot distance in what felt like a single stride. And then my dad said something I've remembered all these years: "Son, you may have taken your eyes off me, but I never took mine off of you."

This is true of all good fathers. It's true of our heavenly Father as well.

A BLESSING FROM PAM

*May you rest in the ever-present protection
that God in heaven affords you every day.*

Taught by God

Jesus went throughout Galilee, teaching in their synagogues,
proclaiming the good news of the kingdom, and healing
every disease and sickness among the people.

MATTHEW 4:23

For four years during my 20's I was a high school teacher, and I learned two important things from teaching school: first, nobody chooses a career in teaching to get rich. And second, no profession requires greater patience than educating children who are only partially interested in learning what you're trying to teach.

Jesus fulfills many roles in the life of the believer: Lord, Savior, Master, Rescuer, Presence, Protector, Friend. But my favorite role of his is that of Teacher. With impossible graciousness and patience, he *teaches* us how to follow him.

Everyone has a favorite teacher from their schooldays. Maybe yours was a teacher who cared deeply about your progress, even when you'd given up on yourself. Or who helped you keep the big picture in mind when you were feeling stressed out. Or who kept showing up for you day after day, eager to show you something you hadn't known before. Or who high-fived you when you finally "got" something, when that skill somehow magically clicked.

Jesus as Teacher is no different. He does all these things and more.

Here's an invitation for you today: Spend some time thinking about what it is you need to learn, to become a better version of yourself. Have you been struggling with materialism? Do you wish you were gentler with your kids? Are you sick of battling the same addiction but don't know how to break free? Whatever it is you need to learn, Jesus stands ready to teach you that thing.

A BLESSING FROM PAM

May you be taught by your Teacher Jesus today. May you grasp
something for the first time that you didn't understand before.

How to Spot Wisdom

A person of understanding
delights in wisdom.

PROVERBS 10:23B

I met with a group of pastors in Nashville once to discuss key cultural issues that were impacting the church, and while there were plenty of topics that we disagreed on, I came away sincerely impressed with each person there. Let me tell you why. Whenever I'm in conversation with someone who professes to be a follower of Jesus, I look for two things to be true: first, I look for evidence that Jesus is at the center of their life.

We sing a song around New Life that conveys that exact sentiment: "Jesus, be the center of it all …"

As I'm talking with them, I want to know what they're worshiping. Are they truly devoted to Jesus, or is he an add-on in their life?

The second thing is this: As I engage with this person, I pay attention to whether the conversation we're having makes me want to follow Jesus more fully. If the topics the other person is choosing to cover and the posture with which they're engaging make me want to lean in and listen and learn and love Jesus with greater passion, then I know I'm in the presence of divine wisdom. I know that this person is someone I should respect. Those pastors in Nashville? They were people who brought me delight.

Now, the tables here can also be turned. As you go about your daily life, is it evident to the people you talk to that Jesus is at the center of your life? Furthermore, does the way you talk with them cause them to want to follow him? By God's Spirit you can become such a person. You can become such a person today.

A BLESSING FROM PAM

May your words be filled with wisdom today.

The Advice We Entertain

Walk with the wise and become wise,
for a companion of fools suffers harm.

PROVERBS 13:20

When my kids still lived at home I was an unapologetic helicopter parent who knew every one of their friends. I knew where those friends lived. I knew who those friends' parents were. I knew what they were reading and what music they enjoyed. And I knew what they liked to do for fun. Come at me with whatever criticism; I'll take it. To this day, I have zero regrets.

If there was one thing I told Abram and Callie about friendship as they were growing up, it was this: "If you show me your friends, I'll show you your potential." We really are the sum total of the five loudest voices in our lives, and if we haphazardly listen to just *anyone*, we'll become *just anyone* in the end.

I wanted more for my kids.

In the book of Proverbs, Solomon says that if we "walk with the wise," we will become wise. That's not rocket science, right? Yet too often we let bozos into our lives or into the lives of our children and then are shocked when we make foolish choices later on.

Here is some advice that will save you time and energy: seek out wise friends. Teach your children to seek out wise friends. If your closest friends are lazy or apathetic or inconsiderate or irresponsible or constantly pessimistic, it's time to get new friends.

A BLESSING FROM PAM

May you settle for nothing less than deeply wise friends.

What to Ask God For

This is the confidence we have in approaching God: that if we ask anything according to his will, he hears us. And if we know that he hears us—whatever we ask—we know that we have what we asked of him.

1 JOHN 5:14-15

Many come to faith in Christ at New Life, and a topic I'm often asked about by new believers is how to pray. I'll tell you what I always tell them, which is simply to ask God for what he has already promised to give them. God *loves* to answer such prayers.

The Bible is filled with promises from God, which is why it's so critical to make a daily habit of reading God's Word. How can we trust in his promises to us if we don't even know what they are?

A great way to begin a prayer habit is to read God's Word and ask him to fulfill any and every promise you find noted there. Here are a few to start with:

Ask God for *protection*: "The Lord is faithful, and he will strengthen you and protect you from the evil one," (2 Thessalonians 3:3).

Ask God for *provision*: "He who did not spare his own Son, but gave him up for us all—how will he not also, along with him, graciously give us all things?" (Romans 8:32)

Ask God for *power*: "Now to him who is able to do immeasurably more than all we ask or imagine, according to his power that is at work within us, to him be glory in the church and in Christ Jesus throughout all generations, forever and ever!" (Ephesians 3:20-21)

Ask God for *peace*: "You [God] will keep in perfect peace those whose minds are steadfast, because they trust in you," (Isaiah 26:3).

A BLESSING FROM PAM

May you claim God's promises in your life today,
trusting him to make good on every last one.

Peace Begins in the Mouth

*Do not envy the wicked, do not desire their company; for their
hearts plot violence, and their lips talk about making trouble.*

PROVERBS 24:1-2

Every violent act begins with a violent word. If you ask anyone who knew someone
who committed a violent act, they will tell you that the person talked about doing it
first. "Yeah, they mentioned something about being fed up," they'll say. Or, "Now that
I think of it, he'd been ranting a lot online ..."

The heart plots violence before the hands commit it, which is why we must be very
careful with our thoughts and words.

I'm going to tell you a story that may make you think I've fallen into some legalistic
trap. I promise you I haven't. Let me explain what happened, and then I'll make my
case for why it mattered so deeply to me.

I was with some staff members after a meeting, and we were just goofing around. I
asked one of them a question that revealed I'd become aware of a change in her life,
and this person said, "Hey, how did you know that?"

In all good humor, I laughed and said, "Well, if I told you that, I'd have to kill you."

As soon as the words flew out of my mouth, I regretted saying them. "That's not
funny," I then said to her. "I'm so sorry I said that. It's not funny at all."

Was I just joking around? I was.

Did this person know full well that I was kidding? She did.

Did I overreact by recanting as soon as I realized what I'd said? I believe the answer,
truly, is no.

As a kid, I suffered at the hands of violent bullies in school.

As a teen, I saw evil perpetrated growing up because people chose violence instead
of peace.

As a church, we suffered deeply because of violence that came to our campus
years ago.

As a society, we see what violent video games and movies do to desensitize our
minds to violence in every form.

I reacted so strongly that day with that staff member because I want to be different from all that. I want to be a person of peace—in every sense of the word. You know, it's interesting: I can preach about sexual sin from the pulpit, and people cheer. But when I preach about guarding our hearts against violence—including sarcasm, flippancy, crudeness, and the like—things get painfully quiet.

I have no interest in fostering a culture of legalism—I really don't. I just happen to think this proverb means exactly what it says. We can do better than to speak violence to another person, even jokingly. We are called to do better than that.

A BLESSING FROM PAM

May you think peace today. May you speak peace today.
May you be a person of peace today.

A Story to Tell

Moses said to the LORD, "Pardon your servant, Lord. I have never been eloquent, neither in the past nor since you have spoken to your servant. I am slow of speech and tongue."

EXODUS 4:10

When I was pastoring a church in Hereford, Texas, years ago, I asked Pam if she'd be willing to lead a small group, and without so much as giving the offer a second thought, she looked at me and said, "No."

Just like that. No explanation. No excuses. No buttering me up before the big let-down. Just *no*. No, period. Sensing she wasn't exactly open to discussing the matter, I decided to pray instead. "Lord," I'd pray, "by the power of your Spirit, please give my wife the passion and ability to tell her story—that's it. I know that if people heard her share her story, they would be drawn into relationship with you."

I prayed. And I waited. I prayed some more. And I waited some more. Still, no movement from Pam.

About six months later, Pam came up to me and said, "Okay. I'll lead a small group. But nobody is going to come. It's going to be awful. But I'll do it because you want me to."

Talk about setting the bar low! I knew that she was wrong.

Over the next ten years, Pam not only led that small group with effectiveness to spare, but she trained fifty other leaders, who launched small groups of their own. She hadn't done anything fancy or elaborate all that time. She'd just been faithful to tell of what God had done in her life, which is all that any of us is expected to do.

What's your story?

Are you sharing it?

Are you marveling at the impact it's having in your circle of influence?

If not, then get going! Get talking. Get sharing. You won't *believe* what God will do.

A BLESSING FROM PAM

*May you find the courage I so desperately needed back then
to share from your heart what God has done.*

Making Room

*"All those the Father gives me will come to me, and whoever
comes to me I will never drive away."*

JOHN 6:37

Every time I stand on the platform to preach, I notice the empty seats. I notice you sitting there, as well! But my eye does land on those empty seats. You might think those empty seats bother me, as though they are proof that we aren't doing our part to get as many people as possible into our building on a Sunday morning, but that's actually not the case.

Here's what those empty seats make me think: *We still have room for more.*

While I don't like having the debt that big churches tend to have, I love that New Life is a big church because we always have room for more. There is room for people to have a place here. There is room for people to hear the good news of the gospel. There is room for people to stand at the altar and surrender to Jesus. There is room for people to be baptized. There is room for people to serve. Of all the things I'm consistently grateful for, high on that list is *space.*

We have room in our church's physical structures; do you have room in your life too?

Do you have room in your home to practice hospitality?

Do you have room in your schedule to sit with people who long to know more about Christ?

Do you have room in your heart to care for people who are hurting?

Do you have room?

Will you make a little room today?

A BLESSING FROM PAM

*May you open yourself to God's divine activity in
people's lives today by making plenty of room for them.*

Holy Expectancy

The LORD reigns, let the nations tremble; he sits enthroned between the cherubim, let the earth shake.

PSALM 99:1

A question, if I may: When was the last time you were on your way to church and found yourself a little shaky, a little nervous, a little undone with expectation about what God might do in your midst?

A favorite author of mine is Annie Dillard, and the best thing she's ever written has to do with this subject of awe. She wrote: "Why do people in church seem like cheerful, brainless tourists on a package tour of the absolute? Does anyone have the foggiest idea of what sort of power we blithely invoke or as I suspect does no one believe a word of it? The churches are children playing on the floor with the chemistry sets, mixing up a batch of TNT to kill a Sunday morning. It's madness to wear ladies' straw hats and velvet hats to church. We should all be wearing crash helmets. Ushers should issue life preservers and signal flares. They should lash us to our pews, for the sleeping God may awake someday and take offense or the waking God may draw us to where we can never return."

She gets straight to the point there, right?

Throughout history, every revival that has ever occurred did so because believers *expected* it to. Which makes me wonder what you and I are expecting, each time we come through these doors.

A BLESSING FROM PAM

May you anticipate greatness today!

We Pick Presence

The LORD replied, "My presence will go
with you, and I will give you rest."

EXODUS 33:14

In the book of Exodus, the prophet Moses is asked by God to lead the nation Israel into the land God had promised them. God saw great leadership potential in Moses that Moses didn't see in himself, so throughout the book we find exchanges between the two, where Moses is pushing back on God's plan.

In Exodus 33:12, for example, Moses said to God, "You have been telling me, 'Lead these people,' but you have not let me know whom you will send with me. You have said, 'I know you by name and you have found favor with me.' If you are pleased with me, teach me your ways so I may know you and continue to find favor with you. Remember that this nation is your people."

In today's parlance, Moses is saying, "Hey, God, help a fella out! Give me the instruction manual on how to lead these people. Just tell me what to do. And by the way, if you don't, then this failure will be on *your* hands. These are *your* people, not mine. Whatever happens here is *your* doing. Just thought you should know."

In response, God said, "My Presence will go with you, and I will give you rest," (v. 14).

Listen, I'm guessing that while you may not be begging God for guidance on how to lead an entire nation these days, you're probably begging him for *something*. For healing. For financial relief. For insight. For a job. For a child to return. For a spouse or a friend to care. The question I have for you is this: If you had to choose between the outcome you're praying for and God's abiding presence with you, which one would you pick?

We want the presence of God. We *need* the presence of God. Without God's presence, we can do nothing. God's presence is always the right pick.

A BLESSING FROM PAM

May you be contented today with God's abiding presence,
as you wait on the outcomes you seek.

Ready to Receive

*"And no one pours new wine into old wineskins. Otherwise, the new
wine will burst the skins; the wine will run out and the wineskins will be
ruined. No, new wine must be poured into new wineskins."*

LUKE 5:37-38

When I talk with people who are middle-aged, I love hearing about how they dealt with the various changes they've likely walked through. If they're educated and married with children, then I start there: "What was it like to graduate from high school and go off to college, your first time on your own?"

"How did you meet your spouse? What were your early days of marriage like?"

"What was parenting like at the beginning? How did you know what to do?"

No matter your age or your life experience, you've surely been through some changes, too. We all went through *significant* change in 2020, as Covid singlehandedly shut down the world. The question to consider is how you managed those changes, how you adapted to the "new wine" that was poured.

In Luke 5, Jesus reminds us metaphorically that our old way of doing things simply cannot accommodate the new he longs to do. We need lifestyles that can flex to the shifts that are coming. We need hearts that are ready to receive.

It's worth remembering that only those of us who have prepared our hearts for new seasons and new things will be trusted with the outpouring of God. Let's ready ourselves by telling God, "I'm ready. I'm in. I welcome the work you long to do."

A BLESSING FROM PAM

*May you receive with gratitude and joy
the changes God brings your way today.*

Divine Sight

*I [God] will lead the blind by ways they have not known, along
unfamiliar paths I will guide them; I will turn the darkness into light before
them and make the rough places smooth.*

ISAIAH 42:16A

A church where I was working at the time had about five hundred people coming
regularly but was growing by leaps and bounds. The other senior leaders and I knew
we'd better secure property to build on, or we'd have no place to put all those
newcomers, and so we decided to purchase land. The price tag was $8.2 million, money
we absolutely did not have.

The elders and we prayed and prayed, and we all kept getting the same prompting
from God: "Do it. I'm in this. I'll provide the funds. Just go."

Are you sure, God? That's a lot of money. Are we hearing you clearly? Are you saying go?

The monthly pull on our finances was almost more than we could bear, and for months
after the transaction was completed we wondered if we'd heard God wrong. But then
came a phone call I won't soon forget, from a man who was brand new to our church.
"I have money I'd like to tithe to the church off a recent business deal," he said. "It's a
sizeable amount, so I was wondering if you could tell me the best way to get that done."

Any guesses as to the amount?

I'm not suggesting that anyone go into debt just for grins. What I am saying is that
when God speaks clearly, go ahead and follow him in faith. Once that man's check
cleared, we paid off our debt in full. That church is *30,000* people strong today—
operating debt-free, I might add.

A BLESSING FROM PAM

*May you be led by divine sight today,
trusting God to lead the way.*

What Greatness Demands

*"Enter through the narrow gate. For wide is the gate and broad is the road
that leads to destruction, and many enter through it. But small is the gate
and narrow the road that leads to life, and only a few find it."*

MATTHEW 7:13-14

Devoted musicians have learned that if you want to compose great music, you must work within the boundaries of scale and meter and rhyme.

Devoted writers have learned that if you want to publish great books, you must work within the boundaries of messages and deadlines and words.

Devoted farmers have learned that if you want to raise great crops, you must work within the boundaries of seasons and rotations and seed.

Devoted athletes have learned that if you want to have set great records, you must work within the boundaries of training and execution and form.

Devoted parents have learned that if you want to raise great kids, you must work within the boundaries of discipline and consistency and time.

All that is great happens within boundaries, within constraints; it's where genius is realized. Which is why very few people wind up living wholeheartedly for Jesus. Along the way, they throw off the boundaries he's set.

Narrow is the gate that leads to life that is truly life.

But how blessed is the man, the woman, the child, who enters through that gate.

A BLESSING FROM PAM

*May you willingly and ecstatically enter
through that narrow gate today.*

Your Purpose in Life

*And now, Israel, what does the LORD your God ask of you but to
fear the LORD your God, to walk in obedience to him, to love him, to
serve the LORD your God with all your heart and with all your soul.*

DEUTERONOMY 10:12

A common question that believers have is how to know what their calling is in life—
or more simply put, what God is wanting them to do. When they ask me about this
topic, I always wish for the ability to look into their future and give them a roadmap
to get from where they are to where God ultimately longs for them to be. I wish I
could point to neon signs that would light their specific course and let them know
they were on the right path.

In fact, something equally as wonderful already exists, which is God's holy Word.
Because in his Word he tells us what he expects of us. He shows us which way to go.

Here is how Moses put it in Deuteronomy 10:12: Fear God. Walk in obedience to him.
Love him. Serve him with everything you've got. What I find is that when people are
faithful to tending to those tasks, God trusts them with additional plans.

If you're feeling aimless in life, may I suggest that you start with these things? Obey
what God has already asked of you before looking for more details from him.

A BLESSING FROM PAM

*May God give you the ability to assess how well you're truly
obeying him, and the boldness to yield fully to him today.*

Apologizing 101

*"For I know my transgressions, and
my sin is always before me."*

PSALM 51:3

I know it's commonly accepted that having to apologize to someone is an agonizing thing to do, but I've put together a three-part script that has made that task easier for me. Sometimes simply knowing the right thing to say smooths out an awkward situation and gives you the confidence you need to resolve the conflicts that always crop up.

You're going to think these are ridiculously straightforward, and you will be right. I didn't promise complexity; I promised effectiveness. See how they work for you.

The first one is this: "I'm sorry."

That's it. Just force your mouth to make those words, and use your voice to push them out. Then, stop talking. (This last part is the key.) When you've messed up, go the person you wronged, look him or her in the eye, and say, "I'm sorry."

If you want to say more about what you did wrong, feel free, but *do not* give excuses or explanations just yet. So, "I'm sorry for being selfish and haughty" is fine. "I'm sorry for being selfish, but you were being rude" is not.

Here's the second phrase: "Please forgive me."

Just that, and nothing more. Forming it as a question is fine—"Will you please forgive me?"—but I wouldn't go further than that.

The third part is a question: "How can I make things right?"

That last one requires next-level spiritual maturity. Asking how you can make things right puts you in a position of vulnerability because you're turning over all power to the person you just wronged. Now, I'm not saying you are obligated to do what they're asking you to do. I'm just asking you to graciously receive their input and refrain from defending what you did. If the person you harmed says, "You know, this whole situation has been so stressful for me. I think what would help make things right is for you to pay for me to go to Hawaii," then maybe don't consent to that just yet. For now, simply say, "Thank you for sharing that with me. I really want to chart a path forward, and I'm grateful to hear what's on your mind."

If you will practice saying these three things, your relationships will work better. You will resolve conflict more quickly and more effectively. And best of all, you'll be honoring God.

A BLESSING FROM PAM

May you boldly take responsibility for your mistakes today
and quickly work to make things right.

The Gospel Breaking Through

"And this gospel of the kingdom will be preached in the whole world as a testimony to all nations, and then the end will come."

MATTHEW 24:14

In 2016 our Global Ministries team was serving in Rwanda and met a man with an incredible story to tell. You may recall that for one hundred days in 1994, an estimated 600,000 members of the Tutsi tribe were brutally murdered by militia from the other tribe, the Hutu. The man our team met had slain a woman's family with a machete as he forced the woman to look on. Twenty-two years later, the man's life was completely different. He had served time for his wrongdoing. He had met Jesus. And now he sought the woman's forgiveness. He wouldn't blame her if she chose to say no.

Not only did the woman forgive him for killing her family, but she welcomed him into her home and into her life. Today, they are close friends. They worship at the same church. Their shared history and their present reality have been totally and completely redeemed.

And we can't get past someone posting something unkind about us on Facebook. Sobering, right?

God is doing big work around the world. The invitation to you and me is to stay fixated on that activity instead of getting hamstrung by personal offense. The gospel *will be preached* to all the nations. The question that remains is if we'll be part of that divine effort or if we'll let ourselves be sidelined by frustration and pain.

A BLESSING FROM PAM

May your testimony today be of God's goodness and graciousness, of his protection and power and peace.

Debt or Delight?

*... choose for yourselves this
day whom you will serve ...*

JOSHUA 24:15

As we enter the final days leading up to Christmas, we have a choice to make. We will either get to the other side of the holiday exhausted and in debt, or we will get there feeling a deeper sense of gratitude to God for this great gift he has sent in his Son. One or the other will likely be true; which will you choose this year?

Christmas does not belong to the marketers, who are telling you to rush around finding the perfect gifts.

Christmas does not belong to the retail industry, who is persuading you to spend more than you have.

Christmas does not belong to the grocery chains, who are making you think you have to spend an inordinate amount of time shopping for and cooking an elaborate holiday meal.

Christmas does not even belong to your extended family members, who are requesting so much of your presence on so many Christmas-break days.

Christmas belongs to your heavenly Father, who knows exactly what you need. Which is why he sent his Son Jesus, to usher in wholeness and holiness and peace. He really is the reason for the season, catchy slogan aside. Return him to his preeminent place, and this Christmas you will know rest.

A BLESSING FROM PAM

*May you enter this year's Christmas celebration
knowing not weariness but wonder instead.*

Endurance and Patience

*For this reason, since the day we heard about you, we have not stopped
praying for you. We continually ask God to fill you with the knowledge of his will
through all the wisdom and understanding that the Spirit gives, so that you may live
a life worthy of the Lord and please him in every way: bearing fruit in every good
work, growing in the knowledge of God, being strengthened with all power according
to his glorious might so that you may have great endurance and patience, and giving
joyful thanks to the Father, who has qualified you to share in the inheritance
of his holy people in the kingdom of light.*

COLOSSIANS 1:9-12

A great benefit of being a pastor is having people pray for me. I'm not talking about having someone say, "Hey, Pastor Brady, I've been praying for you this week." More times than not, when someone says that to me, I wonder if they prayed at all.

What blesses me is when someone says, "Pastor Brady, the Lord woke me up early this morning to pray for you. I prayed to God that you would be given supernatural wisdom as you go through your week this week. And that you'd have discernment and strength to face challenges that come your way."

It's a wonderful thing to have another believer claim God's promises on your behalf. Test me in this, and see if what I'm telling you is true. This week, pray the passage above on behalf of a faithful believer you know. Then, tell them what you prayed. You will be encouraged. *They* will be encouraged. And God will be delighted to fulfill your heartfelt requests.

A BLESSING FROM PAM

*May you be filled to overflowing today with the knowledge of
God's will through the Spirit's wisdom and understanding. May you
live a life worthy of the Lord today and please him in every way.*

Steady On

For the word of the LORD is right and true;
he is faithful in all he does.

PSALM 33:4

Throughout my ministry, there have been many seasons when I felt overlooked, abandoned, neglected, and spiritually opposed.

I wanted to be faithful to God in my life. I wanted to be steadfast in my daily disciplines. I wanted to stay planted on the path of righteousness. I just had trouble staying the course. It felt like life was out to get me ... have you ever felt that way?

On many occasions I would wake early, slip into the living room, settle into a comfortable chair, and stare at this particular psalm. And I'd let the reminder wash over me. I'd let the truth of it build me back up inside, brick by brick and belief by belief.

"God, your word is right and true," I'd whisper to my heavenly Father. "You are faithful in all you do. You can be trusted to come to aid when I'm distressed and channel your power through me."

Nothing especially exciting happened on the heels of praying that prayer to God. But as I sat with its reality each time, I'd be strengthened from within. God's word really is right. His word really is true. He *can't not* be faithful to his children.

He will be faithful to us today.

A BLESSING FROM PAM

May you be reminded today that God invites your tough times
and faltering steps. He can handle your stagnancy and doubt.

Ordering Our Affections Wisely

Set your minds on things above,
not on earthly things.

COLOSSIANS 3:2

Last year after upgrading to a new smartphone, I sensed a prompting from God one day to consider my phone usage afresh. I should say here that I'm not anti-technology. If anything, I love it too much. Smartphones are *amazing*. I could run 99.9 percent of my life from my phone and never have to get out of my chair. Love, love, love the smartphone.

The problem? It doesn't love me. So, the prompting.

One afternoon when I was hanging out at home, the Lord whispered, *Hey, Brady, there's nothing necessarily evil about that device in your hand, but it sure is taking up a lot of your time.*

By that point in the day, Pam had walked right by me a hundred times. Abram and Callie were around, but I hadn't talked to them. All of a sudden, I had one of those moments where you see yourself in your situation, as though you're observing things objectively for the first time. I saw a husband and father who was totally ignoring his family, obsessively checking scores from the previous night's games instead.

I handed my phone to Pam. "Delete any app you see fit to delete," I said. "I mean it. Clean the thing out."

Having Pam press, hold, and confirm deletion for the next ten minutes felt about as pleasurable to me as having a few teeth extracted without Novocain. But the process was beneficial. It's tough to get lost in a smartphone when that phone has been rendered dumb.

I don't know what has you distracted today, but my guess is, something does. Go ahead and lay it down now. You won't ever regret that move.

A BLESSING FROM PAM

May you carefully reserve the top spots in your life today,
prizing your Father, your family, your friends.

The Messiah has Come

Therefore the Lord himself will give you a sign: The virgin will conceive and give birth to a son, and will call him Immanuel.

ISAIAH 7:14

I was talking with a rabbi in town, and while our conversation was congenial, I had an honest question I'd always wanted to ask a practicing Jew. I took the risk with him. "Rabbi," I said, "why is it difficult for Orthodox Jews to believe that Jesus is the Messiah, given that he fulfilled every Old Testament prophesy there is?"

Jewish people do not believe that Jesus is the Messiah their people were always waiting for; they believe their Messiah is yet to arrive.

"Well," the rabbi said, "we believe that Jesus set things up such that he was in the right place at the right time but that he is not, in fact, the Messiah."

"You believe that Jesus was a fraud," I clarified, to which he said, "Yes, that is what we believe."

This didn't square with me. It was prophesized that Jesus would be born in Bethlehem. How could Jesus orchestrate that?

It was prophesized that as a baby, Jesus would have to flee to Egypt to escape King Herod. How could Jesus orchestrate that?

It was prophesized that Jesus would be raised in Nazareth. How could Jesus orchestrate that?

I said as much to the rabbi, who then changed the subject on me.

It is my firm belief that if you and I simply pay attention to the myriad prophesies announcing Jesus' birth, detailing his life, describing his death and resurrection, and predicting how his kingdom would be ushered in, we will see clearly the spiritual reality that Jesus is Messiah, that Jesus is Lord.

A BLESSING FROM PAM

May you have eyes to see the truth of who Jesus is today,
and why it matters that he has come.

Easy to Lead

Today in the town of David a Savior has been
born to you; he is the Messiah, the Lord.

LUKE 2:11

More than two thousand years ago Jesus arrived on the scene, his very appearance toppling empires, his very presence shaking things up. But of all the power systems Jesus has short-circuited, the toughest one to bring down has always been us. Stronger than even the Roman Empire is the obstinate empire of *self*.

On this Christmas Day, the most important question you can ask is a question you ask of yourself: Who is on the throne of your heart today?

Who is leading your empire of self?

Throughout the scriptures, God has searched high and low for a people who are easy to lead. They might be flawed. They might be fickle. They might have short attention spans. But despite their shortcomings they are devoted to God. They consistently *allow him to lead*.

Today, regardless of everything else vying for your attention, let that be your number-one goal. *Father, I will be easy to lead today. You're in charge of my every step.*

A BLESSING FROM PAM

May we be fully directable today.

His Name On Us

You shall not misuse the name of the Lord your God, for the
Lord will not hold anyone guiltless who misuses his name.

EXODUS 20:7

I grew up in an era when you'd get a bar of soap in your mouth if you were caught cussing, and to this day when I think of the name Lifebuoy Soap, something in me wants to throw up. That soap had actual coal tar in it; if parents made their kids suck on that stuff in this day and age, they'd have a lawsuit on their hands.

But I digress.

My point is that for most of my life I thought the third commandment was all about cussing, in that we shouldn't use God's name as a curse, instead saying something like, "Gosh darn." But as I matured in my faith, I realized that something deeper was being required.

By way of context, the people who were given the Ten Commandments had lived for many generations as slaves in Egypt but now were living totally free. What God wanted them to understand was that he was assigning them a new identity now: no longer slaves, but daughters and sons. He wanted the world to know they were his, alone, and so he sealed their identity with his name. What they did with that name mattered.

What we do with it matters too.

A BLESSING FROM PAM

May your attitude be one of total reverence
whenever you speak the name of God.

How We Got Here

"Nazareth! Can anything good come from there?"
Nathanael asked. "Come and see," said Philip.

JOHN 1:46

Sometimes when I'm back in East Texas to visit my mom, I drive across the river separating Texas from Louisiana to visit the place where I grew up. Just outside of Logansport, on Marshall Highway at mile marker six, is where our house once stood, the place that was the center of my universe for years. These days whenever I'm out there I feel like I'm standing on the edge of the Earth. It's a tiny, remote town that GPS can't get you to, because GPS doesn't reach that far.

The last time I was out there, I started thinking about New Life, and about you. I thought about all that God had done in our midst these past fourteen, almost fifteen years. I thought about the impact we have in our city, and about the work we support all around the globe. And then I looked at that little plot of land that I came from and shook my head in awe. I was a little boy in the middle of nowhere, with no special training and no pedigree. No resources to speak of. No prospects as far as anyone could tell. And yet God in his graciousness chose to put his hand on my life and do something special with me.

As I drove away that day, I had to laugh. "God, how did you find me here?"

He'll find you where you are too, you know. He'll lay his hand on your life if you'll let him. He'll give you a special assignment that will rock your world and leave you shaking your head in awe.

A BLESSING FROM PAM

May you trust God fully with your story today, believing that he can bring something wonderful out of the place where you are from.

Blissfully Secure

*No weapon forged against you will prevail, and you will refute every
tongue that accuses you. This is the heritage of the servants of
the LORD, and this is their vindication from me," declares the LORD.*

ISAIAH 54:17

Over the years as your pastor, I've taken quite a few hits, and while some of them were warranted, most were unjust. (When you take a fair wage and then have people with posters protesting your "rampant greed" right on your campus on a string of Sunday mornings, you can't help but think it's unfair.)

A friend at church asked me one time how I dealt with those jabs, and I said in all honesty, "I never enjoy it, but it just doesn't rattle me."

Even on the days when I get raked over the coals, I sleep in perfect peace that night, and it has everything to do with the promise we find here in Isaiah 54: for the believer, our heritage is peace.

If you are being unfairly criticized these days, please receive this encouragement from me: the tongue that accuses you will be refuted. The Lord is here to defend your case.

You don't have to fight back or explain yourself.

You don't have to sink or hide or feel ashamed.

You simply need to trust God to do what he has promised to do, which is to vindicate you in the end.

A BLESSING FROM PAM

*May you walk with head held high and confidence sure today,
as you stay the course in fighting the good fight.*

How to Win in the End

You were running a good race. Who cut in on you
to keep you from obeying the truth?

GALATIANS 5:7

Back when I coached basketball for a school that was attached to the church where I pastored, the track and field coach unexpectedly got fired. The athletic director reached out to me and said, "Hey, since you're always up for a challenge, how about taking on the boys' and girls' track teams for us this year?"

A week later I stood in front of the student body to recruit track-and-field participants. "If you like to run and jump, come talk to me," I said.

After assembly, two young men approached and said they were interested. I could tell they had zero athletic experience, but given I had zero experience coaching the sport in question, I figured we were evenly matched.

"How about you guys do the mile?" I suggested. They thought that was a great idea.

Day one of practice, I exhausted my knowledge of coaching milers with this: "Run hard. Bear left. Keep going until you've done four laps. Get back here as soon as you can."

After lap one they were huffing and puffing. I figured they just needed reps.

At our first meet, my poor charges finished last and next-to-last. What their coach had failed to sort out for them was that it didn't matter how they started the race; what mattered was how they finished.

This is what the apostle Paul was scolding the Galatian believers about. They'd started so strong! But now they were totally petering out. They'd let distractions cut in on them. They'd been outpaced by other gods.

We have to run smarter than this, believer.

We must run with the end in mind.

A BLESSING FROM PAM

May God empower you today to stay focused on running the course he has set before you,
never wavering, never becoming distracted from that which he's called you to do.

Your Work Matters to God

Therefore, my dear brothers and sisters, stand firm. Let nothing move you. Always give yourselves fully to the work of the Lord, because you know that your labor in the Lord is not in vain.

1 CORINTHIANS 15:58

One Sunday I was moved by God's Spirit to speak a word of encouragement over us as a church body, and as I surveyed the congregation, a flood of thoughts washed over my mind. I saw moms and dads and teachers in our district and prison chaplains and city servants and New Life staffers who were "off" that weekend but were there just worshiping God, and here is what I said to them all:

> *"You are a good parent.*
> *You are a loving spouse.*
> *You are a patient teacher who makes room for kids of all kinds.*
> *You are a creative and life-giving part of this ministry.*
> *You have survived ridiculously difficult circumstances in our city.*
> *You are a wise and godly part of your team.*
> *You work hard.*
> *You love well.*
> *You live well.*
> *And all of it matters to God."*

I bring you the same encouragement today. If you are working diligently as a student, well done. If you are carefully planning your family's highly complex fall schedule, well done. If you are filing your expense reports with integrity and honesty, well done. If you are patrolling our streets, looking for ways to protect and serve, well done. If you are crafting messages that will honor God, well done. Whatever you're doing, if you're doing that work as unto the Lord, *well done.*

Such work is never in vain, I'm telling you. So: keep going. Keep creating. Keep applying yourself. Your work is not in vain.

A BLESSING FROM PAM

May you sense the delight of your heavenly Father today, as he relishes in your magnificent work.

A Life Well Lived

*"Very truly I tell you, whoever hears my word and believes him who sent
me has eternal life and will not be judged but has crossed over from death to life."*

JOHN 5:24

A truly beautiful aspect of the gospel message is just how straightforward it is to understand. No matter your background, your ethnicity, your language, your race, your family of origin, or your so-called earning potential, you can grasp and respond to this message. You can say yes to Jesus today.

On many weekends at New Life, we close our services by asking anyone who wishes to receive Jesus to pray a simple prayer with us. Even when I'm not leading this prayer, I pray it aloud with great enthusiasm, just to remind myself that this life is not my own, that I have yielded it fully to God.

Wherever you are and whoever you're with, whether for the first time or the thousandth, I invite you to pray this prayer now.

*Father in Heaven, I'm so grateful for your resurrection.
I'm grateful that you did not stay in the tomb but instead rose,
just as you had promised.
I'm asking that the same Spirit who raised Christ from the dead
would empower me now, that you would take up residence in me.
I acknowledge that I need rescue from my sinfulness, and that I
cannot save myself.
Jesus is the only one who can save me, and I call on his name
today. Please forgive me, Jesus. Please be Lord of my life.
In Jesus' name I pray,
Amen.*

A BLESSING FROM PAM

*May you be refreshed today in your relationship with Jesus,
and may you spend a lifetime joyously serving him!*